The Documented Child

The Documented Child

MIGRATION, PERSONHOOD, AND CITIZENSHIP
IN TWENTY-FIRST-CENTURY U.S. LATINX
CHILDREN'S LITERATURE

MAYA SOCOLOVSKY

THE UNIVERSITY OF
ARIZONA PRESS
TUCSON

The University of Arizona Press
www.uapress.arizona.edu

We respectfully acknowledge the University of Arizona is on the land and territories of Indigenous peoples. Today, Arizona is home to twenty-two federally recognized tribes, with Tucson being home to the O'odham and the Yaqui. Committed to diversity and inclusion, the University strives to build sustainable relationships with sovereign Native Nations and Indigenous communities through education offerings, partnerships, and community service.

ISBN-13: 978-0-8165-5401-0 (hardcover)
ISBN-13: 978-0-8165-5400-3 (paperback)
ISBN-13: 978-0-8165-5402-7 (ebook)

Cover design by Leigh McDonald
Cover background text is from H.R.2202 - Immigration Control and Financial Responsibility Act of 1996. Public domain.
Typeset by Sara Thaxton in 10/14 Warnock Pro with Garamond Premier Pro

Publication of this book is made possible in part by the proceeds of a permanent endowment created with the assistance of a Challenge Grant from the National Endowment for the Humanities, a federal agency.

Library of Congress Cataloging-in-Publication Data
Names: Socolovsky, Maya, 1973– author.
Title: The documented child : migration, personhood, and citizenship in twenty-first-century
    U.S. Latinx children's literature / Maya Socolovsky.
Description: Tucson : University of Arizona Press, 2025. | Includes bibliographical references
    and index.
Identifiers: LCCN 2024016864 (print) | LCCN 2024016865 (ebook) | ISBN 9780816554010 (hard-
    cover) | ISBN 9780816554003 (paperback) | ISBN 9780816554027 (ebook)
Subjects: LCSH: Children in literature. | Immigrant children—United States. | Hispanic American
    children. | Children's literature—21st century—History and criticism.
Classification: LCC PS231.C45 S63 2025 (print) | LCC PS231.C45 (ebook) | DDC 813/.6093523—
    dc23/eng/20240922
LC record available at https://lccn.loc.gov/2024016864
LC ebook record available at https://lccn.loc.gov/2024016865

Printed in the United States of America
♾ This paper meets the requirements of ANSI/NISO Z39.48-1992 (Permanence of Paper).

In memory of my mother, Fanny Socolovsky

CONTENTS

ACKNOWLEDGMENTS

This book was supported, in part, by funds provided by the University of North Carolina, Charlotte, at several stages of its writing. I received a Faculty Research Grant in the summer of 2018 for work on an earlier version of chapter 4, a semester of research leave for work on chapter 2, and a College of Humanities & Earth and Social Sciences (CHESS) small grant for help with indexing. I was also awarded a Children's Literature Faculty Research Grant in the summer of 2020, from the Children's Literature Association, for work on the manuscript.

Earlier versions of some chapters of this book appeared originally in various journals. An earlier version of chapter 1 appeared in *MELUS* 43 (2018), as "Material Literacies: Migration and Border Crossings in Chicana/o Children's Picture Books," and chapter 4 appeared in *The Lion and the Unicorn* 46 (2022), as "Borderland Ethics, Migrant Personhood, and the Critique of State Sovereignty in Jairo Buitrago's *Two White Rabbits* and José Manuel Matéo's *Migrant: The Journey of a Mexican Worker.*"

This project has also benefited from the contributions of several individuals who over the years have provided encouragement and motivation. At the University of North Carolina, Charlotte, my department chairs Mark West and Paula Eckard gave sound advice and support. Paula Connolly's book *Slavery in American Children's Literature, 1790–2010* first inspired me to consider a more innovative framework for critically thinking about children's literature and immigration, and her unwavering belief in the importance and necessity of the project helped sustain my confidence in the work. At the University of Arizona Press, I was also very fortunate to work with many talented people, including Kristen Buckles, Amanda Krause, and Elyse Lyon. Their commitment to and enthusiasm for the project turned the publication process into a truly collective and enjoyable endeavor. Finally, I am grateful to the anonymous reviewers of the manuscript for their critical and informative feedback.

I would also like to thank my family: my partner Gordon Hull, for his ongoing intellectual companionship, his cooking, and his steadfast emotional support; my children, Ilan, Amia, and Gali, for reminding me of how and why stories matter; and my sisters, Merav and Mirit, whose compassion, understanding and encouragement have always held me close.

Finally, this book is dedicated to my mother, Fanny Socolovsky, who passed away as it was going to press. She was originally from Argentina, and during her life crossed many borders and migrated between four continents. No matter where she landed, books and reading were her constant companions, comfort, and intellectual passion. Her love of stories, and of the journeys in them, will always inspire me.

The Documented Child

Introduction

Documenting Latinx Children

In February 2017, 84 Lumber—a Pennsylvania-based chain of lumberyard and home improvement stores—bought ad time during the Super Bowl and ran a short commercial it called "The Journey Begins." The commercial features a mother and daughter setting off from a Mexican village before dawn, traversing land, wading through a river, sitting by a fireside, hiking the desert, and crossing mountains. It ends abruptly with the pair walking away from the camera hand in hand, toward the desert horizon. A caption then invites audiences to "see the conclusion at Journey84.com," and on Super Bowl Sunday itself, more than two million viewers visited the site. By March 7, 2017, there had been approximately fifteen million combined views of the revised and original full-length commercial ("The Entire Journey"). At almost six minutes long, the uncut promotional film, according to YouTube, shows "a mother and daughter's symbolic migrant journey toward becoming legal American citizens" and "contains content deemed too controversial for the original ad and banned from broadcast."[1] Indeed, in 2023 the *Independent* (of London) called it "one of the 10 most controversial Super Bowl ads ever" (Clark). The ensuing social media buzz generated far more attention for the company than most Super Bowl ads. Demonstrating how citizenship and national identity play out through territorial boundaries, the commercial and responses to it tapped into some of the United States' most salient preoccupations about immigration, such as border crossings, national security, and the innocence—or criminality—of young migrant children.

In an effort to capture the "authentic emotions" of the journey, 84 Lumber shot its ad entirely in Mexico using "95% local cast and crew" (Deppen). The uncut version of the journey begins with pastoral depictions of rural Mexico and soft background music that creates, as Litzy Galarza and Lars Stoltzfus-Brown put it, "a carefully and beautifully constructed pathos-based appeal" (45). At moments, the mother picks up her child and spins her around playfully and lightheartedly; they also walk hand in hand across fields and sit by a fire, where the mother gazes wistfully into the flames while the girl sews. During the journey north, the girl picks up bits of trash (for example, cloth material, buttons, candy wrappers), and throughout, viewers see close-up shots of her "hopeful, smiling face" that present her as an "optimistic and innocent adventurer" (45).

These journey scenes alternate with brief scenes that show construction workers unloading lumber and building equipment at what we later understand to be the United States–Mexico border. Finally, the mother and daughter arrive at an enormous and impenetrable gray brick-and-steel wall that breaks the land into two, blocks out the sunlight, and casts a shadow on the Mexican side. After a despondent moment, the girl presents her mother with the small woven-together item she had earlier sewn out of her collected scraps of trash, which turns out to be a ragged but clearly discernible American flag. The flag seems to inspire determination: they embrace, run a little farther along the wall, and find themselves before a huge set of wooden doors, with a crack of sunlight peeping through into the Mexican side. They are able to easily push open the doors and walk through, and as they do so, sunlight fills the landscape. The scene then cuts to a lumber truck, and the commercial ends with the slogan "The will to succeed is always welcome here. 84Lumber. Journey84.com."

The sheer volume of media responses to the 84 Lumber Super Bowl ad was testament not only to the power of its emotive messaging but also to the ideological ambiguity of that messaging. No one could completely agree on the actual meaning of the ad, and this ambiguity contributed to the viral nature of the responses, which extended the life of the commercial far beyond Super Bowl Sunday. Rather than pushing its product, the company seemed to have attached itself to a social issue, and critics and viewers relished the opportunity to rehash a familiar topic—"one of the most combustible topics in the country today" (Heath)—in an unexpected context. The contradictory messaging was, ultimately, a reflection of the contradictory nature of immigration policy and rhetoric; as Galarza and Stoltzfus-Brown note, "the advertisement's messages are indicative of greater discourse about immigration" (41). Both during and after the Super Bowl, the company itself joined and redirected the conversation, in effect adding a fallout version of the commercial to the original version. The director of marketing, Amy Smiley, stated that "the message was clear that 84 Lumber was hiring" and that "anyone with grit and determination had a place at 84 Lumber" (Anderson), while CEO Maggie Magerko provided platitudes about the characteristics of ideal (immigrant) workers, contradictory disclaimers about her personal political beliefs, and defensive explanations about the company's hiring needs.[2] Ultimately, Anderson notes, the real "hang-up" was that people could not decide if the company was promoting illegal or legal immigration and whether it was inviting people to circumvent the system. Magerko later publicly stated that the commercial was not intended to be proimmigration and stressed that although her "brand" is pro-Trump, prowall, and anti-immigration (Pekala), she did not intend "to take a political stand" with the advertisement (Bomey). Ultimately, it seems, everyone saw opposite meanings at the same time and was equally convinced that the commercial reflected their beliefs: "pro-immigration and anti-Trump viewers [see] in it an affirmation of their belief in inclusivity, equality, and open borders, while others saw a primetime embrace of one of the more controversial components of Trump's campaign and early presidency" (Deppen).

Because of their simplified and symbolic nature, both versions of 84 Lumber's journeys romanticize the experience of border crossing and depend on viewers' familiarity with iconic markers of United States–Mexico migration. The desert crossing is not harrowing or even particularly dangerous: when the girl is thirsty (we see this once), she is quickly handed a bottle of water from a sympathetic fellow crosser; a silhouette of a coyote appears at one point in the distance, but no actual animals approach the crossers. In fact, based on the actors' expressions, many shots depict the journey as an opportunity for personal contemplation and thoughtfulness. There are challenges, but in keeping with the company's slogan about the will to succeed, overcoming them is a matter of individual strength, perseverance, and determination. In thus sanitizing the reality of many United States–Mexico border crossings, the commercial is able to neatly avoid any acknowledgment of the United States' systemically violent and militaristic approach to the border and its established use of the harsh terrain itself as a deadly deterrent.[3]

The commercial's markers of migrant border crossing—the wall and the flag—all clearly feed into the polarizing discourses around immigration policy and national identity before, during, and since the airing of the ad. The obstacle of the story—the wall—is a likely gesture to Donald Trump's

2015 presidential campaign promise to build a "great and beautiful wall" between the two nations (Demata 274), and to the border as an enduring manifestation of U.S. sovereignty and its security paradigm. The wall's cultural familiarity, in fact, is so pervasive that for most viewers its connotations are immediate: depending on one's ideological position, of course, it signals either an unnatural, inhumane, and unethical boundary between nations or a necessary protective measure against whichever "enemy" is currently "flooding" the nation. The political and cultural context for the 84 Lumber ad matters too: as Massimiliano Demata notes, in 2017 Trump's own "politics of fear" and language on immigration were evidence of the "core ideological tenets only of certain fringe movements" that were now firmly established in mainstream American politics (275).

In this setting, then, such an obstacle can best be overcome with a potent symbol of Americanness, such as the American flag. The scraps (trash, really) that the child picks up presumably strike her in some whimsical way as souvenirs of the experience, but they coalesce productively to form a statement of committed U.S. patriotism. They represent making something out of nothing and building a future American self. The flag, then, is an archive of the (sanitized, romanticized) immigrant child's journey, implying that the American flag (and identity) is indeed a collection of immigrant narratives. It is also a symbol of the girl's own creative and entrepreneurial spirit, as she understands its use value intuitively: it can restore hope at the lowest point of the journey and empowers the migrants to find an opportunity (the door, built by 84 Lumber workers) with which to enter the United States. It appears, in fact, to figuratively open their eyes to see a way into America. The flag becomes a metonymy for the documents that determine so much of the life experiences of actual migrants to the United States but that (along with all the other bureaucratic necessities of authorized migration) are never referenced in the commercial. That is, the flag, as an authorizing document, transforms the pair into "good" immigrants who deserve entry because they are fundamentally American in their outlook and values. In particular, it is the child—with her smarts, her excitement, and her innovative ways—who seems already Americanized, who is compelled to be innovative and solution oriented, and who implicitly educates the mother (the foreign parent) on the importance of patriotism. In this way, the ad might well be suggesting that these immigrants deserve citizenship not because of their humanity (or not only because of their humanity) but because of their perceived American patriotism, "conflating citizenship with assimilation" (Galarza and Stoltzfus-Brown 50). In other words, our obligation to welcome migrants is based on their predestined loyalty to America (even before their arrival) rather than on any broader humanitarian code of ethics.

This "good" versus "bad" immigrant trope perpetuates the nation's rhetoric about who is worthy of entering the country and who has the power to decide that worth. The commercial's use of the mother-child duo is, according to Gretel Kauffman, a "subtly conservative" part of the American dream discourse because "not everyone is a child," "not everyone has a family," and "not everyone looks like the woman and child that are held up as the embodiment [of the good immigrant]" (Kauffman). Even so, the company's attempts at creating "ostensibly nonthreatening bodies of a mother and daughter" also backfired: one online user, for example, posted, "Updated: #84Lumber releases new video today . . . mom has had 4 anchor babies since last filming!" (Galarza and Stoltzfus-Brown 50). The ease with which the mother and child are interpreted and reinterpreted so continually (whether positively or negatively) in these discussions confirms the vulnerability (and instability) of their cultural presence; as Amaya notes, undocumented people "are not subjects; they are objects" (92). This means that the tragedy of migrant crossings can easily be turned into a profit tool and that even in such situations where the emotional appeal is amplified, Latinx bodies "are no longer flesh-and-blood people" but rather "exist as images" (L. Chávez, *Latino Threat* 47). And even with the best of intentions, Latinx identity in the United States is often symbolic and simplified, and "update[ed] in real time through nostalgia, activism, and as a product to be sponsored and consumed" (Villa-Nicholas 9).

In 2017, after the airing of the ad, the chief creative officer of 84 Lumber's ad agency, Rob Shapiro, commented to *Business Insider* that the ad "intended to make a 'patriotic' statement and aimed to make the company a household name throughout the country," adding that "this is a conversation that's taking place in homes across America . . . in Part Two [of the ad] you will see what a beacon of light America is, not just within America but beyond to other countries" (O'Reilly). Here, we see exactly how the topic of immigration inhabits the domestic and private spaces of the nation and appears to belong to everyone (in the sense that everyone feels they own it), sometimes to such a degree that the migrants themselves become images to be manipulated and pawns of the larger political system. Just as the ad elicited contradictory but equally dominant readings, enabled by fast-moving corporate-audience interactivity, so too do immigrants become tropes that are continually documented and redocumented, in both cultural and literary venues, often under public scrutiny. Indeed, according to Eduardo Gonzalez, "the immigrant" as an identity category "has been recreated time and again to serve many political agendas" (51).

This book explores how the documentation of Latinx children has shifted over the first two decades of the twenty-first century in literary texts aimed at children and young adults and looks at how these shifts map onto broader changes in immigration policy and discourse.[4] Through such a critical inquiry, we can see how important legislative and political driving forces have steered public thinking about various aspects of citizenship—legal personhood, social belonging, and cultural membership—and how children's texts reflect and interrogate such thinking. Such literary (and therefore cultural) expressions of migration journeys, and of living with constant fears of deportation, serve as powerful examples of ongoing public conversations about the place of Latinx migrant children in the United States. My purpose in this book, specifically, is to examine how Latinx children are situated in literary contexts and how they thus feature as an always-unfolding part of our cultural norm, particularly given the somewhat contradictory narratives about the innate value of children and the disposability of migrant bodies.[5] The story in 84 Lumber's ad and the multiple interpretations that followed it are exemplary of the process of interrogation, documentation, and redocumentation of Latinx children that takes place continually in the nation and that greatly determines dominant ideologies about migration. No representation of undocumented children can remain neutral; every act of writing and rewriting takes a position, whether implicit or explicit, on the child's presence in the nation. Here, I use the word *documentation* intentionally to show the acute importance of certain papers in the nation's definition of presence and personhood. As Orduña explains, "To not have papers is to be marked as someone who is banned. And to be banned in this way is to be made the walking, breathing expression of sovereignty" (34).[6]

Personhood, Citizenship, and Biopower

My reading of both the 84 Lumber ad and the conversations around it demonstrates how immigration is a personal, immediate, and urgent matter that plays a central role in the nation's perception of itself. These discourses of national branding raise compelling questions about how migrant personhood is valued and, in particular, how migrant children—as indisputably important symbols of the future—are valued. Lisa Cacho notes that the term "illegal alien" invokes images of, but is not a fixed signifier for, Latinxs. Writing in 2012, she points out that different racial and ethnic groups have been associated with "illegality" throughout U.S. history but that what has remained consistent from the late nineteenth-century Chinese Exclusion Act to the 2001 USA Patriot Act is the "legally recognized nonpersonhood of the racialized 'illegal alien'" (112).[7] The Immigration Reform and Control Act of 1986, for example, provided a path toward legalization and citizenship for a specific contingent of undocumented immigrants but did not change or decriminalize the "rightless state of the 'illegal alien'" (5). These sorts of exceptions to immigration law (including multiple attempts to pass the Development, Relief, and Education for Alien Minors, or DREAM, Act, and the 2012 Consideration of Deferred Action for Childhood Arrivals, or DACA, policy) retain the status quo in which "permanently criminalized" groups of people are "ineligible for personhood"—they are populations subjected to laws but "refused the legal means to contest those laws as well as denied both the political legitimacy and moral credibility necessary to question them" (6). For Cacho, being ineligible for personhood is a form of social death that defines who does not matter; undocumented immigrants are "a population that never achieves, in the eyes of others, the status of living" (7). It is worth underlining the fact that in the United States, full legal status for a citizen—the status of living, in effect—means that the state cannot remove you, and that having "personhood" means having the right to move around within the nation. For undocumented migrants in the United States, this lack of legal personhood (which includes the constant risk—if not actuality—of deportation) means that even after building a history in the country and making meaningful social and cultural connections, protected membership and belonging remain limited.

The pertinent question, of course, is how migrant *children* fit into this discourse of personhood, and to fully understand this, we must first briefly explore critical connections between citizenship and biopower. Biopower names a series of governmental practices and theories first emerging in the eighteenth century that treat the population as an economic and political entity, a "composite body" rather than a collection of individual citizens (Inda 136). The logic of biopower stipulates that "in order to fortify the well-being of the population, the state and its apparatuses often strive to eliminate those influences deemed harmful to the biological growth of the nation" (135). The migrant, deemed by many as harmful to the well-being of the nation, is thus repudiated. Attempts to exclude the immigrant from the body politic imply that "illegal lives are expendable—that the lives of undocumented immigrants and their children are not quite worth living" (135). Under this logic, modern forms of government continually make decisions on the value and nonvalue of certain lives, and ultimately, as Inda notes, "the death of the other" (the immigrant) is necessary because it makes life (for the citizen population) "more healthy and pure" (138). The death, it is worth noting, does not have to be direct; it can be the act of exposing someone to death or of increasing the risk of death, or simply "political death, expulsion, rejection, or exclusion" (138). Thus, the Southwest desert terrain where the U.S. border control practices "prevention through deterrence" is a place where life can be taken without apology, "classified as neither homicide nor suicide" (Doty 129, 130). Even cultural differences are construed as incompatible and a "threat to the national body" (Inda 140), making it necessary to reject the foreigner who does not participate in the common language, traditions, or beliefs. In these ways, the state constructs illegal immigrants as undesirable and judges them to be expendable (149).

While this dynamic helps explain national discourse and policy about the migrant population in general, our cultural understanding of childhood as a time of innocence means that migrant children are sometimes presented as exceptions to the logic of biopower. Migrant children are generally presumed to be vulnerable victims and are thus documented in more sympathetic and humanitarian terms.[8] Most important, ideological notions about their impressionable and unformed minds (a legacy of Enlightenment and Romantic notions of childhood) positions migrant children's foreignness as a temporary condition rather than predisposing them to an expendable life. It is worth noting, however, that their state of exception is also used to maintain the overall equilibrium of biopower, because the child's status as a "good" immigrant (and thus their potential eligibility for personhood) confirms their parents' criminality and continued ineligibility. In a neoliberal environment, too, the value system interprets "illegal" status as being a "choice made by rational individuals" and speculates about one's future value by recounting a person's useful assets and talents (Cacho 19, 161). A child who has crossed into the United States with their parents (or in some cases alone, because of their parents' absence) is not seen as having made that choice for themselves.[9] Thus, the little child in 84 Lumber's ad, for some viewers, fulfills the criteria for being a "good" immigrant: she presumably did not choose to make this journey herself, and she already exhibits some important American values (creativity, determination). But under the logic of biopower, the very criteria that permit the child's life to be potentially valuable are also the ones that categorize her mother as disposable; the health of the citizen (or in this case, the child citizen in formation) is fortified by eliminating what is considered harmful to the nation.[10]

Immigration Policy, Border Militarization, and Latinx Literary Responses

The picture books, middle-grade stories, and young adult novels I analyze in this book were all written between 1997 and 2020. This time frame is intentional because from the 1990s onward, going after immigrants became "locked into the political lexicon" (Frey 56). Writing in 1997 specifically, George J. Sánchez notes that "most social commentators . . . identify our current historical moment as one experiencing a particularly sharp rise in American nativism" that is unparalleled since the 1920s, that intertwines in a variety of ways a "new American racism" with traditional hostility toward new immigrants, and that emerges from both sides of the political spectrum (1011).[11] It is also worth noting the connection between xenophobia and criminalization: as Rosaura Sánchez explains, "Criminalization is one key aspect of the current xenophobia narrative as it offers justification for the plot of imminent threat from immigrants" (127). The works selected for this study were thus written during the increased militarization of the United States–Mexico border in the 1990s under the Clinton administration, the escalating deportations of the early to mid-2000s under Bush and Obama, and the explicit xenophobia and nativism of the Trump administration.[12] During this time, several immigration acts drastically changed the way that the United States managed its policies and controlled its immigrants. The 1996 Illegal Immigration Reform and Immigrant Responsibility Act, for example, was a watershed moment for migration policy, as it overhauled immigration enforcement and laid the groundwork for future deportations. Dara Lind argues that it "essentially invented immigration enforcement as we know it today—where deportation is a constant and plausible threat to millions of immigrants" (Lind, "Disastrous, Forgotten 1996 Law").[13] In José

Orduña's words, it was purely a "punitive tool" that created a legal category of "unlawful presence" that was entirely new to immigration law (6).

After the terrorist attacks of September 11, 2001, and the immediate passing of the USA Patriot Act, "the manufactured threat of terrorism coming across the southern border brought 'immigration' under the rhetorical domain of national security rather than just criminality and economics" (Orduña 134). The country's response to 9/11 changed the border landscape and accelerated its militarization, as rhetoric about national security became the main justification for more vigorous immigration law enforcement (Chacón 77).[14] In response to the attacks, the U.S. Congress enacted a wide range of legislation to protect American sovereignty and monitor noncitizens, including the 2002 Enhanced Border Security and Visa Entry Reform Act, the 2004 Intelligence Reform and Terrorism Prevention Act, the 2005 REAL ID Act, and the 2006 Secure Fence Act, which together increased border building and enforcement, pushed migration routes east (sharply increasing migrant deaths), restricted political asylum, and led to more undocumented entry and permanent settlement.

Collectively, the literary texts in this book thus share important concerns, as they are all produced in a time of increased public surveillance and negative rhetoric about migrants' presumed undesirability, foreignness, and criminal status. Endlessly stringent legislation, particularly during the Trump administration, further normalized the notion of the border area as a war zone, while at the same time repeated (albeit failed) attempts to pass the DREAM Act (first introduced in 2001), as well as former president Obama's DACA policy in 2012, recognized the purported value of providing temporary stability for many Americanized undocumented children.[15] It should be noted, however, that even measures that hope to provide a path to legalization do not, as Cacho puts it, "address the fundamental problem of immigration law: that it creates a permanently rightless status" (6). In many respects, the literary texts address these issues in similar ways (critiquing the border, humanizing undocumented persons) to advocate for a more ethical understanding and treatment of migrants. They all highlight the experiential reality of living without rights and strategize ways to make the Latinx child protagonist eligible for personhood, that is, able to become a person defined as having legal rights who is therefore a legally recognized person.

However, over the decades we also begin to see an important change in the literature's strategy. As the border has become increasingly militarized, children's and young adult books have shifted their depictions of the border, personal and national identity, and sovereignty. Given the increasingly harsh immigration policies of the later years and the continued failure of immigration policy to mend itself (or be mended), it is perhaps not surprising to find a changing literary response. In effect, the texts reflect different strategies for making the undocumented Latinx child protagonist eligible for personhood: while earlier texts document the child as a transnational (sometimes global) subject, the later texts also document her as a U.S. national subject. Specifically, the scope of citizenship (understood as social and cultural membership) has changed from a celebratory hybridity to a more anxious hybridity that is part of a carefully curated American self.[16]

This change is a necessary survival strategy. The United States–Mexico border, when understood as permeable, vulnerable, and therefore in need of around-the-clock military equipment and tactics, represents the ways in which violence structures the nation. José Orduña describes the patting down and manhandling of migrants at the border as "an act of empire-building" because "here, in this zone and on these bodies, America defines itself by what it's not. Each rejection, each death in the desert, is a rearticulation of our foundational violence. This is America" (178). It is the border, too, that reduces migrants to bodies: "working bodies, warm bodies on surveillance cameras, bodies held in captivity and exchange as commodities, dead and missing bodies in the desert" (Magaña 151). In the texts I explore in this book, the border is a place of uncertainty, death, disappearance, and terror, where the state decides who belongs and who does not—in other words, who has value and who is expendable. In the earlier works (chapters 1–3), that belonging is achieved when the dominant culture recognizes, accepts, and even celebrates cultural differences and national interdependence, symbolically legitimating the migrant child's presence in the nation. But in later works (chapters 4–6), the more explicit terror and trauma of border crossing and undocumented life shift the concern: now, even when cultural difference is embraced, it does not give the migrant child the same value awarded to a citizen child. Under these conditions, cultural hybridity and transnational identity are not sufficient stand-ins for the stability and security of legal personhood. Transnationalism is a figurative concept rather than a literal practice, as crossing back and forth across the United States–Mexico border becomes more difficult and dangerous, and therefore less desirable.[17] The literature reflects this by showing less transnational deterritorialization and more documentation of the undocumented child as essentially American and thus worthy of life.

Literary Constructions of Childhood

Understanding how children have historically been written into society, and how childhood has been constructed, helps situate the specific dynamics of contemporary Latinx child "documentation"—and the implications of that documentation—in its broader ideological context. Childhood studies scholars often begin with Philippe Ariès's 1965 volume *Centuries of Childhood: A Social History of Family Life*, which claimed that childhood was an invention of modern Europe. Prior to that, children were depicted as small adults, but this changed when adults began to think of children as different and to treat childhood as a special stage in life (Grenby 7). As Paula S. Fass puts it, "Childhood began with a new sensibility about the young that resulted in a view of children as requiring particular and elaborate treatment" (2). While recent scholars have to a degree contested Ariès's view, his general observation that children "gradually became the object of greater paternal and societal solicitude and psychological interest remains convincing," particularly as the population growth and demographic shifts of the eighteenth century led to a society "increasingly . . . concerned with children, and willing to invest in them both economically and financially" (Grenby 7). Fass notes, importantly, that some children have had much more access to a "childhood" than others because "modern childhoods and children's experiences are deeply affected by circumstances such as status, class, wealth, and poverty" (2). Nevertheless, the story of childhood as a privileged state has been, since the nineteenth century, the dominant paradigm, which has deeply influenced literary writings for and about children and has established certain moral codes to do with child-rearing.

The paradigm of childhood that frames today's Latinx children's literature emerges from a long cultural and social history, beginning with John Locke's seventeenth-century notion of the child's mind as a blank slate and extending into the Enlightenment and Romantic periods' understandings of childhood as a time of innocent sanctuary before the hardships of adulthood.[18] To help young people attain reason, compulsory education would train them as future citizens of the state (Schmidt 175), and the "value" of children began to rise in the late nineteenth century as they became treasured "for their emotional contribution to family life rather than for the market value of their wage labor" (Gutman 253). Because children (prized for sentimental reasons) were irreplaceable, "their value increased, and laws, policies, institutions, and places emerged to protect them as 'priceless children'" (253). These developing notions of a child's intellect and innocence, of their economic and emotional value, and of the family unit as a stabilizing social force are the legacy we have inherited. This legacy provides the lens through which we still interpret and understand children and assess the normative and healthy functioning of the nation, and it takes on new relevance when applied to migrant children.

Literature written for children, long understood as both entertaining and educational in its instilling of societal norms and ethical values, has historically presented various tropes that become particularly nuanced in the context of Latinx children's writing. Some of the traditional child archetypes that have evolved over time, for example, also work as models for documenting the Latinx child protagonist: the Romantic/sacred child (virtuous, innocent) is the vulnerable victim; the sinful child (corrupted by original sin, exemplifying cultural and personal fears) is represented by the child's "illegality"; and the working child (economically valuable) is symbolized by the laboring migrant child.[19] Most intriguing is the orphan archetype, which fascinated Victorian-era writers because of how cultural systems placed the notion of the family as a building block around which society was framed. Thus, the parentless children, on the outside of this organizational social structure, represented an interesting and complex version of childhood (Smallman). The orphan archetype, however, also predates the nineteenth century, "reflecting archaic rites of passage when young people were removed from family and placed in unfamiliar situations" (Nikolajeva, "Children's Literature" 321). Within literature, traditionally, orphans symbolize the other: they are outsiders who resist or seek incorporation into normative society, they are perhaps lonely and solitary, but they also sometimes have special powers that will help them achieve social inclusion and happiness (Smallman).

The standard explanation for removing parental figures from a story (whether physically or emotionally) is that it allows the protagonist to test their independence and the readers "to have a vicarious experience of freedom" (Nikolajeva, "Children's Literature" 322); but it is our obsession with the orphan as other, I believe, that makes it such an enduring literary symbol. It is also, of course, an apt archetype for an unaccompanied migrant child crossing the border, or for various permutations of that plot that we see in the texts discussed in these chapters. The child's possible integration into American culture, for example, where they figuratively leave behind their "foreign" parents, represents a kind of orphaning that the nation regards as valuable for assimilation, but the traumatic experience of family separation and the child's status as parentless (losing the structural foundation of a family) are also uneasy reminders of how a broken immigration system is ultimately a reflection of a broken society and broken children. The orphan protagonist needs protection and is also something to be protected against; similarly, the migrant protagonist seems vulnerable but also explicitly represents a foreign threat and potential for disruption. Susan Terrio notes that like street children, "child migrants cause fear . . . when they cannot or will not fulfill their expected roles within the normative realms of family, home, and school" (49). Thus, as a response to increased xenophobia and nativism, the foreign migrant "orphan" necessarily becomes rebranded as an orphan who seeks (rather than avoids) incorporation into the new society.

The Place of Latinx Children's Literature and Scholarship

Children's literature offers an important space for interrogating and reimagining nationhood in part because the intended readership is still solidifying its social attitudes.[20] It is generally recognized as "an important vehicle for ideas that challenge the status quo and promote social justice" (Mickenberg and Nel 445), because children can "effect necessary cultural and social transformations" (Rebolledo 280). Historically, however, Latinx literature and scholarship have been proportionally underrepresented in children's literature as a discipline. Jaime Naidoo points out that initially children's books published in the United States were written mostly by "cultural outsiders" and "did not reflect day-to-day experiences of Latinos" ("Symbolic Violence" xi). In the 1990s, a new wave of Latinx literary production (particularly Mexican American) presented a more complex and informed picture of Latinx experiences, but critics still caution that underrepresentation persists and that such literary exclusion continues to devalue and marginalize Latinx experiences (Barrera and Cortes 143).[21] Frederick Aldama also notes that while important inroads have been made in the academy in the study of children's and young adult literature by and about Latinxs, these changes remain largely confined to education (rather than English or Spanish) departments ("Heart" 10).[22]

While these challenges remain significant, several recent developments have helped move Latinx children's literature into a more central position both on school and library bookshelves and in the academy. In the first place, socioeconomic factors have resulted in an increase in literary production by "insiders"; according to the 2010 census, one out of every six people in the United States is Latinx, and more access to education has meant that a new generation has the "energy, time, and choice to write fiction—and not work in factories and fields" (Aldama, "Heart" 13). Concurrently, various publishing marketing strategies and the creation of library-recognized national awards (such as the Américas Award, the Tomás Rivera Mexican American Children's Book Award, and the Pura Belpré Award) not only "celebrate and affirm Latino cultural experience in children's and young adult literature" but also "bring visibility to the artist" (9). Writing in 2018, for example, Alamillo et al. note that publishers are providing "intentional spaces" for publishing literature with Chicanx themes and that while the present moment is "rife with continued anti-Mexican sentiment," it has also given rise to "our first Chicano National Poet Laureate, Juan Felipe Herrera" (x). Materially speaking, these awards also increase sales, place these books on the radar of librarians and teachers, and help sustain the small presses that "have historically been the ones to take the risks in publishing stories by Latinos and with Latino themes and characters" (Aldama, "Heart" 9). There have been more calls for Latinx studies and children's literature scholars to engage more inclusively across fields, as critics recognize the important role of academia in legitimating these texts.[23] Phillip Serrato argues that children's literature scholars can help effect a shift in how Latinx children's literature is regarded and handled, as "we work with large numbers of students maybe considering a career in teaching" and so "can expand how people perceive Latinx children's books more generally" ("Working").

Although children's literature and ethnic studies have to an extent operated in isolation, Marilisa Jiménez García explains how the two fields converge in significant ways. Acknowledging the historical lack of intersectional work and disparities between the founders of children's literature in both the humanities and ethnic studies movements, she nevertheless argues that they *should* be aligned, because demands for ethnic studies by communities of color have depended on arguments that are directly tied to issues of

educational equity and classroom outcomes. Scholarship in Latinx literature for youths, for example, has its roots in education and library science
scholarship and "necessitates active engagement in interdisciplinary and
comparative approaches" ("Side-by-Side" 116). Both fields still bear the legacy of having been historically marginalized by academia (some argue that
they continue to be marginalized), producing "side by side histories" that
have "collided in the twenty-first century call for diverse and 'own voices'
in literary studies" (114).[24] Asking critics to consider what story such scholarship tells about what we value and what we centralize, Jiménez García
positions Latinx children's literature as a countercanon that not only "publicly amplifies voices of people left out of canons" but whose intersections
also challenge "our understanding of factors that shape scholarly and literary
canons" (117).

By amplifying some of the marginalized voices of Latinx children's literature, then, we can newly understand the structural forces that have
shaped the social and literary experiences of the nation's immigrant children. Clearly, Latinx children's literature resonates powerfully with both insider and outsider groups of readers, reflecting the "myriad of experiences
of young Latinos in the United States" and also "invit[ing] others to share
in these experiences" (Aldama, "Heart" 3). Latinx children gain legitimacy
and belonging because of such literary representation: they are more motivated to stay in school (Naidoo, "Opening Doors" 27), to develop feelings of
self-worth (Mathis 191), and to understand structural and historical oppres-
sions (Mercado-López 6). Most important, perhaps, the intersecting fields'
material and interdisciplinary foci mean that they are directly tied to the
world (for example, through education, child readership, and library studies), where representation can become a form of intervention and where, as
Katharine Capshaw puts it, the future appears both expansive and inclusive
(251). Latinx children's literature and scholarship, then, have the potential
to be socially transformative, to impel "equity [and] social change," and to
have an important effect on language policies and the social and educational
marginalization of (for instance) Chicanx youths (Alamillo et al. xi).[25] In addition, there is a strong argument to be made for the formative influence of
children's literature on social relations, as Capshaw Smith explains: "telling
stories to a young audience becomes the conduit for social and political revolution" (3), particularly as the political implications of Latinx writing can
reach an audience still in the midst of its intellectual and social formation

(Mercado-López 6) and can transform the corrosive effects of racism and marginalization (Terrones 47). It is with this in mind that the representation of migrant experiences in children's literature becomes so important.

This book is not intended to be a comprehensive review of Latinx children's and young adult literature but rather takes a closer look at representative works that are part of a larger conversation about Latinx child migration, citizenship, and belonging in the United States. For clarity, each chapter addresses a distinct area within the field of children's literature (picture books, middle-grade stories, and young adult novels), but the literature is presented chronologically to demonstrate changing responses, over the decades, to the nation's anxious relationship with immigration. This organizational structure foregrounds how the literature responds to dominant narratives of migrant expendability and how it asserts the value of the migrant child in different ways. Because of this framework, I also do not categorize the texts by the ethnic groups or origins of either the authors or the characters, although I am attentive to those details within the chapters when relevant. While the majority of the texts feature Mexican or Mexican American protagonists, authors, and illustrators, they also represent a range of backgrounds, including Cuban, Colombian, Argentine, and Dominican. Given this diversity, together with my book's interrogation of U.S. national identity and dominant culture's interpellation of Latinx migrants, it is most logical to collectively think of these narratives through the pan-ethnic designation of Latinidad.

This book is divided into two sections. The literature in chapters 1 through 3 depicts empowering transnational spaces within the United States, shows the child subject's hybridity, and celebrates that hybridity as a path to personhood. Chapters 4 to 6 show an increasing terror of the border and more efforts to rebrand the child protagonist as American, particularly with the Dreamer narratives in chapter 6. Thus, chapter 1's analysis of three picture books written between 1997 and 2002, which all focus on literacy, shows how they renegotiate experiences of reading and writing and expand "literacy" so that it is more culturally inclusive. The picture books' attention to literacy both as a subject matter and as an activity validates the migrant child protagonists' presence in the United States, as they variously engage in their own reading and writing practices within the action of the stories. In Pat Mora's *Tomás and the Library Lady* (1997), Luis J. Rodriguez's *América Is Her Name* (1998), and Amada Irma Pérez's *My Diary from Here to There* (2002), migrant citizenship is documented and legitimated through multiliteracy (the use of more than one mode of communication), which is, I argue, a politically significant strategy as it can counter prejudice and validate the child's sense of belonging. Just as multiliteracy is an interdependent mode of communication (as the children engage with oral, aural, and tangible forms of self-expression), so too is the nation expanded, figuratively, into a more transnational space.

In chapter 2, I explore the connections between citizenship and farming in two middle-grade novels, Cynthia DeFelice's *Under the Same Sky* (2005) and Julia Alvarez's *Return to Sender* (2009), both of which reimagine and politicize the American farm landscape. I discuss the ways in which geography and land cultivation have long been measures of national and cultural character and look at how farm labor in particular has played a central role in constructing national identity. Traditionally, the iconic American farmer has been positioned as an abstract white male citizen who farms his own land, and in this cultural paradigm, farm labor is valued as both virtuous and indicative of citizenship. Under the new cultural logic presented in the stories, however, where family farms are cultivated by Latinx workers who are marked by their race, ethnicity, and foreignness, the labor of farming becomes demeaned. In my analysis I show how the novels intervene in classic understandings of American farming narratives: they see the landscape as politicized and traumatized by migration, they expose the instability of the immigration system, and they ultimately assert the demeaned laborer's personhood. The novels' explorations of farm landscapes reveal discourses about immigration and citizenship that have been, up to this point, invisible to the white child protagonists, who through a process of maturation begin to challenge the dominant ideologies that operate through those landscapes. Ultimately, the "new" American farm is presented as a space of global, transnational citizenship and belonging.

Malín Alegría's 2008 young adult novel *Sofi Mendoza's Guide to Getting Lost in Mexico*, which I turn to in chapter 3, similarly celebrates transnational interdependence, but it does so as a fictional travelogue that emphasizes the heroine's bicultural identity. As part of an especially marketable genre ("chica lit"), it also uses its commercial appeal to deliver a clear moral message that presents new ways for Latinx youths to imagine and practice social justice. The novel shows how Mexico is created in the U.S. literary imagination and redefines ways of knowing Mexico. My argument explores how a long history of U.S.-centric definitions of Mexico (and Mexicans) that are based on neocolonial and asymmetrical power dynamics depend on discourses of shame and illegitimacy, which market the place and people as commodities and make any "real" or authentic experiences of Mexico disappear. They also play a part in the shaming of both undocumented and documented Mexican Americans in the United States. In the story, Sofi's role as a Mexican American tourist-traveler (who is unauthorized in the United States but initially unaware of her status) requires her to gradually move away from binary models of nationalism and toward a more complex and healing transnational and hybrid identity. Transnationalism, however, not only celebrates blended cultures but is also politically significant as it resists the sovereign state. In this chapter, then, the amalgamation of Mexican and American (Sofi as a "hybrid border girl") creates a healthier subject and also ensures her personhood.

As we turn to the literature—all written between 2011 and 2018—in chapters 4, 5, and 6, we see a shift in the way personhood is strategized. The picture books in chapter 4 (Jairo Buitrago's 2015 *Two White Rabbits* and José Manuel Mateo's 2014 *Migrant: The Journey of a Mexican Worker*) represent important interventions in how the United States defines itself through borders, as they deconstruct those borders and demonstrate urgent social injustices such as the separation of families, poverty, and the push-pull factors of immigration. I argue that these picture books take on an ethical stance where all individuals have a right to rights and where belonging is about moral personhood. Through both the writing and illustrations, the texts show an ethical gap between what is and what should be: they critique the state's surveillance of migrant border crossers and respond to Gatekeeper-era policies by showing the border's material effects, such as disappearances. Although they are ostensibly picture books written for very young readers, as cultural products they demonstrate the United States' exclusionary practices of sovereignty, and they challenge that with discourses about how migrants—as persons—matter.

Chapter 5's analysis of Alexandra Diaz's middle-grade novels *The Only Road* (2016) and its sequel *The Crossroads* (2018) more explicitly shows how when violence structures a nation, some lives become expendable and killable. In the novels, the undocumented child protagonists' unaccompanied journey from Guatemala to the United States becomes an explicit journey of terror as the story examines what it means to be "disappeared" (to be dead, missing, or neglected). Like the earlier texts, these books deconstruct borders and interrogate the exclusionary practices of the nation as a way to document the children's visibility and personhood, but they also validate some principles of national sovereignty and belonging. That is, the stories depict two kinds of assimilation narratives (that of passing and that of conversion) that present "foreign" children as deserving and essentially American, even while the protagonists retain a connection to their homeland. There is tension between these displays of foreignness and of passing, but such displays also interrupt the fixity of national identity and invite a more ethical understanding of migrant personhood.

Finally, the texts in chapter 6 investigate this assimilation narrative even more directly through the Dreamer generation, representing the ways that the Dreamer movement has shaped political discourse since 2001 and transformed national belonging and citizenship into commodified American brands. In the chapter, I explore how the chosen works reflect and build on the Dreamer brand and consider what kinds of new scripts allow them to articulate their personhood. Alberto Ledesma's young adult comic book memoir *Diary of a Reluctant Dreamer: Undocumented Vignettes from a Pre-American Life* (2017) brings together a range of art (doodles, comics, sketches) and writings (ruminations, diary entries, remembrances), while Maria Andreu's young adult novel *The Secret Side of Empty* (2014) recounts an undocumented teenager's personal experiences during her senior year of high school. In his work, Ledesma questions what the political and personal function of the Dreamer brand has meant to him personally, to Latinx youths at large, and to the United States; Andreu shows the devastating consequences of living without the Dreamer brand, and the inevitable need for its collective identity and the political opportunities it offers. I use these texts to argue that this collective identity, in which youths offer up their own brand of normative market citizenship (based on storytelling) in exchange for public recognition of their American identities, is essential for building legitimate belonging and personhood as we move deeper into the twenty-first century.

CHAPTER 1

Material Literacies

Migration and Border Crossings in Pat Mora's *Tomás and the Library Lady*, Luis J. Rodriguez's *América Is Her Name*, and Amada Irma Pérez's *My Diary from Here to There*

In his 1997 afterword to the thirtieth-anniversary edition of *Down These Mean Streets*, originally published in 1967, Piri Thomas considers the status of minority children as citizens of the nation, writing, "When we hear society expressing that 'the children are our future,' many of us ask, 'Whose children and whose future?'" He continues, "I believe every child is born a poet" and wonders, "How can any child be considered unimportant and dehumanized, relegated to being a minority, a less than?" (335). The rhetoric of nation and citizenship has long pervaded children's texts, which, as discussed in the introduction, are recognized as culturally, educationally, and socially formative, while ethnic children's literature in particular shapes and determines children's discourses of nationhood and difference. Although critics understand the high stakes in ethnic children's literature, as it explores intercultural relationships and differences for a readership that is still solidifying its racial attitudes, minority children's experiences continue to be underrepresented and hard to access.[1] How then do children on the margins, particularly undocumented Latinx migrants, participate in and respond to literary expressions of nationhood? In what ways do the stories that we do have about immigration allow a migrant/immigrant child reader to identify with the material, and in that sense, to believe that they belong to, inspire, and are part of the nation's literary, cultural, and creative identity?

One of the biggest challenges posed by literary representations of immigrant experiences is the tendency toward monolithic stereotyping. As Phillip Serrato argues in his blog post "Working with What We've Got," school reading lists are "risk-averse," tending to offer a standard "go-to" Latinx text (such as Pam Muñoz Ryan's *Esperanza Rising*) and precluding "any opportunity for readers to chance upon and explore something new, something different, something out of the ordinary that . . . might prove to be extraordinary." The three picture books I analyze in this chapter, however, do present something different. Written during a time of rising nativism and punitive, anti-immigrant policymaking, the social realism of Pat Mora's *Tomás and the Library Lady* (1997), Luis J. Rodriguez's *América Is Her Name* (1998), and Amada Irma Pérez's *My Diary from Here to There* (2002) gives readers "extraordinary" material that can begin to push back against the political environment. Specifically, the texts overturn some commonplace expectations for children's experiences of literacy by disrupting the traditional thematic quest narrative that determines the structure of so many children's books.[2] The traditional story often follows a pattern of home–adventure/school–return home, but such linearity, of course, does not always fit experiences of migrancy and undocumented residency. When there is no stable home, when the very notion of a return to it implies continual movement away from it, and when the school or institution is just as likely to perpetuate feelings of dislocation and nonbelonging as it is to offer safety and citizenship, how can these picture books build personal and national identity, and develop literacy, for their marginalized audience?

Here, I argue that Mora's, Rodriguez's, and Pérez's books all document immigrant and migrant belonging by demonstrating the acquisition of literacy through multiliterate experiences, as their protagonists continually renegotiate their own relationships to reading and writing. According to Georgia García, literacy itself is a set of practices that develops to meet the needs of a particular culture (3). Literacy studies researches classroom instruction and canon development, conducts national research reports, and engages in national and state educational decision-making but has been slow to embrace diversity (1). The term *multiliteracy* was coined in 1994 by the New London Group (a group of scholars and teachers) to develop a new approach to literacy pedagogy. In this new approach, "authoritarian" literacy would be replaced (or supplemented) by broader modes of representation that reflected increased linguistic and cultural diversity and adapted to rapidly changing technologies of writing (Cope and Kalantzis, "Multiliteracies: The Beginnings" 5).[3] As Elizabeth Boone notes, "We have to think more broadly about visual and tactile systems of recording information, to reach a broader understanding of writing" (3–4). The pedagogical theory of multiliteracy has thus, since the late 1990s, advocated using more than one communication mode (visual, aural, oral, gestural, spatial) to make meaning, in turn expanding "literacy" to include broader textual practices that are also more culturally inclusive. The approach emphasizes the importance of oral vernacular genres and believes that reading is a critical, social, and ideological practice that impacts canon choices and at times disenfranchises certain population groups. Mora's, Pérez's, and Rodriguez's picture books, then, present multiliteracy as a politically significant strategy for the entire community, one that can counter prejudice, stabilize identity, and forge belonging and thus serve as an apt "reading" experience for validating and recognizing migrant life.

In general, picture books are a natural space for multimodal representation, as their visual illustrations, as well as their tactile, oral, and aural features, require readers to engage in more inclusive modes of communication. In addition, these picture books highlight the difficulties of labor conditions, border crossing, and immigration and thus represent migrant and undocumented children's experiences of journeying and literacy as alinear rather than linear. Such alinear patterns encourage synesthesia and imagine a child reader who can move between these modes of communication to re-represent the same things. According to Bill Cope and Mary Kalantzis, much of our everyday representational experience is in fact intrinsically multimodal (gestures may come with sounds; images and text sit side by side on pages; architectural spaces are labeled with written signs), and children in particular have natural synesthetic capacities ("Multiliteracies" 179, 180). This recognition of broader literacy practices coalesces with recognizing the cultural, political, and economic realities that shape minority students' literacy acquisition, as texts imagine "a sophisticated and multiply literate ethnic child reader" who can move fluidly between genres and modes (Capshaw Smith 7). Potentially, such privileging of multiliterate communication offers children the ability to heal from difficult experiences and the stability of "complete literacy," which Rodriguez himself, in his memoir *Always Running*, defines as the ability to participate competently and confidently in any level of society that one chooses (9). In thus bringing together questions of national belonging and new practices of literacy, the texts normalize alternative strategies for storytelling and play a crucial role in shaping all future citizens, motivating migrant children and—one hopes—encouraging empathy in nonmigrant children.

Tomás and the Library Lady

Pat Mora's *Tomás and the Library Lady*, an English-only picture storybook published in 1997 and illustrated by Raul Colón, is a semifictionalized biographical account of the life of Tomás Rivera, who was born in Crystal City, Texas, in 1935 and became a writer, professor, university administrator, and national education leader. Set in rural Iowa in the 1940s, the book tells the story of Tomás, the young child of migrant farmworkers who run the migrant circuit, working summers in Iowa and winters in Texas, helping farmers harvest their fruit and vegetables. When the story begins, Tomás has learned all his grandfather's oral stories and with the help of an Anglo-American librarian discovers books, thus opening up new stories and worlds. On the most obvious level, the story teaches children about the importance of libraries and literacy and the liberating possibilities they offer, but more interestingly, it also establishes a reciprocal relationship with its child reader, who participates, alongside the child protagonist, in the transformative experience of reading. Although the text might be considered risk averse and, as I discuss below, has been critiqued for romanticizing the migrant experience, I argue that by presenting reading as a visual and oral activity and by highlighting books as material items of worth, the text also redefines literacy more broadly, allowing it to address the hardships endured by migrant farmworkers and to provide some model of stability for children affected by those hardships.[4]

In some respects, the illustrations in *Tomás and the Library Lady* present an idyllic narrative of migrant labor. Scott Beck argues that the story does not go far enough in its portrayal of the difficulties of migrant life; the visuals romanticize the family's experiences and cast them in the realm of bygone days, thus failing to address the issues of farm labor as an ongoing and contemporary concern (107). Specifically, Colón's circular patterns, his use of framing, the chosen colors, and the balanced composition all contribute to the story's romanticized ambience. According to Perry Nodelman, the use of circles or curving in picture book illustrations creates reassurance (72), while framing the pictures creates detachment (50). In *Tomás*, the dark yellows, muted golds, and browns of the color palette establish a warm, yielding, and unthreatening tone. In addition, a balanced composition in each picture, where most of the images are arranged with little tension in terms of the configuration and placement of figures, creates a sense of symmetry. Taken together these visual narrative strategies connote stillness and stability, which would seem to be at odds with the unsettling experience of migration.

However, certain instabilities in the visuals also disrupt this idyllic representation of migration: Colón's use of broken frames where the picture spills out of the frame, and the use of close-up shots and character placements that disturb the balanced visual weight of the picture. Both of these heighten the story's dramatic tension and undo the objective distance between reader and character, creating a more immediate connection to and empathy for the protagonist. These kinds of visual disruptions are evident on the first page of the story, which shows Tomás in the car, setting off for Iowa. Various shapes (the car's body and window frame; the moon, hills, and the roof of a house; Tomás's face; the terrain; and the clouds) are all rounded and curved, setting up the story's unthreatening tone. These features are repeated throughout the book. However, Colón breaks with picture books' conventional placement of characters that depart on a quest. Nodelman explains that readers usually identify and empathize with objects on the left-hand side of the page, and that ordinarily protagonists are placed there and move off to the right as they journey, following what he terms the "glance curve," that is, the path of our visual habit of looking at pictures from the left foreground to the right background, which also mimics the Western reader's learned practice of reading from left to right (135).

In showing Tomás's departure, Colón places Tomás (featured close up) and the car he sits in on the left side of the page, increasing the reader's empathy, but the car faces (and moves off to) the left rather than the right. Tomás stares out of the window behind him, toward the right-hand side of the double-page spread. Breaking with the strong convention of voyaging away from home to the right suggests that the character's progress is impeded (Nodelman 164). Thus, Colón depicts the journey as a reluctant migration rather than an adventurous individualistic quest; his protagonist casts a sad look behind him, the car does not seem to move forward into an eagerly awaited future, and the illustration's stillness (connoted by the curves) reiterates his desire to remain where he is. Moreover, although the picture shows a framed window, which in picture books is traditionally interpreted as an invitation into a world beyond (Nodelman 81), the window in question is in a car rather than a house. The world from which Tomás sets off on a journey, then, is founded on movement, not on the stability of a building one might return to. And although the entire illustration is framed, the bottom part of the frame is broken as a car is shown driving away. This broken frame indicates that migrant travel cannot be contained or rendered as a distant experience; instead, it is a continuous part of the present.

The book's written narrative also describes the challenges of the migrant circuit: the car is "tired" and "old," and Tomás himself is "hot and tired" and uprooted, missing his own bed in Texas. On the next page, accompanying an illustration that shows the car nestling in the rosy hills, we read that "year after year they bump-bumped along in their rusty old car." The contradictions between the written and visual narratives create tension, drawing out some of the instabilities in the illustrations, undercutting their romanticized tone and creating an ambiguity that reflects the broader story's difficult task of representing traumatic experiences to a very young audience.

The story's ambiguous representation of poverty and farm labor also hinges on this incongruity between the visual and written narratives. At the town dump, where Tomás searches for books, his brother for toys, and his parents for iron to sell, the illustrations detract from the written text's message of poverty, showing everyone standing on what appears to be a soft hill, patiently rummaging through trash (which is not immediately recognizable as trash; the details are softened and faded out), and successfully finding what they have been looking for. Similarly, when Tomás's parents go to pick corn, he and his brother, Enrique, carry water to them and then play with a ball, which their mother has sewn from an old teddy bear. The words describe the harsh heat and sun—"All day they worked in the hot sun"—while the visuals show contented workers standing in a clearing, smiling as they pick corn, with Tomás and Enrique happily kicking the ball. But despite the muted yellows and golds and the circularity of various objects in the picture (Mamá and Papá's hats, the ball, the curve of bodies playing, the baskets of corn, the trees on the horizon, and the swirls of the ground itself), the bottom left-hand side of the picture's frame is once again broken, showing Mamá holding a stalk of corn and walking toward the edge of the page. Like the car in the earlier illustration, the character's breaking out of the frame destabilizes the idyllic contours of this picture. In refusing containment, the text creates a more immediate connection to the harsher realities of farm labor and their relevance outside the frame of the story.

As a counterpoint to the instability of migrant life, rendered implicitly through visual and written cues, the text explicitly shows how literacy—storytelling, reading, and books—can strengthen and lend stability to Tomás's experiences. In particular, the story's blending of oral, visual, and print mediums positions multiliteracy as the most apt "reading" experience for validating migrant life. The text's first example of storytelling is oral, when Papá Grande tells his grandsons a familiar story. Even in his sitting position under a tree, the grandfather is disproportionally oversized, indicating his central role as the purveyor of imaginative exploration. The picture, neatly contained inside a frame, suggests stability: the two listening boys and the grandfather form a triangle shape whose base sits firmly on the ground. Here, the narrative communicates the fundamental power that stories can offer. However, it also indicates some of the limitations of oral storytelling: while the written text recounts the story that the boys hear in some detail, the accompanying illustration shows us the story*telling* activity most vividly, rather than the events of the story itself, which are faintly camouflaged inside the tree.

In contrast, in later depictions of Tomás reading his library books, the written text recounts what he reads and the illustrations also explicitly depict it. The words describe his immersion in the story: "He'd look at the pictures for a long time. He smelled the smoke . . . He rode a black horse across a hot, dusty desert." But in addition to the imaginative visualization of the events, we also see Tomás himself, off to the side, reading the book and breaking the frame that contains his storybook's events. Here, Mora emphasizes Tomás as both a reader and a participant in the world he reads about. The broken frame shifts the status of the protagonist and of the child reader and transforms literacy into a communal and multimodal activity. Tomás the protagonist becomes a reader; simultaneously, the child reader of Mora's book becomes (figuratively) the protagonist, as their experience of reading the story and their imagined participation in it are blurred. As both character and child reader engage in acts of reading at the same time, literacy seems to transcend the printed page to encompass broader practices of communication and representation. In fact, much of Tomás's "reading" is multisensory: as he looks at the pictures in the book and "see[s]," "hear[s]," and "feel[s]" the characters on the pages, he engages in visual, aural, and tactile modes of literacy. When he does literally read the stories, it is out loud to his family: "In the evenings he would read the stories to Mamá, Papá, Papá Grande, and Enrique," and as his family comes and sits near him to "hear" his story, he roars "like a huge tiger" and elicits laughter from them. Reading here is not a solitary and silent activity but a collective shared one, and literacy is expanded to encompass a multisensory and performative experience that recalls and retains the pleasures of oral storytelling. By extension, the child reader of Mora's picture book can participate in a similarly multiliterate experience of reading, especially if the story is being read out loud to them. Although the story that Papá Grande recounts earlier on does not reach us through the illustrations, the text validates oral storytelling and, by extension, multiliteracy by showing how the successful and rewarding dissemination of book-stories depends on many of the original markers of oral narrative.

In this way the narrative demonstrates how storytelling and acts of literacy can extend one's experience of personhood, belonging, and home, and it culminates in the acquisition and ownership of books themselves. Tomás's initial quest in search of stories (a journey that takes him to the library for the first time) is a quest for the stability offered by storytelling. His reward is almost immediate, as the library space is welcoming, visually inviting him in with the softened curves of arched entryways, the librarian's smile, and her kind face. Books are valued for their physical presence as well as their literary content. When Tomás enters the "huge" library for the first time, he looks "at all the books around the room," which are piled in the librarian's arms, fill shelves in the background, and are stacked up at the forefront of the page. In this space, books provide sustenance. The librarian offers Tomás cold water to drink; notably, the library and its offerings of books present an antidote to the thirsty and hot labor of a migrant farmworker's child.

Although the hardships of migrant life in the story are presented implicitly, the story does directly reference a number of physical discomforts (the hot sun, the heat, the bump-bump of the car, the small cot Tomás sleeps on, the town dump). It thus symbolizes, at least for an adult mediator of the text, the physical harshness of migrant life. To endure this physicality, suggests Mora, we need to experience not only stories but also the materiality and physicality of books, and for a migrant farm boy, owning the book (rather than just borrowing it) is significant. When Tomás finds books in the dump, he puts them in the sun "to bake away their smell," creating something new out of them and altering their status from items of trash into items of utility and luxury. The reconstituted, recovered book is a valuable object that offers stability. More explicitly, at the end of the story, when the family leaves Iowa, the librarian's parting gift to Tomás is a "shiny new book," a luxury commodity that he initially "holds" rather than reads, as if to experience its value through touch. The presence of the book also establishes a contrast between the two journeys taken by Tomás in the story: the trip away from Texas to Iowa and the return to Texas. In the first journey, Tomás stares sadly out of the window as the car moves through the landscape. In the return trip, we have zoomed so far in to the interior of the car that it is barely recognizable as a vehicle. Here, instead of foregrounding the experience of migration, the visual closes in on the family group—the grandfather and mother gazing at Tomás—and the overly large book that Tomás holds. While the first car journey shows a moving vehicle with a lone child inside it, the second one centers a smiling family group around a book, minimizing the migratory part of their journey and suggesting instead the healing and communal power of literacy.

The visuals on the last page of the story emphasize two things: Tomás as the owner of his new book about dinosaurs, and Tomás figuratively participating in the events of his book by imagining himself riding a dinosaur. Unlike the previous illustrations, this one does not show Tomás reading but instead shows him in a separate frame, hugging the book tightly to his chest with his eyes closed. Such ownership, where the book becomes an extension of his body and where he imaginatively inhabits the book even when he is not reading it, implies real literacy. Owning and holding the book allows him both a memory of his reading experience and an anticipation of future reading; the physical book's presence alone offers enrichment, allowing him to benefit from the experience of "reading" at all times, beyond the moment of reading itself. In that moment, the utility of the book and its resourcefulness for a migrant child who is on the move becomes evident: being able to recall and immerse himself in an imaginative journey allows the literal journey to become less restrictive and both journeys to become integrated. For a child reader of Mora's picture book, of course, the paralleling of both journeys validates Tomás's experience as a migrant quest narrative that must be told.

So, what are the implications of *Tomás and the Library Lady*'s presentation of multiliteracy and migrant identity? All the "reading" activities that Tomás engages in during the story extend literacy by moving it into a realm of communication that encompasses orality, visuality, and performance, which fully engage the physical body. In addition, the visual and written narratives foreground books as objects that the reader, and Tomás, engages with in a tactile manner. Such attention to the physical, and to literacy overall as a physical activity, suggests that Mora's picture book is addressing the hardships of and antidotes to migrant life in a more pressing way than first appears. It documents the ways in which a book—the very object that the child reader and child protagonist hold in their hands—can provide stability in an unstable life. Given how intertwined the child protagonist's body is with his books, the story's attention to the physicality of his books also draws attention to his physical body, suggesting that the physical stability represented by the books can also stabilize the migrant body. Furthermore, because literacy operates both within the space of the imagination during storytelling, and within the larger space of the nation by forging cultural legitimacy and belonging, the picture book's engagement with the topic of literacy signals its broader impact. Outside the text, a child reader that identifies with the material undergoes a process of belonging: the story's migrant tale lets the reader recognize that their experiences are shared by others, while its emphasis on multiliteracy valorizes the varied ways of disseminating such diverse experiences as an essential part of the nation's cultural identity.

América Is Her Name

Luis J. Rodriguez's 1998 picture book *América Is Her Name*, inspired by the author's experiences working with Spanish-speaking children and their parents in the Pilsen barrio of Chicago, takes more explicit risks than *Tomás and the Library Lady* in addressing issues of migrancy in the United States. Unlike *Tomás*, whose Mexican American protagonist is American born, this story directly grapples with the eponymous protagonist América's undocumented status in the United States and foregrounds the hardships of living in the shadows of the system. The story traces nine-year-old América's difficult life in the Pilsen barrio and her transformation into a budding community poet.[5] Just as *Tomás and the Library Lady* very clearly advocated literacy and libraries for its young readers, so too does *América Is Her Name* send an unmistakable message about the way in which artistic creativity can assert and legitimate one's personhood in the midst of a culture that often criminalizes undocumented Latinx children. That is, in both stories, multiliteracy counters prejudice and stabilizes identity. Specifically, Rodriguez is interested in exploring the materiality of literacy—writing in particular—as a mode of representation that can transcend one's political and national identity and forge belonging.

These issues—the materiality of literacy and the forging of belonging—are further supported by Carlos Vásquez's boldly colored illustrations, which highlight the picture book's own physical presence and draw attention to its tactile quality. Serrato argues that Rodriguez modulates "the ambitious spirit of new realism into the picture book genre," thus breaking new ground and speaking to the fact that many Chicanx childhoods are "distinguished by experiences with different forms of hardship" ("Conflicting Inclinations" 192). Although the experience of belonging is often considered to be one of rootedness, here the illustrations' use of lines and sharp angles conveys movement, energy, and disorder. Belonging is reinterpreted as an experience of motion and action; more pertinently for an undocumented immigrant trying to valorize her voice and story in her new home, belonging comes about through acts of change and subversion. Throughout, the color pictures are all outlined in black, creating an effect similar to that of cartooning art, where movement is suggested through the lines. As Nodelman notes, cartooning is "a static representation of the body in motion" (97); in the context of Vásquez's work, such movement allows borders to be transcended. At the same time, that motion is stabilized by the solidity of Vásquez's bold colors and images. The picture book thus presents a form of transcendent belonging—movement to elicit change, and stability to create a platform for expressing that change—that allows América to be a creative and productive citizen of the community and the nation.

Rodriguez does not shy away from showing readers both the broad and the specific struggles of living in the barrio, ranging from poverty, unemployment, and alcoholism to the social stigma of being undocumented and the lack of opportunities for youths. Of course, he pitches them at a child reader's level, so that the information is conveyed in snatches, through overheard conversations or indirect implications, in matter-of-fact tones. For example, América overhears her father "yelling" because "he has been laid off from the factory" and her mother telling him "I was called a 'wetback' at the market today. No matter what we do—we don't belong." Thus, the story establishes the tension in América's home environment and her own isolation, as she is now "in a strange place she can't even pronounce" where she has also "lost [her] voice." At school, too, an important site for the validation and legitimation of the child self, the teacher Miss Gable is frustrated, authoritarian, and threatening toward the children.[6]

The narrative also emphasizes the barrio's entrapment. After América's father discourages her from writing because it won't pay the bills—"Don't waste your time. Where are you going to go with writing?"—and advocates that she should instead learn to clean the house and care for her siblings,

América wonders sadly if she is destined not to write but just to passively "wait for the factory to feed us." She contemplates the faces around her, seeing the untapped creative potential of the community in "the desperate men without jobs standing on street corners" who "all seem trapped, like flowers in a vase, full of song and color, yet stuck in a gray world where they can't find a way out." Given Vásquez's bold hues throughout the story, América's thoughts here imply that the acquisition of voice and the acquisition of color go hand in hand: that is, creativity nourishes the self and the community. The use of color in the picture book itself, then, is not just intended to catch the attention of a young reader but is also a statement about the necessity and validity of voicing the story of undocumented migrants in the barrio.

To an adult mediator of the story, these are all indications of epistemic violence predicated on the abjection of the undocumented migrant's body, and they help contextualize the story's single but glaring recounting of street gang violence, with its explicit physical threat. The episode is startling, as the preceding page shows América walking through the barrio on her way to school and smiling at the ice cream man from Guerrero, the barber from Michoacán, and the teenagers who—perhaps with retrospective menace—are "standing around with nothing to do." As América rounds the corner (and readers turn the page), she witnesses a sudden shooting between a group of boys and another boy armed with a gun. The written narrative describes the violence matter-of-factly, as if to emphasize the quotidian nature of the barrio's physical dangers. After the shooting, "the others run but América just stands there. Nobody is hit."

The writing's insistent realism as it documents street violence is matched by the visuals' critical presentation of it, in terms of the placement of the characters, the manipulation of our gaze, the use of thresholds, and the attention to reading as a tangible experience. The illustration shows the "corner" that América has just turned quite literally, with lines drawn in at an angle as she stands on the left-hand side of the double-spread illustration and looks over at the opposite page, where a boy walks along a slab of sidewalk beside a wall. He aims his gun at the group of boys who occupy the top right-hand side of the page, forming, with América, a triangular shape that stands on one of its points rather than on its base. In terms of the composition of characters on a page, Nodelman argues that a triangle configuration standing on its base creates balance and order, but a disrupted configuration (e.g., a triangle that stands on a point) creates tension (130). In the text, the overturned triangle creates an unbalanced composition, which increases the dramatic tension, emphasizes instability, and demonstrates América's uneasy status as both witness and participant.

The illustration also manipulates the spectator's gaze—ours and América's—in an unsettling and disruptive way. América looks at the gunman, who points toward the group of boys, who themselves look in various directions, trying to escape. Similarly, there is no clear direction for the reader's eyes to move across the picture: because of the sharp angles and reflecting gazes of the characters, our own gaze bounces back and forth. Reading this page is thus unsettling not only because of the content (the shooting) but also because of the disorderly motion that forces our eyes to keep moving without settling on any one part of the image. The sensation of entrapment is further exacerbated by Vásquez's depiction on this page of the barrio's sidewalks and walls. Drawn at slanted angles to one another, the sidewalks and walls also look like doorways, thresholds into another world. América appears to have walked through a doorway when she rounds the corner; the gunman appears to be walking on a door. However, because these thresholds are not actual doorways but just resemble them, the visual message is that these characters cannot leave their dangerous world. They are not invited out over a threshold; rather, the danger enters their space uninvited, so that unlike the symbolic entrances and exits represented by doorways in traditional picture books, the ones here symbolize the persistence of violence in barrio life.

This realism moves beyond the picture book itself as the group of boys tries to escape through an opening in the wall. In their escape they seem to be stepping out of the pages of the book, diminishing the line between the story's fictional content and the real world that it represents and emphasizing the materiality of the book that we hold. That is, as the boys try to disappear beyond the pages, we are made to notice their tangibility. In the case of this picture storybook, then, any attention to the book's own tangibility is a reminder of the realism beyond the pages of the book. The visuals are thus both artistic and tactile, documenting rather than merely representing the violences of the barrio. And although this episode is presented as a single fearful event that the story never returns to, it does not function in isolation. Rather, its explicit physical violence is repeated through the story's epistemic examples of violence: the family's despair, the teacher's threats, and the neighborhood's ambience of hopelessness. There is something violent, the book suggests, about not offering support and opportunity to these lives.

In thus depicting the multilayered violences placed on unauthorized migrants in the Pilsen barrio, Rodriguez and Vásquez's narrative draws attention to the abjection of those unauthorized bodies. The story critiques such abjection by repositioning the bodies as transnational subjects who belong to the nation because both their ethnic and creative identities transcend political borders. In terms of ethnic identification, América and her family are presented as Mixtec rather than Mexican, marking their ethnicity through an Indigenous ancestry that transcends national and political borders, rather than by the national—and often racial—markers that dominant culture places upon Mexican and Mexican American migrants.[7] This panethnic label allows new forms of identity to be constructed based on transborder social communities, which challenge traditional concepts of cultural identity that are linked to location, because, as Lynn Stephen notes, Mixtec are frequently part of the fabric of daily life in more than one nation (21). In a world of borders and nations, their lives are shaped by more than one political, social, and economic system. Rodriguez's assertion of the family's Mixtec ethnicity is politically significant, as according to Michael Kearney, such ethnic identification tends to emerge as an alternative to nationalist consciousness precisely in areas where nationalist boundaries are ambiguous or contested (129). Facing down racial epithets of nonbelonging, as América does in the story by referencing her Mixtec identity, exactly pinpoints the way in which her very presence in the United States threatens certain nationalist ideologies.

Both the written and visual narratives positively highlight América's Indigenous identity: she is described as "a Mixteca Indian girl" who "has honey-brown skin and elongated eyes that are large and dark; her thick hair is in braids," and there is no mention of her Mexican nationality (or of Mexico) other than the fact that she speaks Spanish. Repeatedly the narrative suggests that the family's Mixtec ethnicity renders them transnational: even though the United States–Mexico border demarcates them as "illegal," their cultural identity is not limited to geographic place and can be, in Chicago, reaffirmed collectively and creatively. Such transnational belonging is asserted at the moments when América or her family's presence in the United States is abjected. When her teacher Miss Gable whispers about her "She's an illegal," the text describes América's thoughts: "How can that be—how can anyone be illegal! She is Mixteco, an ancient tribe that was here before the Spanish, before the blue-eyed, even before this government that now calls her 'illegal.'" Similarly, when her mother recounts being called a "wetback," her uncle asserts, "We belong anywhere, everywhere."

The narrative's rhetoric of transnational belonging also legitimates América's abjected body by combining her Indigenous personhood with her poet's personhood. When Mr. Aponte, a visiting Puerto Rican teacher and poet, tells the class that "there's poetry in everyone," his words are doubly inspirational because they are both oral (immediate) and written (permanent). Within the action of the story, the words are spoken, but for the reader of the picture book, they are also part of the illustration, printed inside a frame that looks like a book. This effectively creates a small book within a book. Thus Mr. Aponte's oral lecture to the students is metatextually preserved in book form for the child reader. He encourages the students to write in Spanish and reassures them that it's "okay" if they can't write very well, noting that this will come later. He adds, "You are a poet, and poets belong to the whole world." Like the Mixtec, poets cross national borders, which is also why in this moment English loses its absolute authority in the classroom. At the end of the story, the two kinds of transnational identities are validated together, as América (together with two important authority figures in her life, her father and Miss Gable) finally accepts her own creative potential: "A real poet. That sounds good to the Mixteca girl, who some people say doesn't belong here. A poet, América knows, belongs everywhere."

The poet's ability to create belonging and to provide both stability and transformation for the lives in the barrio is also shown through the story's depiction of writing as a physical and collective experience. As in Mora's *Tomás and the Library Lady*, where reading was a multiliterate experience, so too Rodriguez and Vásquez's narrative shows writing as an activity that moves beyond the purely literary realm into a space of orality and performance. When América steps up in Mr. Aponte's class to recite poetry, she "closes her eyes and rocks with the rhythms of the Spanish words she recites." Her performance elicits enthusiastic interaction from her listeners: the class "explodes in applause." Such multiliteracy, the text implies, is politically significant: it legitimates Spanish; validates her body through sound, music, and movement; and releases América's voice in a way that sets her on the road to writing. The experience transforms América into a dynamic and "active designer of meaning," as she engages in a pedagogical process that is not only innovative and creative but also potentially "emancipatory" (Cope and Kalantzis, "Multiliteracies: New Literacies" 175).

The illustrations also show how América's emancipated voice (her literacy) has moved away from just reading or writing. In them, her voice is depicted through swirling lines that emerge from her mouth and form various images (such as flowers and animals); the movement and energy of the lines visually reflect the creative movement of her live performance. Similarly, throughout the story América's poetry is never shown as writing per se, because the illustrations never show her putting words or letters on her sheets of paper. Instead, her "writing" (mostly memories of Oaxaca) is visually depicted as illustrations that fill the pages of the text. When she touches her pencil to the paper, the pages before her remain blank, connected to images of Oaxaca through strong swirling lines that run between her paper and the space around her. The lines do not indicate a particular direction for the reader, so it is unclear whether the memories pour out of her, metaphorically bringing Oaxaca into the United States, or whether she is gathering the memories around her into the page. Either way, the lines represent writing as an energetic and creative activity that, given the storyline, will upset the balance of her restricted life in the barrio. The lines also present her writing as multiliterate, reaching beyond the literate reader and privileging alternative modes of communication (visual, oral): it is not a static thing but, like her voice, full of movement and texture. As readers, we are thus made to see speech and poetry as they happen, to understand them not only as end products but also as constantly unfolding agents of change.

Through its depiction of América as a community poet, *América Is Her Name* underlies the complexity of minority experience and stories, rejecting the notion of a singular solution to the barrio's troubles. Capshaw notes that there are sometimes generic limitations within children's literature, with a tendency to present, for example, tales of heroic individualism in which "a singular individual battles the evils of racism, solving the problem of oppression" (248). But Rodriguez presents América's poetry as belonging to and coming out of the community. In the story, one of the main conflicts—that América stops writing after her father chides her for its perceived uselessness—is resolved when her mother requests that she "write something for me." In response, América asks that her mother also write something. Eventually they share stories with one another and the other members of the family, forming a small writing community that is for everyone, as "even the little ones join in." This implies that an audience is essential to the production of these stories, turning them into testimonials that need witnessing. The illustrations also show how writing, as a collective activity, illuminates and reimagines the child's creative body as sacred: the illustrations of América sharing her writing with others depict her surrounded by a golden yellow glow that outlines her body and the paper she has touched.

The question of América's collective grace is essential to understanding the final image of the book. Ultimately the story asks, To what extent can this child of the barrio, as a promising writer, help the whole barrio? Perhaps to please the book's young target audience, its critiques of U.S. nationalism and its direct and indirect depictions of migrant hardships are resolved with the last page of the book, a double-spread illustration. In it, the family is centered and nestled safely within the buildings of the barrio, smiling at one another and at the reader, and the composition is balanced and symmetrical.[8] Unlike an earlier depiction of the barrio that showed the buildings from above and created a sense of oppression and vertigo, here the tall buildings are at ground level and tilt toward one another in a friendly rather than threatening way. The ice cream vendor, a teenager, and happy neighbors waving at the windows of the buildings counter América's earlier fear about the grayness of all their lives and imply that a bright future lies ahead for everyone. And when contrasted with the family portrait that appears at the start of the book, it becomes clear that the ending does more than satisfy the child reader's desire for closure. The first family portrait is a sepia-toned (i.e., colorless) sketch that shows only the family, with the baby holding a toy truck. In the final picture, however, the baby grips a pencil. This, together with the picture's bright colors and its inclusion of the neighborhood, sends a clear message about how the acquisition of creativity transforms the entire community. It argues that América's individual achievements and promise have a significant collective impact; potentially, everyone, especially the youngest, can participate in and belong to a multimodal process of representation, thus validating their marginalized experiences as legitimate literary material for the nation's construction of itself. The story's message about writing—that it is fundamentally connected to other forms of representation—becomes part of the story's closure, so that rather than erasing the hardships depicted earlier or signaling an ending, "closure" is reunderstood as a beginning and as the necessary renewal and dissemination of the community's voice.

My Diary from Here to There

Unlike Mora's and Rodriguez's picture books, the migration plot of Amada Irma Pérez's 2002 autobiographical bilingual picture book *My Diary from Here to There*, illustrated by Maya Christina Gonzalez and winner of the Pura Belpré Award, directly features the United States–Mexico border, thus raising questions about how to depict to child readers border crossings and the difficult experiences of immigration. Most of the story involves waiting: Amada migrates from Mexico to the United States with her family but must wait in the Mexican border town of Mexicali while her father, a U.S. citizen, acquires green cards for the rest of the family. As with *América Is Her Name*, writing—in this case, in her diary—helps Amada navigate her experiences of loss and homesickness. Specifically, the story's multiliterate strategy—its presentation of writing as a visual and tangible mode of representation— strongly legitimates Amada's documentation of her border crossing and conveys its continuing relevance to U.S. readers.

One of the text's most interesting strategies for highlighting the materiality of writing is its integration of the story's words into the actual illustrations. Often, the words themselves are framed inside parts of the picture so that they take on the role of ornamental art. This extends the writing into broader systems of communication, as we "read" words not just for their meaning but also for their material presence, their visual placement, and their appearance. When the words become art, their tangibility and materiality become dramatized, and the experiences of migration and deportation that they convey take on an urgent immediacy. The visuals themselves, like Colón's illustrations for *Tomás and the Library Lady*, look like painterly brushstrokes and favor unthreatening curves rather than energetic lines, creating a retrospective tone that seems to memorialize the events in the very moment that it narrates them. Such memorialization is particularly appropriate given how the picture book stresses the process of its protagonist's artistic development. Pérez's book creates a metanarrative in which, as Rocío Davis notes in her examination of ethnic autobiographies, the materials of the past are shaped by memory and imagination to serve present consciousness (139). In Pérez's case, that present consciousness is a writerly one intent on documentation and recording: at the end of the story, Amada exclaims, "Maybe someday I'll write a book about our journey!" (30) as a reminder that the tangible book that we are reading contains and creates the story of its own genesis. Even when she is not shown writing, Amada's diary appears in almost every visual, functioning as a traveling companion, a treasured object, and an antidote to the uprooting of migration.

The narrative shows how the "mediated quality" of autobiographical writing allows the reader "to witness the process that leads to the writing of [the] book," so that "the interaction between the writer and the reader . . . acquires heightened importance" (Davis 141). When, for example, the illustration shows the Spanish words that Amada writes in her diary and the written text replicates those exact words for us ("I know I should be asleep already, but I just can't sleep" / "Sé que ya debería estar durmiendo, pero no puedo dormir" [3]), the bond between the protagonist and the reader is strengthened, as seeing the original diary script makes us recognize the narrative's integrity and authenticity. Amada's voice speaks to the picture book's readers and simultaneously displays itself as a tangible document within the text. Because the protagonist will become a writer, the story also dramatizes the relationship between the experiencing self and the narrating self, closing the gap between the Mexican girl and the U.S. author and between past and present. And because the text focuses not only on immigration and border crossing but also on the process that led to the writing of the book that we hold, issues of immigration are repositioned as continually unfolding and narratable experiences beyond the frame of the story. This is a politically empowering move on the part of the author because it demonstrates an immediate recording of these events and turns the experience into an aesthetically valuable literary event. As the protagonist is destined to become a writer, her migration and border crossing also become acts of literary self-invention.

The diary format itself is, I argue, particularly appropriate for documenting the migrant writer's experiences because its narrative is mediated by interactive and participatory modes of representation. By definition, diary writing continually foregrounds the subject's writerly persona, and because the writing imagines an audience—whether it is the "diary" as a reader or someone beyond that—it is also continually informed by addressee consciousness. Unlike letters, diaries do not expect reciprocity, but they do imagine a reader. The intimacy of voice that we get with any first-person narrative is thus enhanced by the dynamic interaction of the (imagined) reader and writer, which is more materially present in the frame of the story than it would be in a nonjournalistic relation of events. Diaries are also infamously secretive, serving well as domestic narratives of politically significant but dangerous experiences and allowing for the writer's release of emotions, so that they preserve and archive testimonials for future remembrance. Amada is no exception to this rule, exclaiming that "if I don't write this all down, I'll burst!" (3). Because they are private, diaries seem to disclose true feelings, earning our trust. Finally, a diary's voice is both literate and oral, participating in both the standard features of writing—permanence, words separated from their speaker—and the standard features of orality, as it imagines and anticipates an audience in the very moment of its performative utterances. When read out loud as a picture storybook, the diary's speakerly presence and oral literacy function as both recorded *and* oral testimonials that move reading beyond the purely literary realm into a multiply literate space, one that encourages a broadly empathic relationship between the reader and the protagonist.

Given that the whole story ends with Amada and her Mexican friend Michi writing letters, it is clear that the book advocates epistolary narratives—and their inherent communicative exchange—as well as journal writing for its documentation of migration. In one important instance, Amada's journal expands beyond her individual writer's voice to include her father's voice. While she waits for her father to obtain green cards for the family, she receives a letter from him that she pastes into her diary. She announces that she is doing so: "We got a letter from Papá today! I'm pasting it into your pages, Diary" (19), making the reader aware of the production, activity, and work of writing, and in that moment foregrounding herself as a narrating rather than experiencing subject. Like a diary, an epistolary narrative is, of course, defined through its addressee consciousness, but it also depends on reciprocity and an exchange of voices. In embedding the epistolary narrative within her diary, Amada combines the narrative qualities of both forms of writing, creating a patchwork collage of migration made up of collective reciprocal voices (the letter) and memorializing documentation (the diary). The illustration clearly emphasizes the pasting activity, showing a large bottle of glue and her father's letter stuck into the open journal, as well as Amada's own writing implements nearby. The illustration, an idyllic pastoral landscape, appears to contradict the information in her father's letter, which mentions the "hard, tiring work" picking grapes and strawberries in the fields of Delano and cautions that getting their green cards has been difficult (19). However, if we read the written text visually—something we are encouraged to do because Papá's words are decoratively framed by the accompanying pictures (butterflies and brightly colored bunches of grapes)—the contradiction is resolved. Read visually, the words become ornamental, and like a memorializing plaque they emphasize not only his description of the hard labor but also his quoting of Cesar Chavez's "new words" that "hold the hope of better conditions for us farmworkers" (19). Rather than tension, the effect is a reconciliation of diary with letter, visual with written narratives, and childish innocence with adult experience.

The picture book's strategy of making its writing visually arresting thus asks us to read the words for their material presence, not just for their semantic meaning. As the story narrates the journey of migration and the United States–Mexico border, its written and visual texts continue to intersect in ways that foreground the materiality of the book. When the family sets off on their journey in the car, the words (describing the trip as long and hard) spatially combine with the illustration. Specifically, the image shows a close-up of the car moving through a desert landscape, with the words of the story contained inside the picture of the car, Spanish on one side and English on the other. Here, visual and written narratives cannot be separated, suggesting that during migration, the words of the story must be contained and packaged, like luggage. Again, words become tangible and visually important objects. In addition, because the car frames the words we read, it becomes in itself a book of sorts, in that it conveys and carries words inside it and is also, obviously, emblematic of the family's uprooting. When the car (symbolizing the experience of migration) and the journal (symbolizing the narrative of migration) thus intersect, experience and narrative become inseparable.

Later, when Amada's father leaves for L.A., writing and illustrations blend once more: the Spanish written text that describes the father's departure is enclosed inside the part of the road that the car drives away on, while the English text appears inside the window of the grandmother's house. Again, experiences of departure (the traveled road) highlight their own narrative status (the words inside the road). Once the family has crossed the border, Amada's description of how one woman and her children are "kicked off the bus" (27) by the immigration patrol appears on the side of the illustrated bus. For undocumented migrants, the border extends into the entire nation-space, and the book suggests that such experiences of deportation must be communicated in a multiliterate way: the words are visually and dramatically framed and literally documented on the side of the bus for everyone to see.

The book's depiction of the border itself presents the ambiguous separating and joining of U.S. and Mexican identity constructions. As if to reiterate the point that the border is real and cannot easily be crossed, the story shows the family driving *along* it for a long while. But at the same time, Amada comments that "Mexico and the U.S. are two different countries but they look exactly the same on both sides of the border" (13), and the illustration shows an identical topography on both sides of the border, teaching the child reader that the political border is an artificial construct. The border region's complexity is even more evident when the story describes the family's border crossing, because the actual moment of crossing does not get recorded in the present. Amada's diary begins, "My first time writing in the USA!" (25), and explains that they are in California waiting for the bus to Los Angeles. Amada then goes on to describe the border crossing, but it is a retrospective narrative written from within the United States, after the event. Although the illustration of the crossing shows Amada's red diary peeking out of her bag, implying her potential recording of this experience, her inability to write from within the experience itself suggests something of its traumatic nature; the border zone resists narrativization. Amada's family crosses legally, with Mamá holding their green cards "close to her heart" (27), but the experience is nevertheless frightening: "Crossing the border in Tijuana was crazy. Everyone was pushing and shoving. There were babies crying, and people fighting to be first in line. We held hands the whole way" (25). The accompanying visual, however, shows a group of orderly and smiling people waiting calmly.[9] Even in a child's picture book of authorized crossing, then, the border is a site of ambivalence: it both is and is not a specific place that can be easily identified and marked; it is both undialectical and narratable; it is a place of danger (if you do not have the correct legal status) and joyful anxiety (if you do); and it is both a line and an entire nation.

My Diary from Here to There's use of diary-epistolary formats, its attention to the broader literacy of words, and its nuanced border area all capture the contradictions of migration for its child audience. Furthermore, its bilingualism enhances the complex relationship between protagonist and author that unfolds throughout the story and turns this record of migration into an exploration of connections between national identity and language development. In their examination of the ideologies of language in U.S. children's literature, María Paula Ghiso and Gerald Campano suggest that readers need to notice what language hierarchies are interrogated or reified in the books (48). In this storybook there are visual reminders that the events of the story take place in Spanish, as the illustrations show Amada writing in her journal in Spanish and moving boxes labeled in Spanish. Presumably the experiencing self is a monolingual Spanish speaker; the narrating self is bilingual. Spanish thus brings together the protagonist and author, as it is both the language of origin and the continuous language. But in terms of reading practice, neither language seems privileged: the placement of English and Spanish varies throughout, so that at times the reader encounters English first (on the left-hand side of the page) and at other times Spanish, making the reading a somewhat playful and interactive experience. In this respect, *My Diary* validates the hybrid language practice of many Latinxs, and of course encourages a broader readership of both Spanish and non-Spanish speakers.

The focus on literacy in Mora's *Tomás and the Library Lady*, Rodriguez's *América Is Her Name*, and Pérez's *My Diary from Here to There* represents an important way forward for Chicanx (and, more broadly, Latinx) artists and authors and is significant in a number of ways. First, because the reader must engage in literacy to enjoy literacy as the subject matter of the story, it self-reflexively advocates its own existence. It advocates its own existence in the very moment of its unfolding. Second, as discussed above, it provides stability, vicarious imaginative experiences, and the documentation of migrant experiences. As one of the nation's most powerful cultural products, literacy contributes to the building and making of the child citizen. But the way that literacy functions in these texts demonstrates more than just an interest in motivating and developing young children's reading skills. Because of their presentation of multiliteracy, all the books examined here also advocate the idea of nationhood as an interdependent endeavor. Employing intersecting literacies (reading and writing as visual, oral, gestural, and tactile experiences) is a strategy of interdependence because none of these modes of representation and communication functions on its own. In this respect, the books affirm "an interdependent cultural ethos and legacy that may stand in stark contrast to more self-reliant ideologies of personhood" (Ghiso and Campano 52).

Furthermore, this interdependent cultural ethos allows the books to position Chicanx and Latinx experiences inside the historical narrative of writing and literacies. Damián Baca argues that although Latinxs are often situated outside of this historical narrative, they in fact are heirs to a rich legacy of Indigenous writing: Mexican and Central American codices, which use multiliterate strategies. He describes how Mesoamerican rhetoric required use of the "entire body through choreography, recitation, chanting, and choral production" (72), while coded scripts depend on graphic specific marks such as painting, drawing, and pictography (1). These rhetorics critique enduring power structures and work "to create 'new' literacies: new ways of speaking, writing and reading" (2, 3). As well as advocating interdependent (rather than individualistic) practices of nation building, then, multiliteracy also points to legacies of writing beyond the borders of the United States, suggesting that these picture books represent a new direction for Chicanx children's literature. With this new direction, the authors and illustrators offer young Chicanx readers the possibility of complete literacy. They build personal and national identities through ambivalent migration (rather than the journey model of home-return-home) and recognize interdependent rather than individualistic practices of personhood, acknowledging transnational and hemispheric migrant voices and experiences as part of U.S. culture's ongoing practice of nation building.

CHAPTER 2

"What Should We American Farmers Be Without the Distinct Possession of That Soil?"

Homesteading and the Cultivation of Citizenship in Cynthia DeFelice's
Under the Same Sky and Julia Alvarez's *Return to Sender*

In 1782, J. Hector St. John de Crèvecoeur, a French cartographer and surveyor who traveled widely in the American colonies before settling down to marriage and life as a New York farmer and man of letters, published his famous *Letters from an American Farmer*, which presented an idyll of colonial American life. Broadly speaking, the letters, written by the character James, establish the superiority of small local government over large government and monarchy, but some critics have argued that the letters, in "expressing the spirit of the place," also mark the beginnings of "American literature and the voice of our national consciousness" (Stone 7). Most relevant for our purposes here are the connections forged in this seminal text between the cultivation of owned land and the cultivation of American citizenship. Crèvecoeur was eager to demonstrate how certain fundamental American cultural values—meritocracy, work ethic, and assimilation—are bound up in a specific moral geography, a crucial tie to the physical land itself, and through his descriptions of farming we see how geography and physical place become important measures of cultural and national character. Without a doubt, from the eighteenth century onward, land and its cultivation from wilderness to farmland becomes connected to definitions of political and cultural belonging, citizenship, and national identity. For Crèvecoeur "political felicity" (42) as well as "our rank, our freedom, our power as citizens" directly emerge from and are founded upon the conversion of "formerly rude soil" into "a pleasant farm" (54). Crèvecoeur's rhetoric identifies a connection between geography and nationhood at the precise moment when the American nation was in transition and in formation, shaking off one empire and simultaneously forging itself as one. Thomas Jefferson, in fact, later famously praised farmers as "the chosen people of God" and adapted the ideals of physiocracy—a school of thought that believes that the wealth and virtue of nations reside in the cultivation of land—to the American environment, declaring that "the cultivators of the earth are the most valuable citizens" (426).[1]

It is not, however, just the work of cultivation that forges this national belonging but specifically the cultivation of one's *own* soil. Beginning in the sixteenth century, the British Isles and other areas of northern Europe passed various enclosure acts, which privatized agricultural land and made common land access illegal. This forced peasant farmers off previously commonly held agricultural land, and they started arriving in the United States as immigrants. In the American colonies, they sought to secure land tenure for themselves, creating a system where land became an important commodity for investment and trade. According to Horst and Marion, since then "the value of farmland has been seen as an appreciable asset, apart from its use value for food cultivation" (2). A century later, Crèvecoeur's James, as Crèvecoeur's mouthpiece, describes returning home to his American farm as follows: "The instant I enter my own land, the bright idea of property, of exclusive right, of independence, exalt my mind. Precious soil . . . What should we American farmers be without the distinct possession of that soil?" (54). In this context of the late eighteenth century, the term "American farmer" referred specifically to a freeholder, a man without a master, rather than a tenant that (as in Europe) owed taxes and paid tithes. This "important distinction in the evolving definition of what it meant to be an American" (Manning xviii) has established a powerful legacy of property as sacred, and Crèvecoeur's ensuing belief that when you are an independent farmer who "does not riot on the labour of others," you enable "the most perfect society now existing in the world" (67).

Critical and literary attention to the ways in which farming and farm labor construct national identity shows how the United States continues to invest in a cultural narrative that positions the white male farmer as an ideal citizen and a "paragon of national integrity" (Wald 3). Of course, the actual number of U.S. citizens who work in agriculture has steeply declined over the twentieth century, so that "in the twenty-first century United States, access to agrarian virtue does not require actual agrarian labor" (3). As discussed by S. Bender, at the time of the nation's founding, 90 percent of U.S. labor was involved in agriculture, while today, as corporate agriculture displaces family farms, farming employs only 2 percent of the U.S. workforce. Data also show clear evidence of ongoing racial, ethnic, and gender disparities in agriculture in the United States: a National Agricultural Workers Survey conducted by the U.S. Department of Labor in 2001–2 found that 75 percent of U.S. farmworkers were born in Mexico and 81 percent spoke Spanish as a native language, and that most farmworkers (53 percent) are undocumented (59–60). Because the agricultural industry has long turned to the most vulnerable groups (most recently, Mexicans) for its workforce regardless of their immigration status, farmworkers have, according to Bender, "always struggled to be seen as fully human . . . by farmers, politicians, and the consuming public" (60). In addition, they are consistently excluded from federal minimum wage protections, suffer from seasonal unemployment, and are vulnerable to abuses in pay, housing, and occupational safety (Bender 69).

Given all this, Sarah D. Wald asks, "How can the idea of farming being a sacred calling, the occupation that establishes the virtuous character of the true American citizen, continue to resonate in a culture that also perceives actual agrarian labor as beneath white U.S. citizens and as the natural domain of undocumented labor?" (4). As in the eighteenth century, we can still look at farm labor to understand how narratives of national membership and belonging are established, although now the new cultural logic produces "both sentimentalized depictions of the white farmer as iconic U.S. citizen and representations of Asian and Latinx farmworkers as 'abject aliens,' individuals whose labor is necessary for the nation while their humanity is rendered alien and excluded." In fact, the white citizen farmer persists as an ideal "only in relation to representations of nonwhite farm laborers" as abject aliens (5). The racial scripts that determined Jefferson's understanding of land cultivation—both land and people of color needed to be benevolently conquered by the white farmer—are now "reactivated" in relationship to undocumented Latinx laborers and rest on a binary in which the American farmer is a disembodied and universal abstraction of citizenship, an abstract person that "renders the presumed whiteness and maleness of the citizen invisible." Meanwhile, of course, farmworkers are "inherently embodied" and highly marked by their race, gender, class, and citizenship status (7).

The importance of property, and of being "in possession" of the soil you cultivate, remains a powerful determinant of this dual narrative of abstract citizen versus embodied laborer in both industrial agriculture settings and smaller family farm establishments. As Anne Shea points out, when pushing for exceptions to labor laws or fighting unionizing efforts, today's growers still use the mythologized rhetoric of the all-American farmer: "For the owner of the farm, work seems to ennoble. The growers' labor, read through the filter of American national identity construction, renders the growers as 'industrious': the farmer enriches himself and the nation," while that same farmwork is "demeaning for the hired hand" (131). Although both the farmer and the hired help cultivate the land, owning the land allows that act of cultivation to establish or maintain citizenship. Conversely, demeaned labor separates migrant workers from community membership by reducing their bodies into disassembled parts (tools, hands, commodities). It also allows the romance of the white citizen farmer (particularly the family farmer) to endure: his presumed ownership of the land establishes his personhood, while the laborer's personhood is extinguished by his disassembled and marked body. This is particularly evident, for example, in mainstream celebrations of local and organic produce, which often romanticize family farms and ignore "the labor needs of such farms and their frequent reliance on the same racialized hierarchies that mark industrial agriculture" (Wald 192). One of the most tragic ironies emerging from the intersection of the U.S. agricultural system and the food movement's dietary ideal (which emphasizes fresh fruit and vegetables), of course, is how the laborer has vanished from the moral equation. The laborer's body is rendered invisible, unskilled, and frequently sick by the very work of cultivating and harvesting produce that optimizes the consumers' own physical health and well-being.[2] Moreover, the laborer's body is often racially and ideologically marked as innately suited to stoop labor. Such visible invisibility is indicative of the symbolic violence of U.S. immigration policies, which enable workplace vulnerabilities and a labor system in which, as Bourgois notes, migrants are disposable, replaceable, and deportable (xiii). For such workers, land labor creates prejudice and illegitimate belonging instead of national membership.

The two middle-grade novels I explore in this chapter, Cynthia DeFelice's *Under the Same Sky* and Julia Alvarez's *Return to Sender*, represent an intervention into classic American farming narratives, demonstrating how farm landscapes have become politicized and traumatized by the dynamics of migration, and acknowledging the impact of that politicization. They force a cultural shift by exposing the instability of the system and the mutual vulnerabilities of both farmers and laborers and counter the cultural abjection of and prejudice toward demeaned laborers by asserting their personhood and humanity. In both texts, farmland, initially unmarked by anything beyond the white protagonists' own narrow experiences, is reimagined as they bear witness to the experiences of migrant laborers and undergo their own maturation process. Through these experiences, the landscape becomes an explicit site of political and cultural disruption that allows both American and migrant characters to connect to, and also become severed from, the nation. This politicization of farmland is not new, of course—Crèvecoeur himself imagined that through farming, individuals of all nations would be transformed and naturalized, "melted into a new race of men" (70)—but rather than the farm establishing and cultivating citizens, it now often questions or denies American citizenship. At the same time, the paradigm of belonging shifts, as the farm becomes a space of transnational or even global identity and an expansive place of multitudes, with connections that reach beyond the nation's political borders. Place, for Doreen Massey, is made up of social relations that extend beyond *this* place: it is "a site of meaning and subjectivity . . . not bounded or counterposed to abstracted space" (294). This paradigm shift impacts readers too: in making the farm a transnational site for the protagonists, both texts potentially position readers "across locations and times, making visible contemporary overlapping politics of border crossing, global markets, and cultural production across spaces and its implications for transmigrant communities" (Brochin and Medina 4). They thus draw attention to the "often ignored relationship between children and globalization" (A. García, "'We'" 105). As in the eighteenth century, twenty-first-century literary depictions of farming still depict it as a transformative experience, one that enables a process of maturation for children that is deeply connected to acquiring a new cultural and political literacy and becoming educated about the relationship between land, property, and national belonging.

Under the Same Sky

Cynthia DeFelice's 2003 novel *Under the Same Sky* has attracted a number of positive reviews but has not received much critical attention.[3] It nevertheless represents an important contribution to children's writing about migrant laborers because, as Loewen notes, literature for children "systematically erases and silences the migrant experience," which means that "for the vast majority of us, migrants are hidden behind heroic-like oversimplified and culturally iconic white farmers" (19). Both *Return to Sender* and *Under the Same Sky* provide counternarratives that, among other things, fracture and complicate the iconic farmer figure, and both do so in part through the perspective of a white protagonist. *Under the Same Sky* is narrated by fourteen-year-old Joe Pederson, the son of a white farmer in upstate New York, who gradually develops the more mature ethical stance of a white adolescent ally. The first-person point of view creates an "engaging narration that immerses the [adolescent] reader and creates empathy with illicit action" as "readers actualize the narrative for themselves as for the characters" and learn that they too have agency and can disrupt the social system if they choose to (Wylie 192). In the novel, Joe spends his summer vacation working alongside the Mexican laborers on his father's farm in order to earn enough money to buy himself an expensive motorbike. Initially, he is resentful and unskilled, but over time he gains new perspectives due to his experience laboring in the fields, his exposure to the problems and fears that the Mexicans live with every day, and his growing attachment to the workers. The story culminates with Joe playing a pivotal role in helping two of the undocumented migrants escape to a different farm in order to evade the Immigration and Naturalization Service (INS). By the end of the novel, DeFelice's new farm landscape has transformed into a complex politicized space of both transnational belonging and national estrangement.

Citizen Farmers and Demeaned Migrant Laborers

In the novel, the binary of citizen farmer and demeaned migrant laborer operates out of a set of economic, cultural, and social conditions that reflect the realities of life in small American farming towns since the late 1990s, when a combination of factors (an increase in agribusiness and declining numbers of farm children remaining on the family farm after high school) exacerbated the worker shortage problem. The Pederson farm, in other words, faces economic challenges, while the Mexican crew hired to work and live on the farm must grapple with the challenges of being ethnic and racial others in upstate New York. At the opening of the story, Joe feels no emotional attachment to the farm and is actively resentful of his ancestral connection to the soil: "Nobody had ever asked me if I wanted to grow up on a farm eight miles from town, in the middle of nowhere. My dad was born here, and so were his father and grandfather and probably his great-grandfather too," but "I hated it. Town was where all the action was. If I never saw another cabbage field or apple orchard in my entire life, it would be just fine with me" (3–4). Predictably, then, the idea of laboring all summer sounds like "my worst nightmare. Working for my father, doing some hot, boring farm job like hoeing cabbage" (8). Joe's restlessness is a marker of his immaturity and inexperience; even Crèvecoeur, it should be noted, recalls that "when young, I entertained some thoughts of selling my farm" because "I thought it afforded but a dull repetition of the same labors and pleasures. I thought the former tedious and heavy, the latter few and insipid" (52). While many maturation stories depend on the trope of a journey away from home for the protagonist's growth, DeFelice's novel, perhaps following in the literary footsteps of *Letters*, shows the maturity, growth, and transformative belonging that occur when the child "journeys" by attentively and critically staying in place.

Several critics have also discussed the agricultural industry's inability to attract U.S. citizen workers to the fields, a topic explicitly addressed in the novel. Both Pitt and Wald describe the United Farm Workers' 2010 "Take Our Jobs" social media campaign, which, in an effort to prove that the food supply chain depends on undocumented individuals, offered to find farmwork opportunities for all interested U.S. citizens and permanent residents while also cautioning applicants about the physical challenges of the work. Pitt notes that the campaign attracted a lot of media attention but little interest from job seekers (19), thus exposing, as Wald puts it, "the disdain white people hold for actual stoop labor, as opposed to the idea of farming" and reclassifying undocumented labor as "necessary for the nation" (4). Exactly reflecting this, Joe's mother explains the family's need for Mexican laborers: "The truth is that farmers in this country, including us, couldn't survive without the labor of people like Manuel and the crew . . . It makes me so mad when people fuss about how the foreigners are taking American jobs. From our experience, that's just not true. We've tried running ads for local workers, and not one person has ever even called. . . . Nobody around here is willing to do that kind of backbreaking labor for what they consider such low pay" (116).

Throughout, the story demonstrates how the binary of white citizen farmer versus demeaned laborer plays out, as Joe's father represents mascu-

linity, strength, and a good work ethic, while the Mexican laborers are frequent targets of town prejudice. Dad's beliefs establish a specific pedagogical
framework within the story that aligns normative values about masculinity,
hard work, and the value of money with a deep connection to the land. According to Joe, Dad "took farm work pretty seriously" and "was always saying
farming was the best way for a man to make a living" (64) because "his ancestors did it" (15). He believes that Joe must "find out what a real day's work
feels like" (8) and downplays the danger of farmwork for children, "always
going on and on about the good old days, when he did a full day's work in
the fields starting at age ten" (9). Although their mother worries about the
risks, she too is a "good farm wife" (100) who understands, as Joe puts it, how
"growing food to feed the world was the most noble, honest labor there was,
blah blah blah" (17). And rather than physically weakening and psychologically demeaning him, Dad's years of laboring in the fields have strengthened
his body and energized his soul: "His face was *rugged* from years of working
outdoors, and his eyes *blazed* a startling blue" (5, my italics). Joe's dismissive rejection of the farm and his mocking insinuations that such narratives
are tedious, irrelevant, and outdated ("going on and on," "blah blah blah")
position him perfectly for a series of teachable moments and transformative
experiences over the events of the story.

The ideal of the white citizen farmer is maintained by immigration policies (both as enacted laws and as practiced by agricultural growers) that
establish certain cultural and societal norms for how laborers can be treated.
Anne Shea explains how "agricultural interests have had their hand in immigration legislation throughout the twentieth century," at times pressuring the
state to open borders and at other times calling for increased enforcement
(126).[4] Immigration law, with its long history of racial discrimination, creates
an explicit and implicit juxtaposition of laborer against citizen/owner, so that
the laborer comes to be categorized and conceptualized, discursively and
ideologically, as a noncitizen, outside the rights of citizenship and outside
national definition (129–30). As Steven Bender points out, such attitudes
permit dehumanized and harsh conditions for the migrant labor workforce
(61) because of how labor power is embodied and marked by ideologies of
race and inferiority (Mitchell 10). Mexican farmworkers, in other words, are
vital workers whose racial and ethnic otherness makes them particularly
suitable for field work, while rendering their eligibility for citizenship, belonging, and property rights always suspect.[5]

The text shows multiple ways in which Mexican migrants suffer both linguistic and physical violence that is always closely tied to the fact of their field labor. Town prejudice against Mexicans, according to Joe's mother, happens simply because the locals do not personally know any of the workers (101); to an extent, even Joe initially finds the Mexicans unknowable. At first, they are unimportant and interchangeable: he remarks "a bunch of them came every April and left around November, when the harvest was done. I didn't pay too much attention" (10). When he imagines working alongside them, he more closely confronts what it might mean to engage with a group that up until this moment has only been, quite literally, part of the farm landscape: "Suddenly I saw in my mind a group of dark-skinned, dark-haired, raggedly dressed people . . . moving slowly down long rows of plants, their backs bent, their bodies swaying with the movement of their hoes" (15). Joe cannot imagine himself "in the middle of that scene" (15); the stereotyped view of dark-raced bodies performing stoop labor presents a picture of demeaned servitude that has nothing to do with the white citizen farmer's son. Nevertheless, he goes from ignoring them to gazing at them: "It was something I'd seen on farms all around us for as long as I could remember, but for the first time I was really *seeing* it" (15), and while his gaze is objectifying and voyeuristic, it makes the migrants visible and is an important first step in recognizing their personhood.

An even more significant cultural construction of the demeaned laborer lies in its association with criminality. Steven Bender notes how the subhuman construction of "illegals" or "illegal aliens" does not stop with immigration status but rather "extends to their supposed propensities, once in the United States, toward criminal behavior" (38) and that "stereotypes against Latinos/as have been routinely employed to resist measures to benefit field workers" (72). In the text, field labor is consistently associated with criminality: Joe's friend Randy remarks that Joe will be spending the summer "on one of your father's chain gangs" (13) and refers to the work as "slave labor" (14, 20), while Joe himself anticipates that the summer will feel like "a prison sentence" (16). When Joe uncomfortably corrects Randy—"they're not chain gangs . . . they're work crews"—Randy retorts, "But aren't all those guys, like, greasers?" (13), perpetuating the correlation between criminality, ethno-racial othering, and farmwork. The correlation is so strong that Joe himself, his friends jokingly insinuate, will become Mexican and foreign through doing such labor. In other words, the only way for the children to rationalize and understand Joe's work is to interpellate him as Mexican, through a framework of humor that not only maintains stereotypes but also separates Joe from his peer group. For the humor to work, it must depend on a shared understanding, and when Joe ignores their jokes or refuses to laugh, he refuses to participate in the group's linguistic xenophobia. Part of the humor also rests on the unspoken incredulity of the situation: the epithets suggest that the boys don't see the Mexicans as human, so to imply that Joe could ever be friends with them, or be like them, is to imply something impossible.

Another part of this "humor" involves linguistic mimicry, as around Joe, Randy begins to deliberately and emphatically overuse popular Spanish words or phrases that have made it into mainstream English. His utterances make Spanish both disappear into mainstream English (becoming co-opted) and display itself as visibly foreign. For example, Randy and the others repeatedly address Joe as "Señor José," mockingly direct racial and stereotypical slurs toward him ("Why you not working een the fields earning *mucho dinero*?") and urge him to quickly learn Spanish "so you can spic to your *amigos*. Get it? *Spic* to your *amigos*?" (14). While Joe is obviously never under any real threat, he is here positioned as a stand-in for their target practice against the more vulnerable population. Their weaponizing of Spanish symbolizes the way that rhetoric normalizes the mistreatment of Mexicans, because on the surface, of course, it also looks like the boys are just playing around with Spanish words. But later in the story, when Randy and his brother, Tony, argue with Joe about the presence of Mexicans in town, they switch from an economic argument to a cultural one—"The thing I can't understand is why people like your father hire those guys, when they could give jobs to real Americans . . . Look, what I'm saying is that they don't belong here. They don't even talk English" (141)—and try to support their claims by spouting defensive platitudes about "freedom of speech" and it being a "free country" (142). Thus, we see how in order to preserve Crèvecoeur's "most perfect society" (which they fear is disappearing), they wield their "power as citizens" and the nation's founding values (freedom, assimilation) to legitimate their aggression. And in this context, where land cultivation is so closely tied to those founding values, the narratives of white farmer (citizen) and migrant laborer (demeaned, undocumented) also rest on narratives of inclusion and exclusion, where "real" Americans are separated from the imposters.

Labor, Masculinity, and Belonging on the Farm

Although the narrative depicts the dichotomy of white farmer / abstract citizen versus demeaned laborer / Mexican, it also challenges it. As a result, the idealized space of the farm becomes disrupted and eventually reimagined as a cultivating ground for transnational as well as national citizenship. These disruptions drive Joe's maturation journey over the course of the story as he learns to navigate the various conflicting ideologies of the landscape, which, he slowly realizes, is the site of unbelonging, trauma, and violence for the Mexican workers (particularly overdetermined by policy and law), as well as the site of his own heroism and transformation into a strong, masculine citizen farmer. A central part of this transformation involves Joe acquiring experiential knowledge of manual farmwork and thus adjusting his preconceived notions that such work is unskilled. This becomes the nexus around which his anxiety about his masculinity and his status as the farmer's son revolve. In other words, the American farm requires the citizen farmer's son to perform field labor with dignity and strength, proving (and providing) a continuity of masculine belonging on the farm and in the nation.

Initially, Joe finds that in the fields he is more of a demeaned laborer than a citizen farmer (or farmer's son). Because he starts off feeling entitled, he is especially appalled at how he is treated: "I, Joe, the boss's son, had to walk [behind the crew in the tractor] in the wet, clumpy soil, racing back and forth across all four rows, checking each plant to make sure it had been securely stuck, right side up, in the dirt, and bending down to replant it if it wasn't. Unbelievable" (32). This particularly grates because "it was my father's tractor, and my father's farm" (34). His own assumptions about the supposed ease of farm labor reflect cultural norms: Klocker et al. comment that the "manual" work done by farm laborers—picking and packing fruits and vegetables and pruning vines and trees—is "widely designated unskilled" and that "in policy, media, academic, activist and everyday discourses, hired farm work is framed as something anybody can do" (463). The "unskilled" label in fact sets a foundation for the exploitation and vulnerability of hired farmworkers "as a disposable workforce" that is also subject to ethno-racial stereotypes that aggravate their exploitation and "deny their personhood," because they attribute certain qualities (work ethic, endurance, stoicism, nimble fingers, strong arms, for example) as "natural 'racial' traits" rather than a result of horticultural experience, knowledge, and skill (464). In the text, Joe too initially assumes that the work will be "no sweat" (23), asking rhetorically, "How hard could it be?" (27), but quickly learns firsthand about the tedium, fatigue, and physical pain involved: "The work was so boring and monotonous that there was nothing to think about except my own misery. My mind constantly went over every little aspect of my body's pain and discomfort" (33–34). He describes dead bugs and straw stuck to his "sweat-drenched skin" that make him itch, blisters that have "formed and popped on my heels" rubbed raw by his boots, and his back "killing me from bending over five billion times" (35–36). His body becomes painfully marked by the labor: he notes how "my shoulders and arms were on fire from sunburn" (37) and, after moving from setting cabbage to the "excruciating pain" of picking strawberries, declares that "every inch of muscle, every tendon, and every bone in my body hurt" (84).

The physical pain of field labor is also compounded by the humiliation that Joe experiences and the emasculation that seems to result from it. He feels like an "idiot" (29) not knowing much about the day-to-day workings of the farm despite growing up on it, and realizes that without the skill and knowledge to cultivate its fields, he is not really in possession of the soil. And not being in possession of it alienates him from the space and from his status as a citizen farmer, as he is surrounded by the Mexican work crew who appear to be more physically comfortable on his homestead than he is and to enjoy one another's camaraderie on it because of their shared cultural identity. While their bodies seem to blend naturally with the landscape (one of them, for example, is described as "really dark, with wrinkles that resembled furrows in a plowed field" [30]), Joe's "gringo face" turns "bright-red-and-pale-striped" from the sun (38). He is also acutely aware of his presence as a symbolic worker rather than a real one ("You've got eight workers and Joe," remarks his father to the crew leader, Manuel [29]) and feels infantilized and ignored by his father: "I didn't like the way they were talking about me as if I wasn't standing right in front of them" (81). Rather than performing the sacred work of cultivation and citizenship, then, Joe takes on the role of a demeaned laborer who experiences pain, otherness, invisibility, and shame.

On the farm, Joe's abjection intersects with his desperate desire to win his father's recognition and approval, most specifically as a strong man. The power dynamics are complicated because Dad repeatedly seems to treat Manuel, the crew boss, as the son he never had—one with a strong work ethic, a mature sense of responsibility, and a skilled body—while Joe looks on jealously: "I watched Dad smile at Manuel and slap him on the shoulder in a kind of man-to-man gesture. For a minute, I hoped that I, too, would feel that same comradely hand on my shoulder" (29). Manuel's physique is impressively manly; in contrast to Joe's pink-striped gringo face, Manuel's back and arms are brown, and "the muscles showed beneath his skin . . . Anybody could tell he was in charge just by the way he moved" (40). He is also superbly skilled: "The motion of his hoe looked smooth and effortless" (60). Noticing how Manuel is positioned as the pseudo-son and longing to hear his father say *"Nice work, son"* (65), Joe becomes determined to work harder and gain the necessary skills to belong: "I wasn't going to give Dad any reason to think I wasn't a 'worker,' just as good as anybody else" (36). In one episode, Joe rushes through picking strawberries to keep up with Manuel's pace and fill his quarts as fast as possible. Consequently, his "work" looks "awful" (87), and he has to listen to his father's remonstrations: "None of these other people . . . would dream of picking a quart of berries that looked like this" (87). After this, Joe is determined to "pick perfect quarts . . . and let that do the talking for me" (91). In this landscape one's labor speaks to one's worth and provides evidence of one's ability and character. In other words, a real worker cares about the quality of the product, and skilled labor takes "years of experience" and knowledge (89).[6]

Here, in an important pedagogical moment where the protagonist (and possibly the reader) learns that farm labor is specialized and intricate, the text mirrors critical scholarship. Manuel Romero, for example, explains how different crops and different stages of growth and production (planting, harvesting, packing) require a varying set of skills that must be taught and developed: "There are . . . a number of abilities needed to do this job. Some . . . are related to the commodity's specification, like recognizing the fruit that meets the required conditions and cutting it without damaging the trees . . . Other abilities are related to becoming adapted to the job and doing it in a less exhausting way" (77). Brown and Duguid elaborate on this, arguing, for example, that factory workers must "exercise insight and judgement based on accumulated wisdom" (45) and that hands-on work involves muscle memory and thinking. The worker, therefore, is "reconceived as a reflective practitioner" (Schon qtd. in Klocker et al. 466). Through Joe's many detailed descriptions of the job, the text elevates farm labor into complex work that requires expertise and is both physically and mentally exacting in various ways. The explanation of how to set cabbage, for example, reads almost like an instruction manual: "You have to move down the row quickly, sizing up which cabbage plants to leave and which ones to hack down . . . and at the same time attack the weeds . . . The idea is to leave behind the sturdiest, strongest-looking cabbage plants, eighteen inches apart, surrounded by nothing but freshly turned soil" (59–60). Joe cautions that "it sounds simple, but . . . it's not" (59), presumably because hearing about it is not the same as doing it. Similarly, harvesting strawberries requires working fast, knowing which berries to pick and which to leave for another day without bruising them (81, 83). Demeaned labor, clearly, is highly skilled work.

However, recognizing such labor as skilled and specialized does not detract from the pain it causes and the danger it presents. Adjusting to physical pain just means enduring it more quietly: Joe notes that Gilberto, who does not seem bothered by being crouched down all the time, gives a "quiet little groan" whenever he has to rise to his feet (83). The story also remarks several times on the predominance of workplace injuries, either as risks or as realities. One of the crew, David, has lost half his arm in a grain silo (62), while Victor, Manuel's father, is back in Mexico after hurting his back from a job picking apples, and might never work again (57). Victor's only apparent asset—his body—now has less value than it did when he was a laborer. Clearly, the politics of immigration dictates that some bodies are more valuable than others. Joe, for example, notes that "we all knew about farmworkers who'd gotten mangled by machinery or kicked in the head by a cow, or who had worked with a dangerous pesticide and gotten sick" (17), and although he might be referring to American workers, because the majority of workers (both within the story and outside of it) are Latinxs, it is statistically more likely that the majority of farm labor injuries happen to Mexican (or Latinx) bodies. Those bodies, already raced as other, are thus more vulnerable to these workplace traumas, indicating yet another way in which they are deemed less valuable by the system. Joe's mother has worried about the risks of letting her children work on the farm, but the reality is that their bodies are valued highly; it is the Mexican children (Manuel and Luisa) who have no choice but to work and are therefore the most unprotected.

In various ways, then, the text begins to provide new narratives through which to understand farm labor, narratives that depart from or complicate idealized conceptions of farming. In a reversal of the expected binary (white citizen farmer / migrant laborer), it is Manuel rather than Joe that exemplifies the American farmer's virtues: he is skilled, experienced, and physically and emotionally strong; he has a good work ethic; and he is a leader. He is even, we discover, studying for his citizenship exam by listening to lessons on tape while working in the fields. In the eighteenth-century narrative of American farms, Manuel would be an ideal citizen farmer in formation, an individual of a nation ready to "melt" into a "new race of men" by cultivating the soil into American farmland and himself into an American. In the twenty-first-century setting, however, the farm landscape is indicative of a much more problematic belonging because Manuel is not in possession of the soil he cultivates so well, while Joe is (potentially) the owner of a farm he has little interest in cultivating (he plans to go to college someday "and never do farm work again" [58]).

The myth of farming is further deconstructed through the novel's presentation of the U.S. food supply chain's vulnerabilities. Despite her belief that they are doing "noble, honest labor" by growing food to feed the world, Joe's mother also explains the reality of having to keep food costs low: "Nobody wants to pay more for their food. . . . The lawmakers and the politicians know that. They know the whole system relies on cheap labor. Which means foreign labor" (116). When Joe learns the monetary exchange value of his physical labor, he realizes how much less he is paid compared to what he produces. Calculating that they are all making about twenty-two cents for a quart of strawberries, he remarks, "It didn't seem like nearly enough. I was beginning to think of each quart of berries as a small carton of gold . . . judging by the labor involved in picking them, each quart ought to cost a small fortune" (85). Gradually, he begins to defetishize commodities, seeing (and counting) the cost of consumer items in terms of the time spent on field labor. Items are translated into congealed labor, where their worth is suddenly not inherent to the item itself but is instead measured by the work needed to afford the purchase. An evening out with pizza and movies, therefore, is now calculated as "two hours of time spent planting cabbage" (39); later, the motorbike Joe planned to buy with his summer money (in order to fit in with his peer group) seems like a frivolous purchase, as it would represent hours of underpaid labor (152).

In this way, the text interrogates the social meaning of objects and how they might contribute to experiences of belonging and national identity. As Joe matures, he must rethink how he wants to belong to the nation: whether as a prejudiced child who fetishizes commodities (like Randy and his friends) or as a person who can recognize the contradictions and complexities of the nation and work toward social justice. Along with Joe, child readers learn about the discrepancies between the labor of farming, the low wages, and the cost of the final product and the way all this contributes to the invisibility and devaluing of migrant laborers, despite the critical role they play in the food supply chain. On a broader level, this provides a new narrative of farm economy for the reader, who comes to understand the extent to which the twenty-first-century landscape of farming is balanced on an unstable foundation where farmers and undocumented workers are in positions of mutual vulnerability. Discussing the dairy farm model presented in *Return to Sender* (in a comment also applicable to DeFelice's novel), Kristin E. Pitt argues, "If undocumented farmworkers are in a precarious position due to their vulnerability to deportation, citizens of the United States are also in a precarious position given their unreliable access to fresh and affordable food. Undocumented and often invisible farmworkers help conceal this vulnerability, so that many residents of the United States fail to observe either the farm laborers or the nation's food insecurity" (19–20).

The Traumatized Farm-scape

A text such as *Under the Same Sky*, of course, reveals much of this concealed vulnerability and invisibility, and through the story's experiential pedagogy, Joe, too, learns how the whole nation is potentially impacted by the farm's shifting political and economic landscape. He thus gradually becomes educated in the role of the "new" citizen farmer who has to negotiate the realities of twenty-first-century farming. One pertinent reality is that unlike its eighteenth-century model, the actual farm is not a desirable long-term home for most of its workers (the migrants) nor a site of family continuity with the land. It does, however, still provide a framework for the process of Americanization. Whether documented or undocumented, the migrants see it as a space from which they can, with hard work and a strong desire to succeed, prepare for a future elsewhere in the United States. They take lessons in English in the evenings, hoping to one day get a "better job. Bigger, more important, more money" (94). The farm functions as a viable foundation for citizenship for documented characters like Manuel and as a springboard for the American dream for the undocumented characters such as his cousin Luisa, who hopes to eventually save enough for the rest of her family to join her and for them all to somehow "be citizens . . . [and] go to school" (164) because she doesn't want to forever "just pick the fruit and plant the cabbage" (95).

The farm landscape is an apt setting for the enduring nature of the American dream, but at the same time, it is an increasingly unsafe and traumatized landscape as some of the town's inhabitants become more aggressive toward migrant workers. The teens' earlier linguistic violence later develops into direct physical attacks, for example, when locals drive onto the farm in the middle of the night, honking their horns, breaking glass, setting off fireworks and stink bombs, and shouting out epithets: "Aliens!" "Go back to where you came from, beaners," and "Hey, Pancho! This is America!" (73). On the farm, symbolic violence manifests as physical violence. Joe worries, "What if the men who drove through the farm had had guns instead of fireworks and stink bombs?" (110), and indeed the land does become politically marked in this way when the INS shows up later in the story. In that scene, Joe and Luisa are horrified by the officer's gun and the way "his hand was inching toward his holster" (107) when he talks to them. Later that night, as Joe tries to sleep, he remembers "Luisa's terrified face, and the INS man's hand reaching for his pistol" (120). The repeated gesture of *reaching* for the pistol represents a continuous political threat, exemplifying how the ideological state apparatus creates and maintains an ongoing level of fear.

In particular, the threatening landscape becomes an integral part of the undocumented migrants' somatic identities, as they physically respond to and absorb various experiences on the farm. Luisa's body, for example, clearly articulates her growing anxiety. Although she is a skilled worker, her body seems more vulnerable to the physical risks of farmwork (she suffers a severe allergic reaction to a hornet attack, which leaves her body "fallen" and weak [54]) and the psychological strain of being undocumented (after a visit from *la migra*—that is, U.S. Immigration and Customs Enforcement, or ICE—she is afraid to sleep from fear [126]). She does not speak much in the story; to a degree, her vulnerability makes Joe objectify and even exoticize her. Her Mexican body, to Joe, seems troubled beyond its years but also mysteriously wise because it is endangered: "She seemed to be seeing past me to another time or place. Wherever or whenever it was, it made her eyes darken with sadness" (80). He often likens her to a deer, a beautiful and vulnerable creature that is easily startled, fears discovery, and must always be on the alert. She stands "rigid and unmoving" when the INS comes, but unlike a fawn cannot camouflage or blend "into [the] surroundings" (171). The analogy, which implies both her natural belonging and cultural otherness on the land, also problematically renders her into a silent hunted animal and Joe (potentially) into a white savior figure who will rescue her.

The INS's presence, and the fear it maintains and perpetuates, is part of what turns the farm into a traumatized border space for Luisa and several of the other migrants. For them, obviously, the entire geographic space of the nation can operate as a political border; as Ong notes, workers' bodies are "physically coerced through systems of control regulating their movement, in the fields, in the camps, and across borders" (73). But Joe is initially surprised that the border patrol has shown up: "Border patrol? What border? We were smack in the middle of New York State, for crying out loud" (106). His assertion to the officer that "this is our farm" is met with the retort "It's U.S. soil" (107). This strange new geography, where the private property of the farm belongs to the sovereign state (the *soil* itself belongs to the political nation) then forces a more mature questioning of right and wrong, because as Joe reasons to himself, "the border patrol weren't the bad guys, they were the law! And the law meant the good guys, right? I couldn't think straight, I felt so confused and scared" (106). With this instability comes a new political awareness, also, as Joe learns that his family farm in "boring old Stanley, New York, where nothing *ever* happened" (70) is indeed a border, insofar as it is the place that brings one's national identity, citizenship, and belonging into sharp focus. Here, the INS officer studies the crew's papers, staring "intently at them for a long time, as if he had X-ray vision for spotting phonies" (108); such scrutiny implies that the documents not only have the power to legitimate or delegitimate one's presence on the land but also somehow contain within them evidence of personhood.

While the real threat is directed at the migrants rather than at Joe (who points out that however much "the fear and paranoia wore on my nerves," it "had to be even worse for the crew" [121]), at times his narrative perspective focalizes his fear in such a way that his subject position seems to move from white child citizen to Mexican migrant laborer. His empathy turns into identification: he can "feel the fear in the air," describes it as "contagious," and wants to run away without quite knowing why (105). All the workers— the white citizen farmer's son as well as the migrant work crew—become fearful and watchful as the politicized landscape criminalizes them. After the INS leaves (issuing warnings about future raids), they are "all nervous and jittery," with Joe looking over his shoulder every few seconds, "dreading the sight of those white vans with their official green insignias" (121). With the farmland so irrevocably marked by the nation's apparatus of authority, DeFelice demonstrates how the psychological fear and trauma enacted by immigration policies can deeply impact both citizens and noncitizens.

The impact of this fear on the white citizen is illustrated through Joe's realization that he too is interpellated as a particular kind of subject in the nation. In other words, his identification with the migrants' fears actually heightens his awareness of his own white privilege, reminding him of his relative safety and his ethical obligations toward migrants. He also comes to understand that his (and his father's) idealized citizen farmer identities are only normative because they are ascribed as such by a particular national rhetoric. In one exchange with Randy, where Randy asserts that the Mexicans "all look alike to me," Joe decenters American whiteness by responding, "Maybe we all look alike to them. Did you ever think of that?" (42). Later, whiteness is further unpacked. After the incident where the townspeople drive onto the farm at night and throw firecrackers, leaving everyone shaken up, Joe feels personally responsible: "For some reason, I felt like apologizing [to Luisa] for what had happened . . . I wanted her to know all gringos weren't all the same, but how do you say a thing like that?" (79). Here, Joe suddenly experiences his subject position (white and American) as a visible and marked ethno-racial category rather than a normative one, and in feeling like he represents all gringos, he understands the implications of being assessed (potentially) on the basis of that subject position. Nevertheless, he also knows that the broader workings of prejudice are what determine the power dynamics of the nation: near the end of the story, when he is pulled over by a police officer for underage driving, he escapes any real punishment because the officer claims that he has "a [good] feeling about you, Joe" (202). The law may be capricious and at times inexplicable, but readers see how it also structurally favors whiteness.

As Joe becomes more attached to the migrants, especially Luisa, he becomes more personally invested in their lives, realizing that even though he has never been actively aggressive toward them (as Randy is), it is also not enough to be a neutral bystander either. When the INS returns to the farm, he exercises his position as a white ally by speaking out, stating angrily, "Why don't you just leave them alone? They're not hurting anybody . . . They're *hoeing cabbage, that's all*" (173). This moment, in which Joe positions the migrants simply as farmers cultivating the land rather than criminals, causes the officer to fall silent, after which he sighs, shakes his head, and acknowledges that he doesn't make the rules and is just doing his job. Joe's small moment of resistance, then, exposes how even those who enact the law recognize the irrationality of a system where the crucial producers in the nation's food chain supply are continually vulnerable to deportation.[7]

An important part of Joe's maturation into a "new" citizen farmer, then, involves understanding the highly politicized twenty-first-century farm landscape so that he can navigate his own subject position within it. Working the land develops his community membership with the workers: with time, his technique improves, his muscles ache a little less, and he begins "to feel more like part of the crew" (61). The Mexicans, who all refer to one another by nicknames, start addressing Joe as "Little Boss," a moniker that makes him feel "proud" and "just like one of the guys" (63). But it is also a continual reminder of his status in relation to the land, referencing his implicit authority over them and hinting at his future rights of ownership to the property. He knows that his leadership is purely symbolic (particularly compared to Manuel's), but the narrative also recognizes the power of such symbolism in maintaining the binary of citizen farmer versus laborer. Even as intimacy and cross-cultural amity build (as Joe eats with the crew [93] and brushes up on his Spanish to better connect with them [66]), a certain rigid hierarchy remains in place, obstructing the development of real kinship. Joe, who longs for more connection with Luisa, notes sadly that "I wasn't part of Luisa's family and, even though I was feeling more like part of the crew all the time, I'd always be the boss's son" (153).

The New Citizen Farmer

To be transformed into the "new" citizen farmer, Joe must not only learn the political landscape but also demonstrate his ability to manage the farm responsibly. When his parents contemplate leaving him in charge of the farm for a few days while they go and visit extended family, Joe for the first time ever talks with his father about the handling of the various crops and notes that "it was a new feeling, a good one, to be talking to him about the farmwork" (149). As his parents hesitate about their trip away, Joe encourages them to leave: "I want to prove you can trust me and that I care about the farm too" (156). Interestingly, this first acknowledgment that he cares about the farm is not couched as a sentimental attachment to the land but rather as an interest in cultivation and an expression of smart husbandry and property management. The anticipation of responsibly managing the property, however, does prompt Joe to provide a rare description of the farm's bucolic beauty too: "maybe because I was feeling responsible for watching over the place . . . because the air was so sweet and rich with the smell of growing things, or because the familiar chirps of the crickets and tree frogs and birds sounded so peaceful. For some reason, I felt I was really seeing our farm for the first time in a long while. I'd so often wished I lived in town that I hadn't paid attention to the beauty of the land and the sky and the water all about me" (162). Here, cultivated land enhances nature with its fertility and fecundity (the "growing things" make the air sweet and rich), as well as making nature a familiar part of the homestead. As a citizen farmer, Joe finally appreciates how cultivated land—and the implied ownership of that land—is a beautiful thing.

As the story draws to a close, Joe is set a much larger task than basic farm management, because during his family's absence he must defend the farm, first from Randy and his brother, Tony, and second from the INS's return. The episode with Randy, who as a "big joke" shows up in the night to set off firecrackers and give Joe and his *"amigos"* a "little thrill" (167), clarifies Joe's own separation from his peers. Joe defends the property (as his father did before him [73]) by standing in the middle of the driveway as the car heads toward him (166), signaling a moment where he rejects the model of xenophobia practiced by Randy, establishes the boundaries of the farm, and cements his connection to it. After this, Joe's awareness of the farm's landscape, as both a physical geographical space and as owned property, seems heightened. When the crew all returns to work the next day, there is no longer any mention of the pain of labor. Instead, Joe notes simply that they "began weeding" and offers up descriptions of the cornfields that border the property and the "big stand of woods" that is "also our property" (170). His demarcation of the farm as a space defined by its boundaries represents his new maturity in the role of citizen farmer, a role where, in taking possession of the soil (in his father's absence), the pain of labor becomes abstracted and vanishes, and where he also recognizes the complexity of state sovereignty's interaction with private property.

Joe's ultimate test as citizen farmer comes when he helps Luisa and some of the other undocumented migrants escape to a safer farm after the INS's return visit to the field. This rescue mission (where Joe drives the undocumented migrants from the woods where they are hiding to a neighboring farm in the middle of the night) particularly highlights the contradictions of the politicized farm landscape: as Joe waits in the house for Manuel to contact him, he is scared and jumpy but also feels "ridiculous sneaking around in the dark like some sort of spy on *my own farm*" (180, my italics). He feels a heightened sense of surveillance both on his "own farm" and as he drives through the night, imagining "a big red arrow hung over us, flashing out the words 'Alert! Unlicensed Driver! Illegal Aliens!'" (191), where all their bodies are publicly marked by criminal status. After the safe delivery of the migrants to the new farm, Manuel turns to Joe and says formally, "We are—all of us—very grateful . . . Thank you, Boss" (204). The night's events, in which the farm is temporarily transformed into a fearful border space, earn Joe the title of Boss and represent a turning point in his identity as a critical thinker. Although he breaks the law and risks his parents' disapproval, "it feels so right . . . It felt right to have helped Luisa and Rafael and Frank" (206). With this new maturity, he confesses the night's events to his parents on their return but also speaks out this new truth, which is that he's "really *not* sorry" about what he did (209). Joe's publicly voicing his ethical stance provokes his father to acknowledge that immigration laws are misguided, harmful, and contradictory and to also refer to "another law, a higher law, that we feel we have to answer to" (210). Dad tells Joe that while he cannot look him "in the face and say it's all right to break the law," he also doesn't believe that what Joe did was wrong: "The fact is, I don't think Luisa and Frank and Rafael belong in jail" (210). He ends by stating "I'm proud of you" (211). All at once, then, Joe's father finally recognizes Joe's maturity because of his thoughtful ethics, which cement his belonging on the farm and his own status as a principled "new" citizen farmer.

The farm's politicized landscape, which Joe has labored on and defended as property, now also holds sacred memories that allow Joe to develop an emotional connection to it. After Luisa, Frank, and Rafael run off into the woods following the INS's visit, Joe notices both the farm's sensory power and how it is irrevocably marked by their absence: "The sun continued to beat down, making the long rows of cabbage shimmer with light and heat. The smells of the chopped weeds and the freshly turned earth, the sounds of the crows calling and the breeze sighing from the trees were just the same. Yet everything was different" (174). When Luisa moves away to the new farm, Joe spends "long working hours trying to picture her in her new life," imagining her playing or working (213). Luisa, who in her undocumented status perfectly embodies the contradictory existence of living openly in the shadows, now haunts Joe's farm with her absent presence, texturing its landscape with the past and expanding it beyond the here, into the elsewhere.

This expansion of the farm beyond its boundaries is, ultimately, the novel's way of presenting a new kind of identity that is both national and transnational. Concurrent to Joe's growing sense of responsibility for the farm, then, is his growing attachment to it as a place that evokes other places. As Luisa has earlier remarked to Joe, watching the moon and stars rise every night helps her feel connected to her family in Mexico because they are all under the same sky. After Luisa herself leaves, knowing she is looking at the same sky makes "perfect, beautiful, wonderful sense" to Joe, who closes his eyes and lets the sun "warm his face" (214). It is no coincidence that this moment, in which Joe feels an elemental and satisfying connection to the farm as a part of the earth (rather than only as part of the nation), is also the moment when the sun warms the farmer's face instead of burning down harshly on the toiling laborer. This is more than just ideal sentimentalism: such a transformation of place allows "people of all ages [to] learn to negotiate with others" (Massey 294) and thus has important ethical implications for the ways that children, in particular, can develop a broader sense of connection, humanitarianism, and social justice toward others. Through Joe's journey of maturation, therefore, and his developing identity as a twenty-first-century citizen farmer, DeFelice shows the farm as a blended space: a place of trauma and labor, a complex political site of national exclusion and inclusion, and a landscape of global kinship and connectivity.

Return to Sender

Compared to DeFelice's *Under the Same Sky*, Julia Alvarez's *Return to Sender* (2009) has received considerable academic and literary attention.[8] It has been the recipient of both the Américas Award and the 2010 Pura Belpré Award, which is presented annually to a Latinx writer and illustrator whose work best portrays, affirms, and celebrates Latinx cultural experience in an outstanding work of literature for children and youths. Alvarez's fiction for both adults and children has been recognized for its contribution to the field of Latinx literature, and much of her work, particularly that intended for adults, has entered mainstream literary circles. Despite the differences in their reception, the two novels share similar plot and thematic devices: *Return to Sender* explores the effects of the changing farming demographics in rural Vermont through the third-person narrative of Tyler, a white farm boy, and the first-person narrative of Mari, the undocumented daughter of the migrant workers on Tyler's family's dairy farm. Like *Under the Same Sky*, Alvarez's novel traces the maturation process of the white child as he navigates the newly politicized farm landscape, and the ensuing kinships that develop through his relationships with the migrant laborers.[9] The novel, which Alvarez's postscript explains is based on the undocumented "underground" population of Mexicans who began moving to Vermont around 2000 to help dairy farmers sustain themselves, draws attention to the plight of family farms, the mutual vulnerability that results from immigration policy, and the impact this has on migrants who live in the shadows of the nation.[10]

The novel shows the conflicts experienced by both white and Mexican children in Vermont and is an important part of Alvarez's "commitment to building a more egalitarian world" and her efforts as a social activist advocating for the rights of Latinx workers in Vermont's farms (Moreno-Orama 73). The text also deconstructs the binary of white citizen farmer and demeaned laborer, challenges prejudices against the Latinx population, humanizes migrants, and reimagines citizenship by showing the transformation of the farm into a complex traumatized landscape that is, in more explicit and far-reaching ways than in DeFelice's novel, transnational and global in its vision.[11] It is also deeply committed to exploring the relationship between personal identity and community in geopolitical terms, as evidenced by its many images of land, earth, and physical geography.[12] The novel, then, more radically reorients the relationship between nation, citizenship, and farming.

As part of this reorientation, *Return to Sender* creates what Andrea García terms a "polyphonic layering of voices" ("'We'" 105) as Tyler and Mari both share the narrative stage. In DeFelice's text, readers can identify only with Joe, leaving much of Luisa's experiences and history unspoken (for example Joe, as Amy Cummins points out, never learns exactly how or where Luisa came into the United States ["Border Crossings" 62]). Some critics note that Alvarez's novel also privileges the white voice by emphasizing the "moral development of the white citizen-son who becomes enlightened by the Mexican other," perhaps because the major target audience for this novel (as for DeFelice's) is clearly nonimmigrant children (Caminero-Santangelo, *Documenting* 138). Nevertheless, Mari's first-person accounts, delivered as epistolary narratives to various family members, resonate throughout the novel with immediacy and intimacy, and function, I argue here, as resistant acts of literacy that help document (and legitimate) her presence in the United States. Those acts of literacy authenticate Mexican migrant presence in the nation in a new way, by moving beyond depictions of Mexican migrants as laborers. Admittedly, Mari is the child of laborers rather than a child that must herself labor in the fields (like Luisa); nevertheless, even her references to her father's life do not provide any detailed descriptions of the farm labor he does all day long. Similarly, Tyler, who does work on the farm, rarely refers to physical farm labor as demeaning or difficult. In *Return to Sender*, literacy has replaced the physical pain and toil of farm labor detailed so thoroughly in *Under the Same Sky* and diminished the focus on the laborer's body. The experiences of schooling and education that migrants in DeFelice's story longed for are realized, and the migrant's body—as a metonymy for manual labor—is rendered more abstract.

The entire novel (through both child protagonists' stories) also presents a strong attachment to the farm and the land (and at times, the nation) that is forged through an appreciation of the pastoral setting rather than through evident toil. Citizenship, then, is nurtured through acts of documentation which displace political and national borders and transform place—the farm landscape—into a site of bucolic transnational and national belonging. Consequently, the notion of property and land ownership shifts more radically in *Return to Sender*. In *Under the Same Sky*, the farm will continue to be cultivated by the white citizen farmer (albeit one with a more complex understanding of national identity) who by the end feels a deep connection to it; in Alvarez's story, the ending shows a more communal way of being "in possession" of the soil one cultivates, as Tyler and his family prepare to let go of working on their own family farm. This means letting go of the farm as place of continuity (land on which their ancestors plowed and toiled) and as a place to nourish future generations.[13]

Sacred Farms, Abstracted Labor

From the outset (and unlike Joe) Tyler values the farm as a space of home that connects him to his ancestors and feels motivated to help out with farmwork because of a strong sense of family and belonging, which is part of the reason why initially having "strange people" working on the farm (3) or "illegal people . . . living on their farm" (56) is such a shock. As the story opens up, readers are introduced to the various ways in which the farm, as a former stronghold of family life, has become the site of several personal, economic, and political changes. In proximity, Tyler's grandfather has died, his father has been seriously injured in a tractor accident and is thus unable to work, and a Mexican family has moved in. Over the course of the story, Tyler's maturation reflects the landscape's transformation, as both become marked by fear, the actuality of loss, and the possibility of future losses. Tyler is particularly traumatized by his father's accident because he saw it happen and afterward cannot "stop playing the moment over and over in his head: the tractor climbing the hill, then doing this kind of weird backflip and pinning Dad underneath. Tyler would wake up screaming for help" (5). It is worth noting that his father's accident, which has left him in severe pain and somewhat paralyzed, does indicate the danger of farmwork (and prompts the need for replacement workers on the farm, setting the events of the story in motion), and in this respect one could argue that the novel does not shy away from honestly demythologizing farmwork. But overall, the novel strongly implies that the only real danger facing the family is losing the farm. Dad's accident is positioned as a singular event, a one-off; despite his trauma neither Tyler nor anyone else ever voices fears about further accidents, and the novel's focus on the farm's pastoral nature remains much stronger. For example, even in his grief over losing Gramps (whose body Tyler found), Tyler notes how the "rolling pastures covered in frost and mist in the early mornings . . . bright stars . . . seem to grow brighter as the cold sets in" (76). As a new site of trauma, full of memories of Gramps, the farm's beauty becomes more intensified and complex.

The novel's premise that the family may have to sell the farm also reflects Tyler's deepest fear. Even though his mother tries to reassure him that they wouldn't have to "leave the place," as they would keep the grandparents' house and a little plot next to it to build a new house, Tyler feels that as a "Boston city girl" his mother doesn't fully understand "what it [means] to be a family farm" (8). The quintessential virtue of American farming life is to improve one's own soil, an almost sacred act that represents the family's longevity in one place, with no migration or movement: as Tyler states, "the farm was not just Dad's, it was the whole family's, going all the way back before Gramps, as well as forward, his and Sara's and Ben's, even if they didn't want it" (9). The farm, which by this definition is the diametric opposite of a migratory mindset or experience, thus becomes a fascinating setting for expanding classic American notions of homesteading and family.

The novel navigates the changing landscape of the farm by showing why it is economically necessary to hire outside workers, and then challenging the derogatory overtones associated with migrant labor, thus maintaining the farm—with the migrant workers as an integral part of the space—as a site of virtue and belonging. As Alvarez explains in her letter to readers, actual American farmers (like the fictional Paquettes) are finding it "increasingly difficult to continue farming" as they cannot find affordable help and have to hire farmers displaced from other lands (322). The genesis of the novel, in fact, comes from her interactions with the children of migrants and American farmers in Vermont as they navigated the various challenges of these demographic changes (Moreno-Orama 75). Thus, in the story Tyler's mother explains to him that all dairy farms are struggling and that hired help is hard to find (7), and the conversations among adults and children move frequently into discussions about the incompatibility of immigration policy with the realities of sustaining a dairy farm. Tyler's aunt wonders "how we're expected to survive" without migrant workers (113), and his grandmother (invoking her late husband's words) tells Tyler that "the cows can't wait for their milking till the politicians get the laws changed. They'd still be waiting" (87), establishing a moral code which allows Tyler, who initially has deep reservations about hiring undocumented workers, to also want "the law to be changed" so that the Cruz family can stay and "help his family as well as themselves" (113).

But even with workers from outside the family and outside the nation, the novel still preserves the traditional mythology of the family farm by depicting the Mexican workers not as laborers but as farmers, a move that in this context assumes sacred overtones. Although we are never shown any real toil, readers are often reminded of the Cruz family's strong work ethic, which is equal or even superior to an American one (206, 304) so that their working the land still ensures a connection and sense of loyalty to the pastoral space. Even after his accident, Tyler's father feels an independent "pride" (15) about not needing any outside help on the farm, but finding Mexican "angels" (14) who themselves were farmers in Mexico helps maintain the godliness and sanctity of land cultivation. Compared to Tyler's obviously problematic narrative of Mexicans as machine-laborers, "special aliens" (32) who just have to be "rebooted at night" and are then "ready to go in the morning" (16), the discourse of Mexicans as angel saviors of the American dream might appear to counter prejudiced stereotypes. However, it also transforms the Mexican laborer into an abstract figure, thus maintaining the classic paradigm in which actual field labor remains invisible and the relationship between citizenship, national belonging, and farming depends on a mythological ideal.

The mythology of abstract farming is also maintained through the novel's few (but important) references to physical labor, which, particularly in Tyler's narrative, is described through carefully passive language. When Tyler recalls the farm (while staying with relatives in Boston), he imagines "the cows being milked or the back meadow being mowed" and can "smell the fresh-cut grass, hear the mooing of the cows as they waited for the feed cart to come by their stalls" (12). Unlike the active work and fatigued laborers of *Under the Same Sky*, here the pastoral scene is rendered through stillness and a sensory appreciation for the natural beauty of the farm. Tyler does mention the Mexicans being "hard at work" (39), even remarking on how after the Thanksgiving meal they all have together, the Paquette family stays at the table while the "Mexican workers head off for the evening milking . . . Their father and uncles won't be done with the milking and feeding and cleanup for another couple of hours" (117). Moments like these acknowledge the time-consuming nature of the work but not any fatigue or tedium. Tyler himself, it should be noted, is no stranger to the realities of labor—like Joe, he has put in many hours doing the same kind of work on the farm as the Mexicans do—but as a citizen farmer with a deep attachment to (and possession of) the soil, he still romanticizes "labor" as enriching and ennobling.

Mari's occasional references to her father's work on the farm do recognize his deep fatigue—"Papá works so hard, and when he gets home, all he wants to do is throw himself down on the couch and watch Spanish channels" (201); "How tired Papá is when he comes in from milking" (95)—but her narrative is more focused on how that the physical fatigue is compounded by the more complex emotional strain of living with a missing wife who is feared dead ("Usually, he is so sad and hardly talks at all" [171]). Like *Under the Same Sky*, the novel endeavors to prove that the labor of farming is not demeaning; but unlike DeFelice's text, *Return to Sender* mostly ignores the physical demands that such labor makes on the body and instead implies that everyone on the farm—migrant and citizen alike—can enjoy an idyllic version of farm life.

In the novel, in fact, labor is actually an essential part of that idyllic life because it establishes a classless community of productive farmers that closely reflects Tyler's ideal. Early in the novel, Tyler imagines traveling to another galaxy, where he would choose "a planet with lots of farms and no borders or bullies bossing you around. His grandmother has told him that's what heaven is like" (120). This exactly blends the traditional notion of the American farm (as heavenly and sacred) with a child's hope for an egalitarian utopia. The farm in the story, then, emerges as a new kind of family farm where labor is shared and there appear to be no differences between citizen farmer and migrant laborer. When spring arrives, the farm becomes an expansive space that is welcoming to all, closely resembling Tyler's ideal planet: "the farm unpacks its animals and its smells and its sounds and spreads out on all sides. Then a farmer's second job begins: growing the food to feed his cows during the fall and long winter" (250). Here, the farm is animated and bountiful, with room for everyone: it "spreads out," turning more of the earth's surface into farmland. And true to form, Tyler skims over the difficulty of planting and describes the additional work (the "second job" of planting to feed the cows) lyrically. Rather than hardship or pain, there is healthy busyness. The homestead "hums" with life as everyone pitches in: Tyler helps his father, Corey (a local boy), and Ben (his brother) at the weekends "out in the fields" and "meanwhile, the milking and barn chores are left for Mr. Cruz and his brother. The two groups cross paths at night as one comes from the fields and the other from the barn" (250–51). They are tired, but there is productive cooperation, with no apparent hierarchy between the owners and the laborers of the farm, as the laborers are now part of the family. While *Under the Same Sky* elevated the migrant laborer figure by emphasizing their skill and experience and their role in filling a massive labor shortage, *Return to Sender* takes it further by depicting the Mexican migrants as noble farmers themselves. Thus, migrant experiences become a necessary part of the virtuous cultivation of American soil because of the transnational agrarian ideology created by the narrative.

The Labor of Literacy and Storytelling

This transagrarian dissolution of the citizen/migrant binary is not just part of the reworked romantic mythology of farming, however. In *Return to Sender*, such strategies also have important political implications, particularly when it is Mari who asserts the strong connections between farming and Mexican subjects through her epistolary narrative. Her letters, written for various recipients within the frame of the story, describe Mexicans' cultivation of the earth as a rooted and essential part of (trans)national belonging and thus legitimate Mexicans as necessary contributors to the wealth and virtue of the nation. When Mari describes her father's kinship with the land in a letter to her mother, noting that he will be "so much happier working on a farm! He often speaks of being a boy, helping our grandfather, Abuelote, farm in Las Margaritas" (19), she indicates the skill, experience, and deep attachment needed for such noble work. Most important, her epistolary voice explicitly documents their status as farmers (and thus "citizens") rather than as disposable unskilled laborers. For the entire story, both Mari and Tyler foster their belonging to the nation: Tyler by "farming" (abstractly, connecting to the farm in a pastoral way), and Mari by writing. Where *Return to Sender* departs most radically from *Under the Same Sky*, then, is by replacing the labor of farmwork with the labor of writing.[14] As farmwork recedes into the background, the active production of literacy, through letters, is foregrounded as a new symbol of connectivity to the nation. The farm thus becomes an important space where the undocumented migrant, as a writer, can narrate her emergent and complex sense of national identity.

As an epistolary protagonist, Mari navigates and challenges the nation's complex systems of power by continually authoring herself into a legitimate citizen of a literary space, if not of the broader national one. The novel thus replaces (or hopes to replace) the metonymy of undocumented alien / demeaned laborer with a newly empowered figure: the self-documenting migrant writer, who produces letters (i.e., documents) about their experience, knowledge, and humanity. Within the frame of the story, the letter, in a gesture of empowerment, operates as a real-life document. When Tyler's father explains to him that Mexicans "need a certain document to be working in this country," he adds, "They all say they have it and that's all you need to know, legally" (56). The documents that *are* visible in the story—Mari's letters and later, her diary—become metonymic markers of the work permits that do not exist. Thus, the tangible letters inside the story establish Mari's writing residency even as they call to mind the absence of official documentation that would establish her legal residency.

For Mari, writing replaces farm labor as a form of homesteading, but it still retains some aspects of that labor: specifically, its physicality and its important relationship to citizenship. Thus, we are reminded of the physical vulnerability of paper itself, which, like a laborer's body, sometimes cannot bear the weight and story of certain memories (as with the family's border crossing [27–28]). The materiality of words themselves is also heightened, such as when they become stand-ins for the undocumented migrant's body. When, for example, Mari goes into hiding after her parents are taken away by ICE officers, she replaces her letter writing with diary entries. She writes, "It feels good to have this safe place where *la migra* can't come and haul my words and thoughts and feelings away" (264), referring both to the diary and her hiding location as safe places for her act of literacy and for her body. She also implies that the words in the diary, as more private versions of literacy (compared to letters), have become physical symbols of her externalized self that, like her externalized self, must now live in the shadows. Related to this is the tiring work of writing itself, too: Mari records, in one letter, the moment when she has broken off from and then returned to writing: "(*Later that same day—as I had to stop. Sometimes I get so sad, even if I'm just writing things down*)" (25). Even "just" writing can push the limits of her emotional and physical strength, in the same way that a field laborer's work can push his body to its limits. That is, in both cases, the work of cultivating "citizenship" is physically demanding.[15]

But the same physicality which can make writing so exhausting is also what allows it to potentially create transformation, and like farming, turn it into a sacred process. The tangibility of the paper itself can be transformative. In her letter to Abuelota, Mari writes, "It feels extra special to send you our greetings in writing and know that this very same piece of paper I've touched will soon be in your hands" (195); to Tío Felipe she rejoices that he can now receive letters (in jail) and so "this one will be in your actual hands" (162). Paper is highly valued in the context of this story: not only does it function as a vehicle for the subject's emerging voice, but it also (in its letter form) carries and transfers something of the writer's touch and environment to the reader-recipient. Crèvecoeur's character James is in fact assured near the start of his narrative that his letters will "smell of the woods and be a little wild" (41); their authentic intimacy will transport some aspect of America, literally, to Europe. In one section of *Return to Sender*, Mari describes her writing as having an almost divine purpose: her letter to Mamá is "like a candle that Abuelita promised to keep lit at her altar until we returned. To light our way back to Las Margaritas. Or now to light your way to Vermont, to a farm owned by a crippled farmer and his kind wife" (31). Here, the farm's safe and welcoming space is a holy destination, and the letter functions as a physical light that illuminates the path toward it, bringing together writing and farming as the foundations of national belonging.

This close relationship between national belonging and literacy has a strong historical precedence in the United States, as literacy has long been a way to measure belonging and membership in the community and thus to establish a migrant's worth and value. The Immigration Act of 1917 (known as the Literacy Test Act) aimed to restrict immigration (and deny citizenship) by imposing literacy tests on immigrants and thus created new categories of inadmissible persons, expanding what was considered "undesirable."[16] Contemporaries writing at the time expressed mixed emotions to the passing of the act; Henry Pratt Fairchild, for example, noted that as a selective measure that would put "the finishing touch to our classification of undesirables," it would affect such a large proportion of the ordinary immigration stream "as to be really restrictive" (452). Homer Hoyt believed that the relationship between illiteracy, crime, and pauperism was not convincing enough on its own but also laid out arguments in favor of the law, noting that it would secure a "better quality" of immigrant by barring the "illiterate immigrant" who is "a menace to our institutions, not only because he cannot read, but also because . . . it is alleged that . . . he is potentially more dangerous to the United States and less susceptible to Americanizing influences than his literate brother" (446). Ultimately, the test affords an "insight into the innate character and fitness of an immigrant" (455). These deliberations about the role of literacy in determining national membership established a legacy that a text such as *Return to Sender* builds on, by using writing as testimonial documentation to record and archive Latinx experiences into the nation's history and landscape.

The novel's use of epistolary narratives is particularly significant for understanding literacy as an act of homesteading and for exploring issues of ownership and property. The sheer range of Mari's addressees (living and deceased family members; spiritual figures; jailed, missing, or distant relatives) creates a readership community that expands the sense of place, where place is understood both as a physical and abstract space. That is, as Mari writes, she textures the "here" with the "elsewhere" and populates the space of her farm-nation by conjuring up her addressees. She points out that "while I am writing [to Abuelita and Mamá], I feel they are back" and when writing to Tío Felipe she feels like she is talking to him face to face (160).[17] Writing letters, which we already know is a physical act of labor, nourishes and nurtures the community of readers in a way that recalls the running of a family farm. The letters cultivate a community of readers just as the farmer cultivates the land;

both involve work and reciprocity to produce stories and food with which to feed the nation.[18]

These collective endeavors also provide a model for reimagining notions of ownership and property rights. In an epistolary setting, where the writing anticipates or at least imagines reciprocity and is shaped by the very presence of a community (even if it is just an imagined community of one reader), the inherent collectivity of an epistolary exchange is evident. Legally, a letter belongs to both the writer and the recipient: its content (the ideas expressed in it) are copyright owned by the writer, but the tangible letter itself is owned by the recipient. Without the physical letter, there is nowhere to record or archive ideas; without the ideas, the physical letter is meaningless. In its entirety, then, the letter is owned by the group, just as the family farm sustains itself through a communal effort. Understanding how the letters function as collective property is important for understanding how they function as documents of (national) belonging in the text. Generally speaking, official documents (passports, licenses, state IDs) are owned solely by the sovereign state and represent the state's power over the person, as it uses them to define and constitute whoever the document identifies. However, *Return to Sender* changes what it means to have one's personhood established through documents, as the characters legitimate themselves through documents (letters) that by definition are collectively owned. When Mari's letter-documents create her membership in the literary landscape, they also create her recipients' membership: the act of writing and the act of reading build a collective national selfhood. Her letters transmit information, experiences, and stories that in their physical form also become someone else's property and so represent the migrant's ability to shape the nation's cultural and literary landscape as a more communal space.[19]

It is important to note, however, that because Mari's letters do not always reach the intended recipient or are delayed, this national landscape is sometimes more imagined than actualized. Even though Alvarez creates the semblance or expectation of an internal community of readers, she also demonstrates the problems of transmission that occur when the writer tries to communicate across the inevitable distances and disruptions of migrant life. All Mari's letters are framed by an anxiety about their eventual arrival at the intended destination: her second letter to her mother, for instance, hangs on the condition of arrival and readership, beginning with her statement "If you are reading these words" (17). She also has to add in a postscript explaining that due to fears of alerting *la migra* to their location, none of her letters to Mamá will actually be sent but that instead she will one day hand them over to her mother in person (35). Although the process of letter writing usually functions as a connector, Mari writes into an empty space, widening rather than narrowing the gap between writer and addressee and shifting the epistolary function of the writing.[20]

These compromised acts of communication also become an analogy for the natural and political landscapes of the nation. Tyler describes a sudden cold front after the arrival of spring as follows: "Like the phrase stamped on an envelope with an index finger pointing back to where the letter came from, this is Return-to-Sender spring. A cold front blows in from the north, dumping a snowstorm. Frost beheads the daffodils. The puddles in the fields turn to ice, reflecting the gray sky" (250). Referring to the dragnet operation carried out by the Department of Homeland Security's ICE in 2006, which raided workplaces, seized workers, and sent them back to their home countries, Alvarez implies a broken community and positions the United States as a literal place of nonbelonging. Depicting the farm's landscape through the failed delivery of letters deepens the connection between literacy and farming as cultivators of nationhood, and referencing the ICE raids in this context, of course, politicizes the geographical landscape. The natural landscape, then, echoes and is marked by immigration policy and workplace vulnerability.

Although the compromised epistolary context might isolate the writer from her textual community, the novel's external audience also comes to stand in as a community of readers for the letters' addressees. As Elizabeth MacArthur notes, "real and fictional epistolary narratives require the reader's active participation. . . . The reader necessarily enters into dialogue with the epistolary text" (273), suggesting that for the duration of the novel, we take the place of various addressees. Through our activity of reading, we figuratively become (among others) Mari's missing mother, her jailed uncle, and her family back in Mexico. Alvarez addresses us as external readers, but Mari addresses us as members of her family and community. In conjuring Mari's own internal sympathetic community of readers, then, the novel also empowers a potentially sympathetic community of listeners outside the text who effect the symbolic, if not the literal, circulation of undelivered letters. The letters' impact, therefore, is multifold; their failure of delivery is also in itself an act of communication about the struggles of undocumented migrants in the United States and thus an act of resistance and agency.

At a broader level, we can also read the novel itself as an act of communication about the power of migrant testimonial and storytelling. This
is most aptly illustrated through the narrative's engagement with Mamá's
experiences during her disappearance, where the novel's multiple layers of
readers/listeners are able to bear witness to the events and enable the story to
operate as both personal and public record. After Mamá is rescued from her
kidnapper-coyote, she suffers severe posttraumatic stress because of the sexual, physical, and emotional abuse she has undergone. Once reunited with
her family on the farm in Vermont, she often wakes up at night screaming
(256) and continues to be "upset and nervous" so that with "any little noise,
she jumps. Any little thing, she cries" (227). After Mamá's arrest by ICE later
on, Mari decides to "offer" her story to an ICE officer in exchange for her
parents' release (287). Mari even hopes that Mamá's experiences, turned into
story, will take on a certain exchange value, thinking that if ICE hears the
"whole truth" then "maybe they'd even give us our papers because they felt
sorry" (280). In this scenario, where she will humanize her parents and prove
that they are "not criminals but hardworking parents with kids" (285), Mari
imagines that the status of Mamá's story can legitimate Mexican experiences
so as to make them worthy of citizenship.

Mamá's story is originally told by Mamá to Mari in the car, immediately
after she is rescued from the coyotes, but that story and its telling are recounted to the rest of the family (and to the reader) in Mari's letter. Its genesis, then, is simultaneously oral and written: the orality creates intimacy,
immediacy, and emotion and allows Mamá some cathartic release. Mari
recognizes right away that Mamá must "tell her story, not to have to carry
it alone inside her" (239) and herself becomes so deeply drawn into it that
she momentarily shifts from listener to participant: "We had both been so
involved in her story, as if we were in that [escape] van together, trying to
breathe enough air" (241). The original telling, though, is also written (in
letter form), allowing it to become (potentially) part of a permanent familial archive. And as with all Mari's letters, here too the external readers can
access the momentum and intimacy of the telling and bear witness to the
events described. Later, Mari shifts from listener to storyteller as she relates
her mother's story to the ICE officer in a more formal setting and then records the entire experience in her diary. Here, the undocumented become
documenters through the empowering synchronism of oral, epistolary, and
diary forms. The testimony she provides is recorded on tape and becomes an

official narrative of border crossing that leads to the eventual conviction of the coyote criminals. It is sent to the regional office and is accompanied by a recommendation to release Mamá (292); it is information that is legible to the state and becomes part of the public archive. The story ultimately turns into official documentation for federal authorities and becomes a permanent part of the public record, but because of its multiple layers of literacy (spoken, letter, diary), it is also inherently democratic, filling the national landscape with all possible modes of story and communication and reaching people in ways that they can hear and understand.[21] This way of creating citizenship through literacy thus reimagines the space of the nation as one of collective and democratic social responsibility.

The "New" American Farm: National and Global Citizenship

Because of *Return to Sender*'s status as a middle-grade children's novel, it focuses in particular on how children, as critical citizens, acquire a sense of collective social responsibility through "empathetic literacy," which Calloway-Thomas defines as "knowledge and information-based skills that help global citizens respond to and manage intercultural encounters caringly and competently" (214–15). The intercultural encounters in the novel lead to close kinship between the Cruzes and Paquettes, which also expands the notion of family and thus the paradigm of what a "family farm" looks like, as new connections develop across geopolitical, cultural, and biological lines. For example, Mari's sisters, Ofie and Luby, think of Tyler's Grandma as their only grandmother ("we are like their family" [200]), as they have never met their Mexican grandparents; Grandma calls the Cruzes her "Mexican family" (252), and Mari tells her mother that life in Vermont provides not only "steady work" but also lets them "live right on the farm with the wonderful *patrones* who treated us like family" (238). Kinship develops between the elderly characters too (toward the end, Grandma's friend Mr. Rossetti and Abuelote meet in Mexico and communicate happily despite language differences [309]), implying that older adults (in addition to children) also play an important role in enabling intercultural encounters. Culinary traditions and practices also easily translate between the two nations, as Grandma exclaims, "You know, I think I must be a Mexican at heart. I like your holidays so much more than ours!" (164). Such relationships and exchanges do more than provide pleasure, though. Clearly, the Cruz family is trying to help save the farm economically (205), but their presence also provides cultural literacy that heals ("saves") U.S. ailments. This is evident in several ways, most noticeably through Grandmother's adoption of Day of the Dead practices (such as an altar), which helps her and Tyler memorialize Gramps. Tyler does not want to "avoid talking about [Gramps] as his mother advises" and thinks "there's got to be a happier way to stay in touch with [him]" (76); the altar allows them both to grieve for him in a more effectively therapeutic way (76).

The family farm, as the site of these intercultural encounters, ultimately becomes a site of transnational citizenship for both children, where global and national identities form. Here, the children experience a kind of idealized global citizenship without borders, even as their national identity is politicized and traumatized by the power dynamics of the state. Over the course of the story, Tyler's critical thinking develops as he navigates the farm's political and cultural changes, while Mari navigates it as an uncertain space of trauma, fear, and relative safety. Farms in the area have become a place where Mexicans hide in plain sight, their physical presence and critical yet invisible role in the food supply chain operating as an open secret. Papá cannot "risk going off the farm to shop" (147), and the Paquettes, in Tyler's words, are "harboring Mexicans" (189), implying that the farm is a sanctuary, but the Cruz family also recognizes that they are living on the "borrowed kindness and luck" of their employers (105) while things "[heat] up for Mexicans in the area" (113).

The farm increasingly seems marked by, rather than separate from, the political nation, even before the ICE raid that renders it a symbolic border site. During the raid itself, the idyllic setting is disrupted as Mari watches her parents struggling with ICE officers, being "herded" and "hauled" off with Mamá screaming (268).[22] Interestingly, the moment of the raid through Tyler's perspective (he gazes at the scene from a distance, through the lens of a telescope) is also depicted as a moment of trauma on the land itself. He initially sees "a clump of stars" that he has never seen before, which seems to blend into the horizon: "Those lights are not in the sky but on the dark edge of the horizon and getting closer" (263). The stars, which up until now have inspired the children to imagine a global "home" separate from the nation's political boundaries, shift, dropping down from the skyscape into the landscape. The farm, then, comes to represent a nexus of global perspectives and national trauma, a site where the children's interest in the planets (their ability to see "the bigger picture" [50]) encourages them to understand their place on earth in relation not to national borders but to a broader transnational space. As Marta Caminero-Santangelo argues, the novel's "language of . . . planetary perspective establishes the ways in which cosmopolitanism becomes represented through the trope of an interest in stellar and planetary space in the novel" (*Documenting* 144).

For Crèvecoeur, the farm is also a place of pedagogy: James notes that "there is not an operation belonging to it in which I do not find some food for useful reflection" (53). In Alvarez's novel, too, lessons about the interconnectivity of the world occur within and outside the frame of the story and so are doubly pedagogical and carry extra authority. The children use the space of the farm to think about what their teacher Mr. Bicknell is "always teaching [them]" about how "we are all connected . . . like an intricate spiderweb," making climate and environmental problems in one nation affect people in another nation (59). But while eighteenth-century farming causes James to "[cease] to ramble in imagination through the wide world" (Crèvecoeur 53), Alvarez's twenty-first-century farm is exactly the place from which to encounter the wider world and also (building on Crèvecoeur's legacy) guarantee one's survival, as Tyler notes, "If the planet gets into trouble, farms will be the best place to be. In fact, farmers are going to be the most important people in the world because they will be in charge of the food!" (64).

Even more than in *Under the Same Sky*, *Return to Sender*'s global perspectives are analogous to the process of maturation from child to adult and encourage the child protagonist and reader to consider their personal growth within a universe-oriented framework of citizenship. As Tyler's mother tells him, "Being an adult is about navigating your way through choices and challenges using the North Star of your heart and conscience" (257). This reimagined outlook invites a rethinking of patriotism, shifting it from a narrowly defined national ideology to a broader moral virtue.[23] Tyler, who initially defines himself as a "patriot" along strictly narrow lines, must eventually wrestle with the concept because it seems to violate humanitarian rights (257). As a counternarrative, the story positions American patriotism as a fundamentally ethical virtue: the town hall meeting about halfway through the story begins with a tense argument about the presence of Mexicans in the town but concludes with people "speaking up and reminding each other of the most noble and generous principles that are the foundation of being an American as well as a good person" (192). Expressing one's attachment to the nation provides a vital rhetoric for expressing global connections, such as when Mari cheers on both the United States and Mexico in a blended patriotism: "Long Live the United States of the World" (72).[24] Ultimately, as Marta Caminero-Santangelo puts it, "Alvarez's narrative works hard to reconcile 'patriotism'—those affective attachments to nation that children are taught from the earliest age—to an expansive, cosmopolitan view" (*Documenting* 147). In the same way that farming is transformed, in the novel, from an American virtue to a more universal virtue, so too does ideological American patriotism translate into an attachment to the entire planet and its inhabitants.

A global perspective is also useful in helping the children psychologically manage the absences created by migration or death. Like Luisa's mother's advice in *Under the Same Sky* that everyone is "under the same sun, the same moon, the same stars" (163), Gramps has told Tyler, "*Anytime you feel lost, look up*" (76–77), enabling a kind of healing reorientation of place and perspective where the here and now is part of an expanding place and time (an elsewhere, the past, and the future). Repeatedly, loss and disappearance are tied to the political nation and its borders, while presence and appearance connect to limitless planetary space and to the narratives of the skyscape. When Tyler tries to comfort Mari over her mother's disappearance, he says, "Maybe it's like the seventh sister [of the Pleiades constellation] . . . maybe your mom is just lost and trying to find her way back to you" (145) and decides to show her "the seventh star reunited with her sisters" (146) through his telescope. Through such stories, the skyscape becomes peopled with figures who also experience family separation, and then reunification and resolution, and thus comes to model a place of home without borders. Mari herself proposes a story-answer to the question of why the seventh sister got separated: "She's crossing the bridge to get back to her six sisters. But when she gets to the Milky Way, there's no bridge. So she asks that constellation that's the charioteer" (144). Here, motivated by her own experiences, Mari replaces nation-spaces, the United States–Mexico border, and coyotes with the sky, the Milky Way, and a constellation, and with this alternatively imagined space of "nation" concocts a new and satisfying narrative of belonging that seems more relevant and updated than the old myths. As Tyler puts it, "Maybe astronomers should hire Mari to make up new stories about the constellations. Hers would probably be a lot better than all those dumb Greek gods falling in love with mere mortals" (145). Here, the farm, as the site of storytelling, enables new literacies that are informed by a blend of the nation's (and the farm's) own politicized landscape and the universe beyond.

Overall, then, Alvarez's novel presents the farm in an idyllic way: it is a homestead without borders; it is the site of newly defined familial kinships, amity, and connections; it offers a window into the universe beyond and a grounding in the fertile land; and it will, according to Tyler, always provide safety, a "room" for Mari and her family, even when there is "no room for [them] in this country" (143). That is, it imagines itself as a separate kind of nation-space within the sovereign state, where acts of literacy can create some kind of belonging and continue the legacy of farming as a virtue that will sustain—and save—the nation and the planet. Although it is a classic symbol of American belonging, the Paquettes' farm is also denationalized, belonging to the planet rather than the nation. Mari has been in the United States since the age of four, but rather than expressing a general attachment to the United States, she admits to especially loving it "here on your farm" (260).[25]

The farm, blending American and global citizenship, is also a site of tension, though, fundamentally part of and apart from the nation-state. What, then, are the implications of an American farm that is in the nation but separate from it, particularly when considering traditional notions of property rights and their connection to citizenship? From the outset, through its chapter titles and structure, the novel challenges the idea that virtue is attained through the cultivation of one's own soil. Each chapter names a season and a year, and then a thematic descriptor for the farm to reflect the events in that section (for Tyler's narratives), and the title of Mari's letter for that chapter: "summer (2005), Bad-Luck Farm, *Queridísima Mamá*," "summer into fall (2005), Nameless Farm, Esteemed Mr. President," "fall (2005), Watched-Over Farm, *Querida Abuela*," and so on. The farm's names thus mirror the continually changing political and cultural landscape and the cycles of nature, rather than the identity of its owners. It is known as the Paquette farm, but the family has never been able to settle on a permanent name, and "since there are a lot of Paquettes, that can get confusing" (45). Alvarez's refusal to demarcate this agrarian space as private property is further supported by the text's inclusion of Native American statements about land ownership. Near the start of the story, Tyler recalls an Abenaki chief's words, "My people believe that our land is not given to us by our ancestors. It is loaned to us by our children" (9), but he initially interprets this to mean that the farm must remain in his family. By the end of the story, he has come to realize that Native Americans "didn't really believe people could own the land" (311). This notion that we are only ever custodians of the land offers a blueprint for the novel's position on property. Virtuous citizenship, then, comes from a connection to the earth rather than the sovereign state, and a *collective* possession and cultivation of its soil.

The novel's ending explicitly demonstrates this communal notion of property. Before returning to Mexico, Mari asks to see the farm one last time, and in keeping with the trope of writing as an act of belonging, she uses her diary to archive "the place and the people I've grown to love," all "stored inside me and here on your pages, my dear Diary" (296). In literal terms, the farm cannot be sustained without the Mexican workers, so the Paquettes cannot continue to farm it (Tyler tells Mari that "things haven't been going well with the farm since your dad and uncles left" [299]). Figuratively, too, it is Mari (the daughter of migrant laborers) that preserves the farm with extensive descriptions of it in her diary. Alvarez's new American farm, in other words, is collectively maintained. The Paquettes, who "won't be farming anymore" (312), plan to lease the farm to Uncle Larry, an arrangement that allows them to continue to own and live on it while Uncle Larry pays them rent in exchange for the right to do as he chooses with the land. Ostensibly, the farm is no longer an expression of Tyler's or his father's identity; instead, it will become (at best) a broader family endeavor. Uncle Larry will be cultivating farmland he does not own; Dad, who will be "quitting farming" (303) and is considering being a field agent and helping other farmers (302), will own farmland that he is not cultivating. Meanwhile, Tyler imagines a wider future for himself than he initially did. Writing in a letter to Mari, he finally speaks in the first person (rather than being depicted in the third person): "Maybe I'll end up being an astronomer or a meteorologist or maybe I'll study Spanish and travel to Mexico and help out all the farmers there so they don't have to leave their land" (300). The story mentions several times that Tyler is not comfortable expressing himself through writing, but here, no longer able to cultivate his identity through farming, he must cultivate it through letter writing, symbolizing the ways in which his rooted connection to the American family farm has been replaced with more migratory and far-flung connections, now articulated through an act of literacy. Some of the sentiment of Jeffersonian farming endures, because there is still something virtuous about working the land (doing so might help to save the planet), but the virtue has become separated from owning any piece of that land. Consequently, the American citizen farmer is reoriented into a citizen of the planet.

In both *Under the Same Sky* and *Return to Sender*, then, the farm remains central to the teaching and preservation of certain fundamental American values (work ethic, meritocracy), which are closely tied to the land and the process of a child's maturation. But what new cultural narrative are the texts investing in, and how do they intervene in the classic American farming narrative? How is the twenty-first-century American farmer's possession of the soil distinct? In both novels, the cultivated soil enables a transformation, for some migrants, into social citizenship but is also a landscape of unbelonging, violence, and disruption, where migrant laborers must remain in the shadows, continually fearing and/or experiencing threats of deportation. Because the mythology of both white citizen farmer and demeaned laborer figure is interrogated by the stories, the romanticized notion of the farm as a site of belonging cannot stand. Instead, it is replaced with a new mythology of the farm as a site of transnational kinship and global belonging; the new "American" farm is a symbol of migration, where rather than constituting himself in terms of a singular American identity, the migrant citizen can become a global citizen. In DeFelice's text, the new farmer still possesses the soil he cultivates but is noticeably principled and ethical in his understanding of citizenship and nationhood, while in Alvarez's narrative, more radical notions of farm cultivation and ownership create a distinctly collective "possession of the soil." If, as Kenneth Olwig claims, landscape is so freighted with unsaid meaning that it becomes "integral to an ongoing 'hidden' discourse, underwriting the legitimacy of those who exercise power in society" (307–8), then the novels' explorations of farm landscapes reveal important discourses about immigration and citizenship and also challenge the political and national ideologies that operate through those landscapes.

CHAPTER 3

Narratives of Shame and Healing

Tourism, Commodification, and Solidarity in Malín Alegría's
Sofi Mendoza's Guide to Getting Lost in Mexico

In Malín Alegría's young adult novel *Sofi Mendoza's Guide to Getting Lost in Mexico*, a "chick lit junior" teen romance, the adolescent Mexican American protagonist Sofi, from Southern California, learns that she is undocumented when she is unable to reenter the United States after a weekend vacation with her friends in the beach town of Rosarito, a popular nightlife destination for young people from the United States. Finding herself trapped in Mexico, Sofi undergoes a perhaps "improbable" transformation (in the space of three weeks) from spoiled American to proud border girl who is newly aware of her more complex cultural identity (Bromann 451). The term "chick lit junior" carries a certain stigma of insignificance, as the genre has historically not been seen as worthy of rigorous study, but Joanna Webb Johnson identifies the ways in which its classic themes (coming of age, identity, sexuality, and material culture) "[build] on feminist children's literary tradition" (141). For Johnson the stories affirm flawed women, acknowledge insecurities involving physical attributes, give lessons in negotiating relationships, and "engage their audiences with perceptive interpretations of the ordinary," presenting everyday superficial details of women's lives that matter to them (142). In drawing attention to the legitimate contribution of chick lit junior, Johnson notes its thematic roots in many of the best-selling novels of the nineteenth century and the ways in which the stories, with their emphasis on solely female experiences, advocate for those experiences. They acknowledge that what seems to be trivial often is not, and with that validation, allow the reader (as well as the protagonist) to perhaps "move toward accepting her own shortcomings" (148). She posits that such works perhaps focus less on changing or controlling the world and more on offering ways to negotiate the world.

Alegría's novel, however, does show readers possibilities for changing the world. In fact, Marilisa Jiménez García explains how the broader category of Latinx young adult literature can serve as an important form of counter-storytelling, introducing (even if lightly) themes of institutional and state power, social struggles, trauma, and history in American culture. Because adolescence is often a time of experimentation and dissent, Latinx young adult authors who disrupt the "single story" about growing up Latinx in the United States can help readers negotiate "new ways of imagining social justice" as well as "alternative, interactive forms of literature and education" ("En(countering) YA" 232). While it may seem a stretch to ascribe so much potential power to the predictable plot and stock characters of Alegría's text, book reviewers and critics also acknowledge the larger social context of the romance story and its emphasis on the heroine's ethnic and cultural identity.[1] In fact, commercially published Latina young adult literature is attractive to non-Latina teen readers because of its attention to common issues and to young Latina readers because its focus on the lives of Latina teens adds "an additional layer of connectivity" (Salinas-Moniz 98). Ibarraran-Bigalondo, for example, claims that the story allows young adults to "evolve a moral conscience" (19) through the "critical witnessing" (23) of life on both sides of the border, noting that in deploying a clear moral message, the story's contemporary and mimetic (rather than fantastic) world setting and its attention to moments of crisis can educate readers. In an interview, Alegría states that her writing is supposed to "fill a void" that she herself experienced growing up, as she did not see role models and mentors in school, books, or the media. She "went through a period of shaming" because of "the color of my skin, my name [and] where my parents worked," and consequently, her writing is intended to "heal those wounds" and allow other young Latinxs to see that their voices and experiences matter (Alegría 35). She also wants to reach out to reluctant readers, and while she recognizes that the commercialization of her work (a "safe diversity that's being packaged and sold") risks diluting the complexity of Latinx lives in the United States, she also sees writing as an important and safe space to express both anger and reality (39).

Felicia Salinas-Moniz identifies the novel's teen "chica lit" status as evidence of the growing commercialization of Latinx youth culture and its ability to offer, in effective ways, both entertainment and commentary on border politics (87). She explains that Alegría's novel fits exactly into the highly marketable genre in which friendships, first romances, relationships with family, and the protagonist's growth take center stage, but that the "fun, self-discovery, uplifting endings [and] relatable characters" are complicated by a "nuanced attention" to issues of class and race (89). While teen chick lit is often trivialized as superficial, Salinas-Moniz contends that this story's infusion of social consciousness gives it more substance while still respecting the parameters of both the genre and the audience's expectations (94). A "seasoned chick lit reader," therefore, can predict at the outset that the self-absorbed attitude of the protagonist will shift and that her "fairy-tale" ending will not turn out as she expects (95). Instead, as Sofi's weekend of partying turns into a longer stay in Mexico, she develops roots in her ancestral homeland and learns to negotiate the literal United States–Mexican border and the figurative borders between childhood and adulthood, demonstrating how the timely issue of border politics can impact youths.

While critics have addressed both the limitations and contributions of the novel's genre and its exploration of political and cultural concerns, I argue here that the novel's negotiation of these issues is part of a broader analysis of how Mexico is understood, created, and consumed in the U.S. cultural and literary imagination. Specifically, *Sofi Mendoza's Guide to Getting Lost in Mexico* is about redefining ways of knowing Mexico—creating a new cultural literacy of Mexico in the United States—along a continuum of tourist encounters that are founded on a long history of neocolonial and asymmetrical power dynamics. Although tourism can usefully produce "knowledge around difference," especially about the other, poverty, nature, and culture, it can also become an exploitative and highly charged encounter that bleeds into "empire building," with "uneven power relations between those who engage in tourism as tourists and those engaged in the service of the tourist industry" (Bender et al. 2–3). In Alegría's novel these tourist encounters are strongly informed by discourses about shame and illegitimacy, where the tourist gaze turns Mexican (and Mexican American) bodies into commodities. Through this framework of tourism, then, the novel interrogates the ways in which sovereign nations perpetuate conversations about national

identity and borders in which certain members of a population are continually rendered illegitimate.

Since the early 1930s, tourism in Mexico has produced a kind of "invisible export" in which the place and people are marketed as commodities for
consumption (Berger and Wood 2). Eric M. Schantz explains how in the
nineteenth century, Mexican border towns were transformed from back-
water ranchos into major cities by the tourist industry: American tourists
visited the border cities "expecting risqué entertainment, sizzling-hot floor
shows, glitzy casinos, and colorful racing culture" (131). Given this history,
the earlier parts of Alegría's novel, which depict teenage tourists drinking,
partying, and gawking at their surroundings, are evidence of racially and
culturally exploitative behavior. For the tourists, Rosarito's residents are
not independent Mexican nationals but sources of entertainment. This has
broader implications, because while the United States–Mexico border is a
physical site of disappearance for migrants crossing north, American tourism is also figuratively enabling disappearance: when tourists only absorb
Mexico's "staged authenticity" manufactured by the tourist industry (Bender
et al. 3), the real social, cultural, and political stories of Mexico are erased.

Against this critical backdrop of the tourist industry, however, the novel
demonstrates more difficult experiences of tourism because Sofi, of course,
is not a tourist in the traditional sense. After being denied reentry into the
United States, she is displaced in Mexico—her birthplace and homeland—as
both a tourist and an exile. Tourism, according to Caren Kaplan, "celebrates
choice" while exile "implies coercion" (27); the former "claims community on
a global scale," while the latter "connotes the estrangement of the individual
from an original community" (27). The two are not mutually exclusive, of
course: Sofi's exile from the United States and enforced time in Mexico provoke an unhappy existential crisis about citizenship and belonging and are
at same time an adventurous sojourn. She is a tourist in Mexico, her native
land, and an unwelcome foreigner in the United States, the only home she
has ever known. Ultimately, her journey forces the question of what (and
where) her "original community" is and encourages a more educated understanding of how her Mexican and U.S. communities intersect. Through
her nuanced tourist encounters, then, Sofi can move away from the binary
model of nationalism offered by the sovereign state and toward the hybrid
transnationalism of her own Mexican American identity, where nationalist
narratives of shaming and illegitimacy are replaced with healing narratives

of transnational membership. With this new cultural literacy, the book thus traces the ways in which tourist gazes can become acts of solidarity and social justice.

Tourist Encounters in Mexico

Most discourses about U.S. travel to Mexico, critics agree, are not just personal but also ideological, a set of practices with "tremendous power to create and shape knowledge formations across cultural, racial, ethnic, and national boundaries" (Ruiz 2). Historically and to this day, Mexico has served as place of escape and self-transformation, and its location in the United States' popular imagination is particularly complex: a 1902 primer for American schoolchildren described it as a "strange land" that is "near home," the country as "familiar and alien, close but inaccessible, desirable and ruined" (Ruiz 2). In Alegría's text, this combination of foreignness and proximity is crucial to the tourist's colonial attitude: the relative ease of accessing the country geographically, against a historical backdrop of American presence in Mexico, creates an expectation of familiarity. For the adolescent tourists in the story, Mexico's foreignness is delightfully familiar, and that familiarity creates an assumption of ownership on their part. Their weekend in Rosarito delivers exactly the contradictions and culture clashes they expect, because even new experiences are manufactured novelties, specific to the consumerist tourist economy.

This dynamic determines and alters the environment in important ways. Bender et al. comment that the exploitative energy of the tourist encounter lies in the expectations imposed on the residents, who are "citizens transformed into hosts." When the Mexican citizen "transforms" into a host, his citizenship and personhood disappear into a space of "staged authenticity" (Bender et al. 3) in which the local population must re-create or perform roles to meet tourists' expectations of a genuine experience. In the story every tourist shop in Rosarito sells the exact same merchandise: corny T-shirts printed with pictures of naked girls or lewd jokes, Aztec artifacts, and Mexican jumping beans (27). The souvenirs narrate a confined set of discourses about the place (sex, commodified Aztec history, et cetera) and continually reestablish an environment determined by the asymmetrical power dynamic of tourist/host. The physical landscape is also commodified for the tourist's consumption: as Sofi and her friends catch sight of the

Pacific Ocean on their drive from Tijuana to Rosarito, for example, Olivia comments, "Beautiful sun, beautiful shore . . . now all I need is some beautiful men, and I'll be happy" (22). This narrative of Mexico erases its complexity, with far-reaching implications: simplifying the narratives of Mexico risks simplifying the narratives of Mexicans in the United States, so that they have no backstory and no history. As Ibarraran-Bigalondo observes, "the frivolous knowledge that [Sofi's] friends have of the country as a vacation space depicts the U.S. adolescents' lack of information of their neighboring country's social reality" (26).

Without this information, too, the girls also cannot understand why migrants risk their lives crossing the border into the United States: when they see a young man dashing out in front of the car at the border, they collectively wonder, "What would make a guy do something as crazy as that?" (21). The teenager tourists' discourses about Mexico as a space "which they consider devoid of a social situation" (Ibarraran-Bigalondo 26) turn every novel encounter into a form of entertainment. Olivia's jokey catchphrase, "Only in Me-hee-co" (20), in response to a billboard for bad perfume, is initially amusing but more inappropriate when she repeats it after the border crosser dashes out in front of their car. The homogenizing tourist gaze simplifies disparate issues, so that the way beauty products are advertised is equated with a migrant running across the border: both exist in order to deliver the uniqueness of Mexico to the American (*"only* in Mexico"). The gaze, of course, imposes its own knowledge and eliminates the need for learning new or challenging histories. In this respect, the tourist gaze is narcissistic, as it is more about the spectator than the spectacle.

The way in which the tourists' "frivolous knowledge" intersects with social reality is particularly evident in the girls' encounters with poverty. Jane Hanley notes that actual travel writing will often "foreground unsettlement through the traveler's confrontation with poverty, and unsettlement is one potential counter to both the traveler's subjective authority and their stable interpretation of the world" (3). It is questionable, however, to what extent the girls in Alegría's text allow this kind of instability to enter their worldview. When a group of Mexican children, "little brown kids dressed in grimy clothes, their hair uncombed," begs the girls for change, they debate what their own ethical responsibility is as wealthy tourists (23). Sofi hands the children seven dollars and wants to give them more, but Olivia staves her off, saying that they "can't start giving out that kind of cash" or else they will

have nothing left for beer (23). Her admonitions reinforce neocolonial rhetoric. She reasons that if Sofi gives the children more money, they will "come
down on us like seagulls and then we'll *never* get rid of them," that "poverty is
bad everywhere," and that her dad "says that what those kids need is to be in
school, not learning how to beg" (23). Even when her friend Taylor protests
"That's not fair . . . you say it as if they chose to be poor," Olivia's response is
"We didn't come down here to feed the children" (23). They are not volunteer
tourists, and the purpose of the trip is pleasure.

Olivia's general universalizing of the scene (it is just another example of
poverty; it is not unusual and therefore not worthy of attention), her deper-
sonalization of the beggars (they are seagulls, not children), and the social
lesson about what *should* be happening rather than what *is* happening in
front of them imply that the encounter has provoked discomfort and, out
of that, distancing strategies. Olivia's narrative animalizes the children (they
invade in hordes) and sees them as contaminants: they will never be rid of
them, and in becoming permanent features, they will spoil the temporary
vacation experience that should not, by definition, be part of the girls' regular
life. Universalizing the poverty means the girls can avoid immersing themselves in this particular context. In fact, in the middle of their emerging critical discussion about their moral obligation toward the children, they become
distracted by the sight of some "adorable" men (24). They thus suspend any
emerging guilt by not engaging intimately with their discomfort but instead,
turning to superficial encounters based on physical appetites and pleasures.
While they feel briefly empathic, they quickly excuse themselves from any
ethical responsibility by remembering that Mexico is a party space, not a
complex nation.

The experience of visiting another country thus does not mature or change
the American teenagers, and any new knowledge, folded into their American
frame of reference, merely reinforces their established ("frivolous") knowledge of Mexico. Toward the end of the novel, the rumors that circulate back
in Southern California about Sofi's extended stay in Mexico further illustrate this: according to gossip, Sofi has either "fallen 4 some hot ass Mexican mafioso" and is now "chilling in cabo sipping margaritas" or she has
been "kidnapped by an antigovernment guerrilla militia" and is "training in
the mountains to start a revolution" (197). These fabrications, produced by
American teenagers who live just a few miles north of the border and have
likely visited Mexico themselves, confirm the limited narratives (those of sex

and revolution) available for speaking about Mexico. In Rosarito, the house owned by one of the American teenagers' parents also illustrates a similarly narrow selectivity of experience: although the decor is a "festive Mexican style" and one of the boys welcomes Sofi and her friends with margaritas and a Spanish greeting (*"Buenos días"* [25]), its location in a secured-housing community reinforces its separation from the social reality of its environs, and the privileged mobility that enables that separation.

The novel's depiction of Rosarito's party atmosphere also supports readings of travel and mobility as forms of "imperial expansion" (Hanley 2). The party scenes underscore the way that travel discourse is "deeply bound to racialized and sexualized accounts of Mexican bodies" and functions as a site of empire (Ruiz 3). When travel is disconnected from the political and economic power that determine who has the privilege of mobility, it further reproduces the histories of colonial discourse within the tradition of tourism (Hanley 2). Alegría's narrative especially foregrounds the American notion of the "disparaging moral geography" (Schantz 147) south of the U.S. border when it describes, at the start of the story, the teenagers' excited expectations for the weekend of partying: "As a graduation present, Steve's folks were letting him turn their vacation home near Tijuana, Mexico, into a wanton wonderland" (1). Steve has promised a party that will be "the hottest thing since the thong" (2) with "plenty of booze, and tons of opportunities for unregulated debauchery" (1). Outside, too, the air of Rosarito is "heavy with desire and the scent of sizzling meat" as "gorgeous guys and scantily clad girls [strut] down the boulevard" (37). Mexico as an adventure playground and a site of amusement becomes permissible through a culturally specific rite of passage (graduation), one that couches worldly independence through the language of eroticization, desire, and consumption.

That language of consumption is especially notable in the depiction of women's bodies as racially inflected commodities of desire. We see this in the way that Sofi's brown body becomes particularly disrupted in the tourist setting. Ruiz, citing bell hooks, explains that representations of racial difference, "even ones that appear sympathetic to those whose racial difference is highlighted," always reflect the power between dominant and subordinate groups (29). Sofi, who for years has been dreaming of a romantic relationship with Nick, "a total Abercrombie babe, with the deepest blue eyes, the sexiest shaggy blond hair, the cutest cleft in his chin, and the most irresistible smile" (1), is initially excited to find herself on the beach with him in what she hopes is a prelude to their first kiss and (in her mind) their entire life together: "Their first dance would lead to their first kiss and then dating, the prom, marriage, and happily-ever-after" (54). However, when Nick calls her a *"Latina caliente"* and tells her that she has "the hottest ass in school" and that he had earlier told his friend "I'd tap dat hot Latin ass by Monday" (55), it becomes evident that in this holiday setting, bodies are purely for consumption (Sofi later says that Nick has "treated her like a piece of meat" [59]).

Nick's racial hypersexualization of Sofi, expressed in terms of conquest and desire, is especially disempowering because it also echoes U.S. dominant culture's interpellation of Latinx bodies as expendable and disposable. She fights him off successfully, but afterward, in her mortification, just wants to "disappear" (57), telling her friends that "he didn't see me. Doesn't know anything about me. It's just so wrong" (58). Nick renders her invisible, and like Mexico, she (to Nick) has no story and no history worth knowing. As hooks notes, "when race and ethnicity become commodified as resources for pleasure . . . the culture of specific groups, as well as the bodies of individuals can be seen as constituting an alternative playground where members of the dominating races . . . affirm the power . . . in intimate relations to one another" (Ruiz 29). This particular thread of the story's romance plot, while predictable, foregrounds for young adult readers the ways in which the personal is highly political, as Nick's hypersexualization of Sofi so clearly intersects with his hypersexualization of Mexico, Mexicans, and Mexican Americans.[2] The aborted relationship between them demonstrates a disruption of the commodifying tourist gaze (Nick's toward Sofi), as Sofi strikes back, but because she has invested years fantasizing about the life she and Nick will have together, the crushing of those fantasies disrupts her much broader sense of personhood and identity. After this scene, she is newly aware of her status as a nonperson, a racially subordinate figure in the adolescent hierarchy of popularity and belonging. This personal disruption and erasure of identity, of course, lays the groundwork for the political nonperson that she will become once she tries to reenter the United States from Mexico.

The text's exploration of Sofi's relationship to Mexico and to the United States ultimately asks what kind of legacy and inheritance both nations can provide for Sofi, given her contradictory feelings of separation from and attachment to them. Before her arrival in Mexico, Sofi's knowledge of it is limited and U.S.-centric. Her parents' stories of their homeland lack nostalgia and situate the United States as a place of advantages and privileges compared to Mexico, "where politicians were crooks, cops abused their power, and if you were poor there was no way to get ahead" (4–5). There are no loving accounts of extended family, either; "the faded square photographs of her mother's family were totally foreign to her" (2), and even the fact that Sofi has relatives in Rosarito is presented vaguely: "Sometimes her dad talked about his sister, who still lived around here. Luisa was her name" (20). Mexico and their Mexican family appear to have been left behind geographically and temporally: the fact that Luisa "still" lives there implies that unlike Sofi's parents, she has not moved forward into any kind of successful American future. Such silencing interpellations of Mexico render it shameful and secretive, a place from which Sofi's parents (and inadvertently, Sofi herself) must dissociate themselves. Mexico, therefore, does not provide a firm foundation for her identity. At the same time, neither does the United States: Sofi says that all her life "I never felt like I fit in [there]" (205), and as Ibarraran-Bigalondo remarks, Sofi's "understanding of her own identity (she is an American) is derived from the construction of the feeling of what she is not, rather than of what she is" (29). In other words, she is American only insofar as she is not Mexican; her belonging in the United States is based on a default sense of not belonging anywhere else.

In Mexico, Sofi's tourist gaze is thus ambivalent and uneasy: she feels "disconnected" from her friends' reactions to their environment, aware of the unbalanced power dynamic created by their presence, and more distracted by and immersed in her surroundings (21). She feels guilty at the stark contrasts between Tijuana and Southern California (17) and at how the border imposes inequity even in the physical landscape: "It changed the air, making it heavy and hard to breathe" (17). She is the only one to wonder why the local children are out so late at night (31), recognizing their personhood beyond their role as local "hosts." Even the way she moves through the streets of Rosarito echoes an undocumented migrant's secret life of nonbelonging in the United States: while Olivia and Taylor take "big, confident strides, stopping every now and then to flirt," Sofi follows behind them "in the shadows" (37). The tourist playground of Rosarito is so Americanized that she still, figuratively, exists in the shadows, and her attempts to mimic her friends only expose the masquerade of her tourist identity: when she decides that she too "is going to strut" like them, she twists her ankle in her borrowed heels (37).

In Mexico, then, she is neither an American tourist nor a native Mexican, although she is intermittently ascribed as both. In many ways, she is othered in Mexico: her weak Spanish manifests physically as she struggles to find the right words ("her tongue wouldn't work" [84]), while the beautiful landscape fails to "lift up her soul," implying that she is "infinitely more American than . . . Mexican" (92). Most aspects of life on her aunt's rancho feel difficult and foreign to her (91, 92, 104, 112). But at the same time, Sofi also connects to Mexico because her racial ethnicity—her physical appearance—is shared by Mexicans around her. This racial affinity plays a key role in disrupting her tourist gaze and building her sense of belonging to the nation. Usually, experiences of tourism have defined parameters, such as the expectation of a return home, and inherent in tourism, according to Berger and Wood, is "a sacredness, a kind of liminality defined by time away from the ordinary" (3). From the start, though, Sofi's tourist gaze is more complex than her friends' because she increasingly finds reminders of her ordinary life all around her: the Mexican children "looked like her with their sun-baked skin and soulful brown eyes" (23); she recognizes the hat vendor "from somewhere" and notices that another woman has "the same harried expression as Sofi's mother" (27). The story does at times uncritically adopt an essentialized view of what it means to look Mexican ("soulful" brown eyes [18], "caramel" skin [135]), but identifying Sofi's connection to the nation through her racialized subject position also indicates how so much of the shame associated with being Latinx in the U.S. circulates around American objectifications of Latinx bodies.

Encountering the Border

In the novel, the United States–Mexico border is the site at which Mexican identity is rendered shameful and illegitimate. Borders, of course, mark centrality, marginality, belonging, and unbelonging, but the United States–Mexico border, at the time of the novel's 2007 publication, saw an increase in unauthorized crossing and was the focus of several ideological as well as physical and spatial concerns prompted by the Secure Fence Act (2006). The act included a systematic surveillance of the border through sensors and satellites, as well as physical infrastructure enhancements, and continued to be essential, as Ibarraran-Bigalondo notes, "in the construction of a very particular border identity, and in the reinforcement of U.S. and Mexican national identities" (20). Under such surveillance, the border constructs the notion of the state, imposing the concept of sovereign territoriality upon the landscape and in many cases changing that physical landscape: "Before

the fence, there is just desert, brush, and land. After the fence, there are citizens, ownership, geography, territoriality, governance, and enforcement."
Consequently, the border also establishes the immigrant as the "constitutive
outsider to the citizen, the other to the state" (Auchter 295). State sovereignty is also constructed by tourism, in the sense that tourism requires
an established and sometimes manufactured national identity (made up of
landscape, topography, and culture) to put itself on display, and the border
often marks the moment where the tourist becomes a tourist and can begin
to encounter the new nation.[3] In this respect, the border represents not only
a new sovereign state but an identity shift from citizen to tourist (and back
again, on the return home). Under ordinary circumstances, the border marks
the temporal and spatial beginning or end of the vacation and the time suspended from reality.

The surveillance and militarization of the United States–Mexico border,
which scrutinizes these various shifts between tourist/citizen, member/non-
member, and outsider/insider, is apparent even as the girls cross into Mexico.
Although they enter Mexico easily (as Olivia remarks, "I don't think Mexico
has an illegal-immigrant problem" [16]), the power imbalances between the
two nations, one a "politically and economically weaker sending [country]"
and the other a "more advantaged receiving [one]" (Croucher 4) are evident.
Sofi notes how northward, "cars were piled bumper-to-bumper . . . scary-
looking agents with guns strapped to their waists directed traffic" (16). She
is hyperaware of the border's significance in her personal family history, so
that entering Mexico, "the land of her parents, without their knowledge"
feels momentous, and she holds her breath, aware that they had crossed the
same border fourteen years earlier (15). More so than her American friends,
Sofi is attuned to the border as highly determinant of one's opportunities
in life, and in that sense, she imposes her own emotional surveillance on
the experience of entering Mexico, understanding how even crossing easily
into Mexico is inseparable from, and overdetermined by, the difficulties and
implications of crossing north.

On the girls' return to the border to reenter the United States at the end of
the weekend, we see not only the imposition of state sovereignty at the border site but also the way that the force of that imposition destroys the myth
of Mexico as a fun, playful place. Because "it seemed like everyone in Mexico
was trying to get out" (61), the amusement site has become a kind of prison,
and the traveler's adventure has morphed into a frightening entrapment.

Furthermore, the moment where Sofi must show her green card shamefully transforms her into a non-American. Even before she learns that her green card is forged, she is "embarrass[ed]" to have to "admit that she wasn't really an American" (63), and this sense of shame is later amplified when she realizes that she has to stay in Mexico: imagining her friends telling everyone at school, she thinks that "this had to be the most horribly embarrassing thing in the entire world" (72). At the border, illegality is created and defined: the immigration officer treats them "as though they were a gang of criminals" (63) and addresses Sofi directly in derogatory terms: "you illegals think you can just fool anyone with any number" (64).

Being "illegal" here does not only mean that she lacks the correct documents but also that she has slyly tried to cheat the system; the "illegal" individual, then, is interpellated as being of a certain criminal character. Initially, Sofi takes offense, asking "Who was he to call her illegal?" because she genuinely believes she is a legal resident of the United States. Her insistence that the label does not belong to her is thus authentic and represents, in a broader way, the text's assertion that the label belongs to no one. Sofi's swift rejection of the term *illegal* implies that illegality is not an inherent quality: she does not *feel* illegal because she has never lived in the shadows and has no experiential knowledge or existential fear of not legally belonging. In contrast to the continuous, often insidious trauma that sometimes accompanies Dreamers' daily lives, Sofi's trauma erupts from an isolated moment at the border itself. In other words, the realization that her documents are valueless and illegitimate happens at the very place where documents hold absolute definitive value.[4]

In this moment of trauma where her Americanness is denied, parts of Sofi's life flash before her eyes as a series of ordinary American experiences (playing at the beach, sitting at her desk in grade school) that she now interprets as a series of lies (65). Given her newly existential nonbelonging, she has no narrative framework through which to structure the history of her past experiences or her present-day identity. The shock of this trauma makes Sofi feel not-human and empty and is reminiscent of narratives of death and disappearance at the border, because figuratively, of course, a version of herself *has* vanished at this border: "Her voice sounded dead to her own ears. She felt hollow, like a gutted fish. She was only going through the motions of a normal human being" (66). This rupture at the border, which establishes her illegitimacy, is part of a continuum of shaming experiences that have othered and objectified her Mexican body, much in the same way that a particular kind of tourist's gaze objectifies Mexico. Beginning with Nick's treatment of her, Sofi undergoes a gradual process of figurative vanishing, as the shame of being rendered illegal—first as racially hypersexual and then as racially criminal—causes self-repulsion and abjection. She wonders how her friends see her now and is unable to look them in the eye, thinking, "Were they disgusted with her? Horrified? Angry? All her ugly dark feelings began to surface like bubbles" (66).

The trauma of Sofi's illegality persists in an insidious way long after the abrupt event at the border and becomes an important part of her emergent, albeit unidentified, status as a Dreamer. After the border moves her from one side of the hierarchical binary system to the other—from legal to illegal, worthy to disposable, and American to Mexican—she vacillates between renewed bouts of disbelief and shock ("she didn't want to know" the truth; her heart races and she feels woozy [133]) as well as worthlessness: "She was not a legal anything of America. Sofi was a criminal" (134). Her only point of reference has been America, and now that point of reference transforms her into a person without value and without, in some senses, an existence. The border has seemingly taken away everything: "Her entire life had fluttered away from her grasp. Sofi was left holding nothing but air" (158). Her American cultural membership has been destabilized, as memories of her life, ambitions, and expectations appear unreal and undeserved: "Visions of high school, her friends, her house, and her warm fuzzy bed dangled before her like a dream" (134).

For the first two decades of the century, conversations and stories about the status of undocumented youths ("Dreamers") were circulating in increasingly public forums and outlets. The DREAM Act failed to pass when it was first introduced in 2001 and was then reintroduced several times over the years. While in 2007, at the time of the novel's writing and setting, public recognition of Dreamers was not as widespread as it would later become, it is clear that Alegría positions Sofi as an early Dreamer. Sofi's realization that all her dreams have blown up, for example, is conveyed as a classic Dreamer moment: her parents had "promised that if I worked hard, I could make all my dreams come true" (140). The term *Dreamer* does not appear in the story, and nor does Sofi identify as one, but for contemporary readers her voice and aspirations are clearly those of a Dreamer. The author's note at the beginning, in fact, contextualizes this pre-Dreamer status, explaining that the book was inspired by a real-life story of two women who were denied reentry into the United States after visiting Tijuana for an afternoon. The women, who were California State University students, had come to the United States as children and lived in California for sixteen years with work permits. Alegría writes, "Martha and Carmelia's story is not unusual on the border. However, their voices have been ignored, dismissed by mainstream media, and overlooked in the U.S. immigration debate" (vii), and unlike the characters in the fiction, they cannot petition for reentry for another ten years. At the time of its publication, then, the novel was part of an unfolding (and still ongoing) narrative that was crucial in bringing previously silenced personal experiences into the public arena of immigration policy and debate. Near the end of the novel, when Sofi's lawyer tells her that there is very little hope for her return to the United States (she does not qualify for American citizenship under any of the usual routes), he adds that there are congressional bills being discussed that might help her (207). Although (in an unlikely plot twist) Sofi's American-born Mexican grandmother will eventually save the day, at this point in the story Alegría clearly highlights the devastating effect of stalled policies on real (and fictional) lives so as to alert young readers to the personal and emotional consequences of immigration law.

Knowing Mexico

The trauma of discovering her undocumented status is both sudden and insidious, turning Sofi into an existentially disposable subject, and the rest of the story then examines the healing that must take place to recover from this trauma. Sofi's maturation journey shifts her gaze so that she comes to know Mexico anew, both by bearing witness to the stories she hears and by having lived experiences that connect her to the nation. Her new cultural and political knowledge about Mexico not only allows her to claim her ancestral roots and to value the plurality and intersectionality of her national identities but also recovers Mexico from the rhetoric of secrecy and shame that haunts Dreamers in the United States.

The trope of Mexico as a healing space for disaffected Americans is itself part of a long literary tradition, which has at times produced stereotypes of Mexico in American writings. Mermann-Jozwiak describes how for modernist writers Mexico became "the site of the bourgeois subject's escape from Western civilization and its neo romantic quest for restoration." Drawing on

Renato Rosaldo's work, Mermann-Jozwiak notes how this view, undergirded by an imperialist nostalgia, sees Mexico, as the antithesis to the United States, as representing authenticity, simplicity, innocence, and an idealized past (premodern) time (95, 96). This "Mexicanism" was a form of primitivism that especially manifested as a fascination with Mexico's contemporary Indian population and a colonial attitude to race. Mermann-Jozwiak points out that as American writers continue to cross the southern border, they "inevitably engage their protagonists in ethnography, the encounter with and representation of others, in this case, an Other that has been marginalized and colonized in the West" and she asks, "What, then are the continuities and discontinuities between theirs and modernist writings about Mexico? How do contemporary authors of Mexican descent portray this journey?" (96).

Insofar as I am treating *Sofi Mendoza* here as a travelogue of sorts (in its effect, if not in its intent), these are pertinent questions to consider. Does the text critique or perpetuate Mexicanism? In the novel, Mexico heals a series of American maladies: emotional deficits, internalized self-hatred, tense parent-child relationships, superficial adolescent values, and dangerous understandings of romance; it even provides a legal path to U.S. citizenship when Sofi's Mexican grandmother reveals she is also an American citizen. The story also presents many problematic binaries, such as superficial American lifestyles versus authentic salt-of-the-earth Mexican lifestyles and characters. By the end, Sofi exclaims that she now has "this big crazy Mexican family" that she loves "with all their contradictions" and that she has "never felt so alive" in her entire life (205). This notion of a contradictory, crazy, and complex Mexico (repeated frequently in the text) reiterates the classic paradigms that Mermann-Jozwiak identifies, and Sofi's embrace of them—the way they fulfill and satisfy her so completely—further perpetuates those stereotypes. However, Alegría also interrogates American neocolonial tendencies toward Mexico, albeit implicitly, in various ways. First, although Sofi has been influenced by American neocolonial discourses as much as other American teenagers have, their exoticization of Mexico makes her uncomfortable and works as a starting point for her maturation journey. Second, the novel does show the cultural interchangeability of the entire borderland area and in this respect disempowers the United States–Mexico border and challenges the sovereignty of individual nations.

As her starting point, then, Sofi learns to identify between disparate versions of Mexico: the commodified one staged for tourists and the more complex one hidden from them. Almost immediately after being turned back at the border, she begins to confront these differences. The taxi ride back to Rosarito from Tijuana takes her via the Mexican national road rather than the scenic toll road she took earlier on (73). The former is free of charge, is heavily congested and traveled by locals, and reveals extreme poverty side by side with wealth: "cardboard-constructed shanty houses with tin roofs hanging dangerously close to the cliff's edge" separated by barbed-wire fences from million-dollar megamansions (73). Traveling "in the wrong direction," Sofi moves literally away from the United States, toward a "mismatched" Mexican town (74), and figuratively toward a more hybrid identity of her own. Here, she begins to critically deconstruct some of the myths of national sovereignty: noticing a billboard ad for Gated American Dream Homes, she wonders "why people would have to come to Mexico to get the American dream" (74). In indicating the irony of the American dream taking place in Mexico, the narrative demonstrates how the space of Mexico is co-opted by American values.

Sofi also realizes that the spatial experience of Rosarito is determined by its temporality: now that the weekend is over, the tourist town looks "all wrong . . . with regular Mexican-looking people in regular-looking clothes walking down the busy commercial street . . . It was all so foreign to Sofi" (71, 74). Later, though, she learns to enjoy the border town's hybridity, appreciating that it "always had something new to show her" with its "layers and layers of different perceptions" (130). The American façade and the Mexican authenticity, then, are both legitimate parts of the city's blended dual identity. The narrative's detailed description of Boulevard Benito Juárez, which teems with American tourists, people who live off tourism, and American expatriates, reads like a mini travelogue that illustrates the town's busy network of global capitalism and intercultural encounters. Beyond the ethnographic engagement of this passage, readers (as well as Sofi) can recognize the improvisational interactions that take place through such transnational encounters. Gilbert M. Joseph discusses the ways that even the power-laden contexts of tourism can yield "interactive . . . possibilities" such as the "making and articulation of national . . . and even international identities" (8). Similarly, Sofi's gaze starts to move away from the asymmetrical power dynamic of tourist/ host and toward a more collaborative dynamic whose personal dimension also has, potentially, more far-reaching political implications.

As part of this more collaborative tourist-host dynamic, the story has Sofi begin to celebrate the shared physical traits that she earlier identified in those around her. When she meets her grandmother, she is pleased to notice that they have the same nose, which Sofi has always hated because it is "not at all dainty like her friends' noses" (219). Now she realizes that she "love[s] it" (219), presumably because it is evidence of an ancestral connection that outweighs the white beauty standards that have othered her. At home she has never liked being the "different-looking one," but now, in Mexico, where her "dark skin, dark eyes, dark hair" are a "badge of pride" (177), "she like[s] blending in" (122). This familial kinship extends to all Mexicans. At the migrant camp that she visits, "everywhere she turned she saw familiar-looking faces" (153), recognizing her mother's strong nose and a man who looks just like her uncle. In this place of poverty, she feels a shared bond with the people because of their Mexican faces: "a new feeling was spilling into her heart . . . a crystal-clear awareness that she was related to all these people. *They are Mexican like me*, she thought" (154). Over time, too, this intensifying nationalism connects her more strongly to the physical landscape: "The turquoise blue sky contrasted with the dark green plants and brown hills. It was a soothing sight and nursed her homesickness" (188). In "nursing" her homesickness, the land of Mexico begins to heal the shame of her "illegality" and the trauma of her national displacement. All these therapies—the connections to family, race, and land—give Sofi a sense of worth because they allow her to construct a new narrative, and through that, to forge membership in a nation that up until now has been devoid of stories.

Along with new physical kinships, Sofi also acquires cultural and intellectual knowledge to better understand Mexico's political, social, and historical realities. This knowledge transforms her, and along with the protagonist, readers also learn from these more explicitly pedagogical sections of the text. Sofi's new friend Andres, for example, offers to show her around and be her "guide" in Mexico (178), providing her (and us) lessons that combine history with current affairs and presenting ethical ideas about how to improve things for the future (180). Sofi's most explicitly transformative experience takes place on her visit to the migrant camp where her aunt and cousin distribute used clothing and stuffed animals. Initially Sofi, thinking about her senior prom she is missing in the United States, resists going and claims it's "so not fair" (148), but almost immediately upon arrival she is shocked and moved. The poverty and desperation around her, and her interaction with the migrants, awaken her moral consciousness.

In this encounter, where she engages in a version of tourist volunteerism, she questions the broader injustices of the system ("How could [the Mexican government] let this happen?" [152]), recognizes that life outcome is an accident of birth and circumstances (*"Why do I live there* [in the United States] *and have everything and more? Why do some children go hungry while others pick and choose what they want on a whim?"* [152]), and acknowledges her own privilege ("[she] felt ashamed. All she could think about was getting home for a big party while others were just trying to survive the day with enough food to eat" [161]). Unlike her earlier touristic interactions with poverty, this time she directly faces it without distractions and finds that "the more she watched, the more questions she had" (153). The pedagogy here encourages questioning and challenging the status quo and shows how, when faced with evidence of injustice, the adolescent's natural sense of justice moves them to act: Sofi later considers organizing a broader social justice movement among her school friends to help the migrant camp more (158). Through Sofi's reaction, the reader sees how a tourist encounter, in its most ideal form, can move from empathy to action. It is important to note, however, that her ability to help still echoes an asymmetrical power dynamic: it is only possible because of her relatively privileged subject position and the children's reliance on her.

Sofi's maturation process is also reflected in the changing narratives of Mexico that she sends to her friends and family back in the United States. Sofi's initial emails to her friends are panicked as she pronounces her experiences as beyond belief and the place as otherworldly. In one, she writes, "You'll never believe what's happened to me"; complains about the bugs and the lack of power, hot water, cable, internet, and phone; and exclaims that she has "woken up in a total nightmare" in which her aunt is a villainous character who treats her "like [a] slave" (127). She ends with a plea that Olivia "make up something cool" when talking to other students about Sofi's time in Mexico. The email's rhetoric and tone are hyperbolic, once again fabricating Mexico in the United States' imagination. It also contains important emotional truths about her experiences: those experiences are shameful because (in her mind) they confirm her illegitimate "illegal" status. Sofi's later emails to her friends, in contrast, are newsy, with information about how daily life keeps her busy. There are few complaints, and instead, she provides details about regular life in Mexico (looking after her cousins, watching soap operas, going to a concert). By now, she has earned the authority to write as both an insider and an outsider—her life is still noteworthy and novel enough to be recorded but not excessively other or foreign. With this balance, the extreme narrative of Mexico in the U.S. imagination is undone: it is neither a horror story nor a fairy tale but rather an interesting account of ordinary life.

These contrasts reflect the different purposes served by the traveler's task of communication. Both, as moments of authorship, assume power, but they wield it to different ends. The earlier therapeutic emails are necessary for conveying the urgency of Sofi's situation, while the later emails, in more measured tones, start to mend the narratives of Mexico abroad. Initially, Sofi writes for catharsis and connection: even seeing the emails waiting in her inbox makes "tears well up in her eyes" because she knows she has not been forgotten at home (127). The therapeutic effect of her early emails comes from being able to control the narrative and exert her authority over that narrative; it is precisely because she has so little autonomy in Mexico that exaggerating her account helps her navigate her environment. Both types of emails are forms of tourist testimonials, as their goal is to tell and record the novelty of the experience, to transport it back home, and to increase knowledge production. The first one, however, emerges from shame and (even if inadvertently) repeats familiar stereotyped accounts of Mexico; the second one, after Sofi's maturation and adjustment, is based on familiarity and connection.

Rites of Passage

The novel also shows how Sofi's time in Mexico reframes her understanding of U.S. adolescent rites of passage. The lessons she learns in Mexico make her reexamine these rites and her relationships with boys and with her parents, and develop a new bicultural self that is focused on self-worth rather than shame. Amy Cummins points out that the topic of living without papers is an especially important one in young adult literature because for undocumented youths, adolescence brings a "transition to illegality" as they are excluded from rites of passage such as driving, voting, and other activities requiring authorized status ("Dreamers" 80, 83–84). In fact, the process of attempting these rites of passage is, for unauthorized youths, a process of becoming illegal; typical normative experiences become atypical experiences of illegitimacy. Sofi's desire to participate in these rites, even before discovering her status, has always felt like a desire to be "normal": going to Mexico and attending the party there fulfils an important rite of passage, because "if there was no Rosarito, then there would surely be no Nick, no prom, no happily-ever-after" (10). Critics also point out the connection between this sort of mobility, class, and race: Berger and Wood explain how tourism has "come to represent a rite of passage to adulthood for those who can afford it" (3), while Mermann-Jozwiak notes that whiteness is the very thing (in literary accounts) that gives characters mobility (99). In the story, normative expectations of travel are enabled through the higher socioeconomic status that has long eluded Sofi, and intersect with her longing for whiteness. It is Nick, after all, who "was going to make all her American dreams come true" (4).

The novel reexamines these normative rituals not only with lessons about the privileges inherent in them but also by exploring their cultural specificity. Because Sofi (stuck in Mexico) cannot attend the established rituals that come at the end of one's senior year (graduation, prom), she feels she has effectively disappeared from the United States. Her maturation involves deciding which experiences actually matter to her, as her U.S.-centric perspective about American rituals is replaced with Mexican customs. On the same evening of her prom, for example, Sofi and her cousin Yesenia gate-crash a quinceañera in Rosarito. A rite of passage, of course, is important largely because it is highly anticipated, because of the community membership it bestows, and because of its promise of transformation and change. While their quinceañera attendance is a spur-of-the moment decision, it turns out to be better than prom (170) and becomes, retroactively, its own rite of passage that allows Sofi a real sense of belonging (171).

For Sofi, time in Rosarito seems to "stand still" while life in the United States continues "at a crazy pace" (217), but once she returns to the United States at the end of the novel, she feels that life *there* has "stood still" (274). Her earlier sense of being absent from her life in the United States was an expression of bereavement about not being able to move forward in the only way she knew how: that is, through U.S.-prescribed rites of passage. Seeing the United States through her new "Mexican eyes" (274), however, she realizes that in Mexico there was a different kind of forward movement continuously unfolding, one composed of unanticipated and difficult experiences that did not already fit into a familiar narrative and that for these reasons were crucial for her maturation. This broadened perspective impacts Sofi's friends in the United States, too: during their high school graduation, in her absence, everyone wears buttons that read "NO BORDERS, FREE SOFI" (271). In thus renewing one of the most traditional rites of passage, they demonstrate the hope that it is the youths who will do "most of the work of revolution" in the nation (Jiménez García, "En(countering) YA" 247). By blending political protest with rite of passage, the adolescents can finesse and wield the power of readily available platforms for more socially relevant acts of justice.

Insofar as the need to partake in a collective rite of passage establishes a kind of group belonging, we can also read the novel's romance plot as illustrative of a rite of passage. Most adolescents are strongly motivated by the desire to belong socially to (and receive approval from) their peer group, but in Alegría's text this desire intersects with questions of political and national affiliations and the existential threat that accompanies their erasure. How Sofi navigates her romantic world, then, indicates how she will navigate her own identity as a politically aware, ethically minded Latina in the United States. The romance plot, too, pulls the reader in. Even after the incident with Nick, and even after Sofi finds herself stranded in Mexico and living in an estranged manner with her relatives there, she continues to pine for true love. For this reason, Rico, the handsome and villainous man who pursues her in Mexico, seems initially to offer a perfect antidote to her shame: he is "perfect boyfriend material" (160) and "the type of boyfriend she would be proud to show off to her friends" (212). The book's moral compass, though, eventually helps readers (along with Sofi) realize that not only is Rico "just a pretty face" with "no depth" (226) but that his hungry gaze, so like a tourist's, dangerously reinforces American imperialist values and violations.

With Rico, Sofi learns how a particular type of gaze creates an exotic other and circulates disempowering tropes of shaming. In eventually rejecting him, Sofi rejects objectified views of her body and realizes that her earlier obsession with Nick was a "false idea" and a "made-up fantasy" that problematically reflected his own "*Latina caliente*" image of her (167). While Rico reinforces modes of colonial subjugation with his attempted rape of Sofi, Andres is the epitome of respectful courtesy, treating Sofi like a friend as well as potential love interest. He also represents anti-U.S. imperialism; although he was born in the United States, he chooses (for now) to live in Mexico and critically resists the incursion of U.S. values upon Mexican life (158). Gradually, Sofi comes to appreciate Andres's intelligence and proactive interest in the world around him: "Andres was a real smart guy. She liked that. Most of the guys at school were just into sports, parties, and hanging out. He was like no one she'd ever met before" (157), and in choosing him, she recognizes her own worth and legitimates her own judgment as valid and sound. Andres's ambitions—he plans to go back to school, enter poli-

tics, and then return to Rosarito to institute all the project ideas he has—
represent the novel's optimism about the revolutionary potential of youths,
who are determined to change the world and understand the importance
of promoting social justice. Andres's passionate words, too, are intended
to inspire readers because of his parallel roles as love interest and ethically
minded youth organizer. When he tells Sofi "We'll get rid of the national and
international chain stores and go local. Go solar. It'll be great. Rosarito will
be the first twenty-first-century economically self-sustaining community in
Mexico. It'll be a model for the rest of the country" (262), he woos her (and
the reader) not just romantically but also politically.

The ethical mindset of the novel's youths is also apparent through Sofi's
renewed relationship with her parents, as her time in Mexico causes her
to value rather than scorn them. According to Joanna Johnson, images of
parenthood in young adult literature usually feature parents that do not understand the adolescent, and this lack or rejection of parenting "becomes a
more serious component because it requires that the protagonist make her
own decisions and act on her own. This movement points to the character's
maturing and severing ties that connected her to childhood . . . [she] must
ultimately face the reality that she is responsible for her own actions" (152).
Anglo-dominant young adult literature is also predicated on a cultural bias
where it is a given that adolescents must separate from parents to grow.
Certainly, Sofi spends most of the story away from her parents, is eager to
leave home and live in a college dorm, and from the outset is already engaged
in classic generational clashes with them over boys, studying, partying, and
various other aspects of American teenage life. To her, they are traditionally
restrictive "old-school typical Mexican immigrants" (4), and she defines herself as American in part by opposing everything they represent.

But Jiménez García warns that "few scholars take into account how racial and national associations complicate notions of adolescence, rebelling,
authority, and maturity central to YA" ("En(countering) YA" 235). Latinx
young adult literature, for example, challenges the notion of separate worlds
for youths and adults (246), emphasizing strong family relationships: "To
separate from the adult world is not protocol in a Latinx adolescent's journey . . . since they live in a world in which adults in their communities are
not empowered in the traditional sense" (235). To this point, Sofi's parents'
control over her is ambiguous, as while they wield some authority in the
household, they also seem vulnerable outside of it. Looking at them, Sofi

feels "shame and pity" (4) because of their disempowerment in the work-place and their discomfort among white wealthy Americans. In Latinx lit-erature, then, there is often an interdependence between youths and adults, who might recognize that they suffer the same racial and social inequalities: while Anglo-driven young adult literature thrives on a rebellious youth fig-ure, Latinx young adult literature, points out Jiménez García, does not always present the traditional agents of repression against which teens must rebel to acquire an identity (239).

Sofi's rebellious act (escaping for a weekend to Mexico) physically sepa-rates her from her parents (with traumatic consequences), but it also even-tually draws her closer to them because it forces an urgent reckoning of her own history and therefore of her own parents' lives in unanticipated ways. In wandering the streets of Rosarito and wondering if they had ever walked those same streets in the past (20), she starts to see them as having subject positions and histories separate from her own and redefines them not just as awkward others in the United States but as citizens who perhaps once upon a time seamlessly belonged in this landscape. Imagining them thus allows her to more fully recognize their personhood, and the complexity of Mexico, and plays a key role in determining how she will heal her relationship with them: she not only develops emotional attachments to their homeland and extended family but also begins acknowledging their shared experiences as products, to a degree, of U.S. oppression.

Ultimately, the resolution of the parent-child relationship in the novel demonstrates both interdependence and independence, showing Alegría's commitment to honoring the blended cultural experiences of U.S. Latinx life. On reuniting with her mother in California, Sofi immediately exclaims, "I learned my lesson all right," and adds, "I'll never leave your side again" (270). Here, Sofi suggests that her detainment was a deserved punishment for trying to separate from her parents in the first place. She understands that she is not like her friends Olivia and Taylor, the Anglo young adult characters who take for granted that they will be allowed to go away to college and who seem to operate under a different disciplinary system. Even though Olivia and Taylor earlier on also broke the law (by trying to smuggle a dog back into the United States, a "serious offense punishable by possible prison time" [62]), they were nevertheless allowed back into the United States and simply grounded by their parents. In contrast, Sofi's "crime" and its effects are more devastating, and in her punitive declaration that she will never leave home, she attempts to replicate the authority of the sovereign state inside her own home. In other words, she tries to restore her parents' authority over her as a kind of gift to them, parallel to the authority of the nation-state, and perhaps also as compensation for their own history of disempowerment. But importantly, the novel provides a happy ending, satisfying readers' hopes that Sofi will still experience some of the rites of passage and cultural freedoms of her peers. Once she is back in the United States, Sofi's parents finally give her the independence she seeks, allowing her to attend the University of California, Los Angeles. Hearing this, Sofi screams in excitement, "UCLA dorms . . . here I come!" (270). Although dorm living symbolizes separation, it comes after an intense journey of connectivity, implying that Sofi will be able to forge a new self that is both independent and collective and more ethically attuned to the specific nuances of her bicultural identity.

Knowing the Border

An important part of the novel's pedagogical intent is seen in its depictions of the United States–Mexico border, which are crucial to Sofi's maturation. The narrative clearly deconstructs the border—almost immediately after she is refused reentry into the United States, Sofi's cab driver refers to a time "before the border, when this was all Mexico" (72)—and it also recounts the material effect of the border on the daily lives of Rosarito's denizens.[5] From various characters in the town, who all "wanted to talk and hang out" (124), Sofi hears testimonials that nuance and texture the narrative of the border: the tradition of hanging a black ribbon on the door when a family member dies trying to cross, descriptions of bodies being returned to their families, and accounts of the vigilante Minute Men (124–25). These stories provide her with accumulated histories and remembered pasts that build a more complete and legitimate sense of identity. Hearing these stories is empowering, as it helps Sofi understand how the shame of illegitimacy that haunts her U.S. identity is based on an arbitrarily established border line and on the nation's exercise of sovereignty at that site. She is also empowered by the intersection of prayer and politics that manifests as acts of resistance and survival in the daily life of the border-town Mexicans. In the botanica that she visits, for example, she learns that there is a prayer, candle, and saint specifically for crossing the border (165). The prayer's wording ("I recognize that I have defied human laws. They arrested me for crossing a line that men have drawn as a frontier" [165]) acknowledges the law but also deconstructs the border as a man-made boundary.

Alongside mitigating the fear of border crossing through resistant prayer, the narrative also offers some alternatives to the American dream and the desire to cross north. Doña Clementina, for example, vividly recounts her own crossings into the United States through a dirt tunnel in Texas and concludes, "I ended up here in Rosarito after my fifth deportation. It's hard living like a scared *pollito* . . . I like Rosarito . . . It wasn't my American dream, but I think I gained much more. I have a nice shop that's close to the beach. There're lots of friends who stop by. Life is good. I don't stress about being deported or about managers trying to cheat me because of papers. Here, I'm in charge of my life" (117). At this point the text highlights not only the difficulty of crossing and then living as an undocumented migrant in the United States, but also reorients what might be considered valuable and worthy by discarding the American dream in favor of a Mexican one.

The most powerfully pedagogical moment in the text, though, comes from Sofi's own experience of unauthorized border crossing when she runs away from her aunt's house in the middle of the night. Earlier on, when she first attempted to reenter the United States with her friends, she was an American tourist who was newly traumatized by the discovery of her fraudulent paperwork, but this time, in her decision to cross north with help from Rico and his coyote contacts, she has abandoned the tourist "scene" and become a Mexican trying to cross into *el otro lado* (the other side [of the border]) (236). She also now carries with her the many stories of danger she has heard: "She remembered María Rita's story and that of Javier's uncle, who died trying to cross. She could be raped, mugged, or even killed" (233). The decision to cross is an explicit rejection of the state's declaration that she does not deserve to be in the United States, so in that respect it indicates a more determined act of resistance, but it also briefly moves the narrative into darker possibilities. She ponders, "Would people put flowers on some unmarked grave if [I] didn't make it?" (234). She pushes the thought away, but the moment of imagining herself as literally disappeared is a grim culmination of the figurative disappearing she has experienced since being forced to remain in Mexico.

Rico encourages Sofi's fears, noting that "there's always a risk. I'm sure you've heard all kinds of tales about the people who get lost in canyons and die of dehydration?" (236) but adds that "everybody has a sob story" and that "most of those people don't know what they're doing" (238). Such circulation of stories about border crossers is important, functioning as a memorial for those who have died or disappeared and foregrounding the insidiousness of border trauma in their daily lives. But Rico's narrative blames the crosser (for being ignorant or weak) rather than the system and attempts to undo the protective role of cautionary tales. His dismissive tone also removes the emotional appeal of such stories and their potential, if disseminated, for making important policy changes to immigration law. Through Rico, a border crosser's inability to arrive safely on the other side is a sign of individual failure and shame, rather than a collective responsibility and tragedy.

The novel, of course, has its protagonist not only recognize Rico's problematic narrative but also triumph and overcome it. It is fitting, too, for a young adult romance novel to demonstrate the violent nature of the border through the framework of domestic assault, as it allows readers to appreciate the intersectionality of the personal and the political. When Rico tries to rape Sofi the night before she is due to cross, she pulls out the border saint statue that she had purchased at the botanica earlier on and uses it as a weapon. Rico's attempt to violate Sofi represents the border's violation of people's physical bodies, and its metaphorical violations too (its attack on their dignity and membership in a nation). In the ensuing struggle, we see a direct correlation between these violations, as Sofi worries that because of Rico's strength, he will succeed, and that everyone will think she has disappeared "like countless anonymous travelers whose bones decorated the U.S.-Mexican desert landscape without markers" (240). In attacking back, Sofi figuratively resists the border's role in establishing and maintaining sovereignty and in establishing and perpetuating the disproportionate power of the United States in relation to its southern neighbor. When Rico, seeing Sofi wave the statue at him, jokes, "What are you going to do? . . . Pray me to death?" (239), he is exactly right: the power of community prayer that is embodied in the statue comes full force in the face of border trauma, as Sofi stabs him in the eye with it.

Because Rosarito's identity is so marked by stories of the border, Sofi's experience now functions as an important rite of passage that signals her stronger belonging in Mexico. The trauma of her near crossing and near rape is like a wound, but the outpouring of grief and testimonials that emerge after it provide growth, maturation, and community. Her aunt, who until now has been singularly harsh toward Sofi, is so relieved to see her return to the ranch that she welcomes her back with an embrace. Sofi's brief dis-appearance reminds Aunt Luisa of her own border-crossing attempt and moves her to speak of it openly: "Words, long held back, rushed out of her mouth like a healthy stream after a storm" (242). By bearing witness, Sofi is able to connect to her aunt and understand the fears that have lain behind her previous rage. In the most telling moment, Luisa asks for forgiveness and confesses that she is "so ashamed" (243) for the way she has treated Sofi. Although both of Sofi's encounters with the border end with her remaining in Mexico, they differ. The first experience leaves her feeling illegitimate and ashamed because of the state's psychological violation of her identity; the second experience ends with her active resistance to violation, allowing her recounting to then shape the frightening experience as one of triumph and strength. Once again, we see how border trauma structures family relations by imposing shameful silences and how sharing those stories serves as an antidote to the shame.

Where, ultimately, does the novel leave readers in terms of its narrative about the border? Eventually, Sofi crosses the border into the United States with legal paperwork, and this, together with her dangerous rite-of-passage border story, indicates the novel's general sense of resolution toward the end. In an unlikely plot twist, Abuela (Grandmother) suddenly shows up with a letter (a "birth statement" [250]) written by the midwife that deliv-ered her in the United States, and the hope is that they will be able to find the woman and/or prove she was a real midwife. Sofi's American lawyer, Mr. Wilcox, tells her, "We may be able to find previous statements that can legitimize this claim. After that, it's all smooth sailing. I'll take your dad's and your birth certificates to INS and get them approved" (259). The novel here departs from what would happen outside the world of fiction: having an American-born grandparent does not, on its own, guarantee legal status for a Dreamer, particularly as Abuela has not been resident in the United States for many years. However, the real-life complications of having such weak documentation are skimmed over, as the book is less interested in providing accurate details of immigration policy and more interested in the broad brushstrokes of the situation, that is, the injustice of Sofi's situ-ation. The fundamental truth at the center of the book's conflict—that she is American in every sense except documentation—provides an emotional appeal that reaches beyond policy details. Her love story also resolves itself simultaneously with her legal status as she recognizes Andres's value and they declare their love; thus, she emerges stronger and more fulfilled, with a sense of legitimate belonging at all levels.

Despite the success of Sofi's last border crossing, Alegría is careful to show how the border remains an anxious site, both because of the arbitrary ways through which it wields its power and because Sofi's happy ending is an exception rather than a rule. As she approaches the border once again, this time with the correct papers, she worries, "What if the documents were fake? Or what if Grandma had been mistaken? She wiped beads of sweat from her upper lip and tried to breathe" (265). When the officer appears not to want to let her in, she is sure it is because "he thought she was a criminal" and panics (266). Even with her newfound strength as a bicultural woman, the border seems once again to suggest the possibility of her criminality by reestablishing state sovereignty and toying with her sense of self. She is in fact allowed to reenter the United States only because of the immediate intervention of her American lawyer and a random moment of goodwill from the border officer. The border officer looks up Sofi's information and finds that she "has a record" and "was excluded from entering the United States before because she had false documents" (266). But after the lawyer speaks up "in an authoritative voice," explaining that Sofi is a minor who believed she had the correct documents and adding that "in the end, she's still a citizen, so let's put that incident behind us," the officer gives Sofi a "sideways glance" and lets her through (266).

Several things are of note here. First, it takes a male American authority figure to legitimate Sofi's documents in person and to speak for her: she is not allowed to assert her own citizenship status. Second, although the officer's decision is the one readers are rooting for, the entire scene is a microcosm of the way that one's life outcomes are often based on the chanciness of an authority figure's mood at a particular place and time. The power dynamics of border crossing, then, rely heavily on the unexpected and on the awareness that one could have ended up with the exact opposite outcome without fully knowing why. Success in crossing, that is, always lies very close to being turned away. Furthermore, the border officer's power rests on the assumption that he is doing the border crosser a favor because granting permission to cross, despite this permission being based on documentation, has become personal. The border crosser is placed in a position of gratitude for something that seems to happen for indistinct reasons. Nevertheless, the officer's eventual acquiescence—"I guess you're right. Welcome home"

(266)—has a powerful effect on Sofi's father, who, driving back through the United States, seems changed, sitting up taller and smiling broadly. The words "welcome home" legitimate the family's presence in the United States but are also haunted by the specter of a hypothetically opposite outcome. Thus, Sofi turns and looks back "to make sure that the border patrol hadn't changed their mind at the last minute" (267).

In this way, the novel demonstrates certain gaps in its plot resolution, which allow readers to critically reflect on how the border still plays a paramount role in establishing power and opportunity. While the details of Sofi's situation are resolved, the text remembers people who cannot enjoy such luck and privilege. As the family drives back into the United States, Sofi catches sight of a man in jeans running and hopes he will make it over the border. This is in stark contrast to her reaction to a border crosser at the start of the novel, when she and her friends gawked in confusion and treated the scene as part of their vacation entertainment. This time, she believes that everyone deserves a chance to "make their dream come true" (267) and appreciates how for every successful story of crossing, there are many more of danger and disappearance.

Speaking Out as a Tourist/Citizen

Throughout *Sofi Mendoza's Guide to Getting Lost in Mexico*, Sofi's more empathic national identity develops not only by listening to stories and lessons about the nation and the border but also by acquiring experiential knowledge that will, ultimately, "set the stage for her eventual self-affirmation as a bicultural young woman" (Salinas-Moniz 97). Of course, she is already on a literal journey in a new country, which means that her psychological maturation is always closely tied to the novel's framework of tourism and travel. This positions her experiences of maturation in an environment of new possibilities, creating a sense of odyssey that can vicariously engage the reader and motivate change and healing outside the text too. Narratives of shame and healing, and their exploration of border and national identities, thus show how Sofi's various encounters with Mexico operate along a continuum of subject positions, ranging from tourist to citizen.

As she navigates new Mexican cultural practices and becomes more comfortable being a citizen subject of Mexico, she finds herself physically healthier too; her national identity and her body seem more synchronized. Mexico, as Sofi admits to her mother later, has been "good medicine" (270). She has become more confident in Spanish, practicing words so they roll off her tongue with ease (188), and as Spanish becomes part of her physical body, she gains the courage to speak assertively and meaningfully enough to her grandmother to heal the family's decades-old intergenerational rift. Similarly, her body is now experientially Mexican, so its ascription as Mexican no longer feels like a misnomer. In contrast to the anxiety-inducing hives she suffered in the United States, her skin is now "clear and glowing" because (she decides) of all the nopales she has been eating (211). The various lessons and experiences that mark Sofi's time in Mexico combine with her innate connection to the nation, allowing her to inhabit a newly healthy body, which replaces the exoticized stereotypes of hot Latinidad that up until now have been the only available narrative through which to express her physical self in the United States. It is no surprise that once back in the United States, she describes herself as "more confident in my own skin" (274), because an integral part of her maturation centers on embracing her physical self on her own terms rather than through the objectification that mainstream culture has historically placed on it.

Ultimately, her transnational identity is most strengthened when she blends her tourist and citizen subject positions. In an important scene toward the end of the story, she wields her American privilege and voice to speak as a Mexican in defense of Mexico. Sofi, wearing her cousin's flowing red skirt, overhears some American teenage tourists commenting, "Oh my God, do you see what that wettie's wearing? Fashion nightmare. Talk about what not to wear" (247). They continue to make fun of her, while Sofi thinks that she is "no wetback. That word was just plain racist and mean" (247). Her clothing attracts the tourists' gaze, ascribing her as Mexican and drawing negative attention to her body at the very same moment that she herself feels "fabulous" about the way she looks (247). Initially Sofi experiences this as a personal slur that she considers letting pass, but then, thinking about her grandmother "who'd been illegally deported because she looked Mexican," she makes the connection between the personal and the political—"ignorant people like these girls did that to her family"—and decides that "she had to do something" (248). She speaks back to them, saying, "I heard that . . . Shame on you" and asks, "Who do you think you are, judging me because of the way

I look? You don't know me . . . You need to learn some manners" (248). The shock of hearing her speak English silences the girls, who in that moment are faced with the unexpected empowerment and resistance of an American/ Mexican voice. Her words redirect the shame toward the tourists and stir within her "a strange but comfortable sense of belonging" as she realizes that "it felt good to defend herself and her country" (248). In this teachable moment, the tourist girls must respectfully acknowledge Sofi's personhood and recognize the limitations of their own outsider tourist gazes.

By the end of the story, Sofi has thus grown into her identity as a hybrid border girl, in the sense that she is neither Mexican nor American but an amalgamation of both. She has learned how her identity as a mestiza allows her to live a "full life" and be part of an "ever-evolving culture" that is "another link in this evolutionary cycle" (167). As a person of value, she is enriched by the wealth of ancestral legacies and is "whole" (205). As a bridge between the two cultures, she combines, in her mind, "the best of both worlds" (276), and the celebratory tone of the story's end strongly legitimates the productive possibilities of such multiple allegiances.[6] Even her return to the United States is not so much a return as a new reckoning, as she gazes like a tourist at the once familiar landscape that now presents a novel panorama. That the United States is now ambiguously foreign and familiar perfectly captures the nuances of her bicultural identity, which can see multiple perspectives simultaneously.

The implications of interdependency in the novel, however, go beyond just celebrating blended cultural practices or multiple national allegiances. Interdependency also has political significance: border towns themselves, as blended spaces, resist the assertion of a single sovereign state, and the border can in fact be a "bidirectional bridge," a rich hybrid space where people, goods, and ideas cross from one side to another and nurture both sides (Ibarraran-Bigalondo 25). Similarly, then, Sofi's hybrid persona also reflects that resistance. The reality of the sovereign state, too, persists, as folded into the celebratory tone at the end is a cautionary reminder that Sofi's story could have ended differently: on the very last page, she thinks about Rico and the black ribbons "that represented death on the border" (276). This reminder of the more marginalized and unspoken stories in the narrative, though, is intended not to invoke fear but rather to fuel more resistance, which is itself fueled by the novel's pedagogical reach. The novel's "didactic purpose" materializes, as Ibarraran-Bigalondo explains, through Sofi's status as a "common Chicana" who undergoes a quest for her personal and cultural identity (30), and the novel's blend of travelogue and quest narratives themselves might help forge a transnational consciousness among readers. The journey, which teaches the protagonist lessons in self-awareness and nurtures a more meaningful ethnic identity, also shows how experiences of U.S. tourist consumerism can become transformed into practices of solidarity and affiliation.

Borderland Ethics, Migrant Personhood, and the Critique of State Sovereignty in Jairo Buitrago's *Two White Rabbits* and José Manuel Mateo's *Migrant: The Journey of a Mexican Worker*

In "Toward a Borderland Ethics," Pablo Ramirez argues that fiction that blends the United States and Latin America, self and other, and citizen and noncitizen demonstrates a "borderlands ethical stance" that produces "new unauthorized truths and relations outside the law and beyond national borders" (49). However, within those national borders and inside the jurisdiction of the law, the belief that only legal residents are rights bearers means that to be "illegal" is to have no legitimate public voice or presence; imposing its own logic, the law's rigid categories make some histories mute (50). Furthermore, because nationalism encourages us to situate ourselves in a determinate manner, the state makes people's histories and relationships intelligible only through the solidification and bounding of national space. Thus, personhood can happen only through authorized attachment to nation, and the nation-state reserves the right to police its boundaries and establish immigration policies. But an ethical stance abolishes distinctions between documented and undocumented residents and asserts that all individuals possess, as Sara Radoff puts it, a "right to rights" regardless of citizenship (439). It argues that the polity of belonging is not attached to the classic nation-state but to moral personhood. And when fiction adopts this kind of ethical approach, it emphasizes the complexity of migrant experiences, reimagines the border, and disrupts political understandings of nationhood, proposing new ways to document practices of belonging.

Jairo Buitrago and Rafael Yockteng's *Two White Rabbits* (2011) and José Manuel Mateo and Javier Martínez Pedro's *Migrant: The Journey of a Mexican Worker* (2014) provide recognition and identification for insider readers and provoke empathy from outsider readers. They also show how nations fundamentally define themselves through borders by deconstructing the nation-state and demonstrating urgent social injustices, such as the separation of families, poverty, and harsh immigration push factors.[1] A number of recent Latinx children's picture books explore social unbelonging through thematically intersecting topics, such as the experience of integrating into school, the stigma of being undocumented, and the power of attaining literacy in order to voice one's identity.[2] While several deal effectively with issues of citizenship, documentation, and parental separation and certainly merit discussion and analysis in a different context, the two I analyze here are particularly salient for their refusal to produce the sort of "palatable" and easily consumable "sense of Latinidad" that Mary Pat Brady believes is too often emphasized in children's narratives (380). She points out that in general, such stories have tended to celebrate quotidian pleasures rather than dangers (380). Both the visual and written narratives of *Two White Rabbits* and *Migrant: The Journey of a Mexican Worker*, however, present a borderlands ethical stance and provide readers with the "edge" and uneasy danger that Brady has wished to see represented in Latinx children's texts.[3] They create empathy and also potentially move readers to consider the connections between empathy, responsibility, and social action and to notice the ethical gap between what is and what should be at the nation's borders. To deconstruct the United States–Mexico border and complicate experiences of migration, they critique the state's narrative tendency to quantify migrants (*Two White Rabbits*) and complicate its surveillance of migrant border crossers (*Migrant*), and they may be able to disturb readers' complacency about the ways in which sovereignty and nationalism determine social and legal belonging.

Contextually, *Two White Rabbits* and *Migrant* are both part of a broader literary response to the mid-to-late 1990s Gatekeeper-era immigration policies, when, according to Marta Caminero-Santangelo, various border enforcement measures, in a renewed desire to solidify the nation's sovereignty, reified the border "as an imaginary line meant to be impermeable" and clearly demarcated "who did and didn't belong in the nation" (*Documenting*

5). Some examples of the Clinton administration's Gatekeeper-era policies, which were an effort to preempt Republicans from gaining too much political traction from the issue of "cracking down" on undocumented immigration, are Operation Blockade in El Paso (1993); Operation Gatekeeper in San Diego (1994); Operation Safeguard in Nogales, Arizona (1995); and Operation Rio Grande in Texas (1997). Together, these increased policing at the border in order to make it harder for migrants to pass through the heavily trafficked crossing points (Caminero-Santangelo, *Documenting* 4). Books published during this period began to emphasize the border's material and concrete effects, replacing earlier representations of it as symbolic or metaphorical with depictions of the journey north, death and disappearances during crossings, the threat of deportation once in the United States, and familial separation (7, 12). Similarly, *Two White Rabbits* and *Migrant* depict the border's concrete realism, featuring a parent and/or protagonist who has disappeared during or after crossing. But the texts also metaphorically reenvision the border, so that it also comes to represent an idealized hope. Materially, the border can be a site of death or disappearance; ideally it can also motivate and inspire a rethinking (perhaps even a transformation) of national, political, and cultural belonging. The books, I argue, are thus an important part of what Caminero-Santangelo terms the "chang[ing] landscape" of Latinx writing (*Documenting* 15). They raise pressing concerns as we enter the third decade of the twenty-first century, continuing to reflect, respond to, and impact the nation's exclusionary practices of sovereignty.

Two White Rabbits

On September 1, 2017, Melania Trump, working with the Department of Education, identified one school per state that had achieved high standards of excellence and sent each of them ten Dr. Seuss books as a special gift to start off the school year. In response, one school librarian in Cambridge, Massachusetts, whose school was a recipient of the gifts, respectfully declined them and attached a list of what she considered to be ten more appropriate books, including Buitrago and Yockteng's *Two White Rabbits*. *Two White Rabbits* has been placed on many annual book lists and been awarded many accolades. It was named a Best Picture Book of the Year by *School Library Journal* as well as *Kirkus* and received USBBY (United States Board on Books for Young People) Outstanding International Books and Notable Books for a Global Society accolades, as well as being a "Commended Book for the Américas Award" (Cummins, "Refugees" 26). In her letter to Mrs. Trump, the librarian identifies the potential pedagogical impact of children's literature on government practices, writing that she hopes her recommended books "will offer you a window into the lives of the many children affected by the policies of your husband's administration" (Soeiro). The story of *Two White Rabbits*, told in the first person by a little girl who is traveling with her father, traces their journey from an unspecified location (presumably somewhere in Central America) across Mexico to the United States–Mexico border. Along the way, the girl counts various things that she sees around her (the clouds in the sky, animals) while crossing a river on a pontoon; riding on top of a train, then fleeing it when police arrive; waiting in a border town; and riding a truck into the desert.

For much of the story, the girl and her father are also accompanied by a dog who is introduced as a *chucho* (mutt) and then featured in almost all the drawings as a fellow traveler. Visually he appears to be both a companion (running or sitting alongside them) and a more sinister coyote that sits in the front of the truck while they crouch in the back. The coyote's ominous presence increases by the end. Even though he does not appear on the last page, the (possible) transformation of the girl and her father into two white rabbits at the end of the story increases their vulnerability vis-à-vis the coyote: in his literal animal form (a dog will attack a rabbit), in his traditional narrative role (in folktales he is a dangerous and untrustworthy trickster figure), and in his symbolic role as a contemporary human smuggler. The simple storyline is accompanied by realistic, expressive line and watercolor drawings (with an emphasis on desert hues of brown and blue), whose thin ink-drawn contours and textured cross-hatching evoke the artistic style of graphic novel illustrations.

Through its illustrations and written narrative, the story attempts to impact different readers in various ways to produce critically thoughtful responses. Child readers (especially, but not solely, those with firsthand knowledge of the events depicted) will infer some of the story's emotional turmoil from its illustrations, although they might need some scaffolding to understand the story's more adult angles. In addition, the story encourages its readers (to varying degrees, depending on their maturity and subject position) to adopt an ethical stance that recognizes the humanity of the protagonist and the injustice of her traumatic experiences. The book's peritextual elements also establish an ethics of responsibility, which asks readers to recognize their own role in a system that ascribes legitimacy to only certain members of the nation's population. Marta Caminero-Santangelo, for example, explains how the move from recognition (which involves a necessary process of identification and empathy) to responsibility (where we hope to find a means to redress the injustices encountered) is complex.[4] Of course, just reading a narrative does not always result in empathic identification, and identification does not always lead to action; empathy itself, while vital, could seem to absolve the reader from any further action.

In the case of *Two White Rabbits*, however, the moving illustrations and the child's innocent narrative voice all but guarantee an empathic response, while the additional editorial and authorial information direct empathic readers toward questions of responsibility. For example, a note at the end of the book from Patricia Aldana, then president of the IBBY (International Board on Books for Young People) Foundation, asks, "What do those of us who have safe comfortable lives owe to people who do not?" In asking us to question our own role in the face of such injustices, the book disturbs reader complacency: we are not allowed to believe that through our reading alone we have become responsible citizens. But the story also recognizes the potentially transformative role of reading, as its dedication page simultaneously demonstrates injustice and tries to correct it. It is addressed to "the invisible walkers through the countries," drawing attention to the fact that migrants' stories have long been silenced and made invisible and to the possibility that they might not even be able to access this story or a platform from which to tell their own experiences. At the same time, the story can and is accessed by migrant children; in such cases, for readers who are themselves (or know of) "invisible walkers," being addressed is an act of recognition and visibility. Thus, the act of turning the invisible walkers into addressees (into readers) imagines a just situation where they could become vocal advocates of their own stories and experiences of trauma. In this respect, the book contributes to the "need to acknowledge Chican@ children's literature as a means to achieve equity and social change" (Alamillo et al. x).

In terms of migration and border crossing, *Two White Rabbits* critiques the nation's practices of exclusion and its marking of migrants according to their nonmembership status, and draws attention to their personhood. As I will go on to show in this section, it does so by disrupting immigration rhetoric that has relied heavily on data about the sheer numbers of immigrants entering the United States and by then reimagining the border itself. Even proimmigration rhetoric (and certainly anti-immigration rhetoric) talks of spikes and rapid increases, using words like "unprecedented numbers" (Lind, "There Is a Crisis"), "off the charts," and "record numbers" (Miroff) in its analysis and scrutiny of border apprehensions.[5] Such counting of people, where official accounts of migrants often rely on numbers rather than humanitarian stories, promotes paranoia and fear. Quantification, of course, is sometimes necessary: quantifying people helps record their presence or note their disappearance, gives them relevance and attention, and raises awareness of the magnitude of a humanitarian crisis. Aldana's note at the end of the book, for example, is effective partly because it attaches numbers to migrants ("millions of people around the world become refugees every year"), and clearly, the little girl in the story finds comfort in initially being able to count what she sees.

Nevertheless, most accounts of border apprehensions are tied to political discussions about the nation's security, identity, or economy. When the nation understands its entering migrant population as quantifiable bodies that need to be counted, it is also reasserting itself as an enclosed and bounded space. That is, because the nation's definition of itself relies on a narrative about borders (which themselves must be defined through acts of exclusion and inclusion), its authority can be sustained only if it documents entering populations as quantifiable members (or nonmembers) of that place. Such statistical data relies, obviously, on mastering numeracy and counting, a skill which *Two White Rabbits* (as a counting primer) begins to teach young readers as the protagonist counts the things around her. But in the story, the child protagonist's counting fails in various ways, raising questions and uncertainty rather than providing answers, and implying that the migrant experience cannot be fully understood just by counting the number of bodies that cross the border. Instead, the narrative presents readers with experiences that need to be represented but cannot be easily categorized or counted, such as the trauma of migration and the vulnerability of immigrants, recognizing migrant identities in a humanitarian way rather than through their unauthorized status. And as part of this recognition, the story also demonstrates its commitment to change by deconstructing the border: although it presents the border as a potential site of disappearance (the father and daughter seem to vanish there), it also reimagines it as a natural landscape without conflict.

Although initially the child in the story is able to count what she sees in a way that satisfies her, she fairly quickly begins to interrupt her own counting with other details, as if to suggest that counting alone is an unreliable and insufficient way of conveying this journey. In addition, the story's written counting games themselves break with certain conventions and create confusion, for example, by identifying some but not all the things that appear in the illustrations, or miscounting what they do identify. Thus, when the little girl states, "I count what I see" and later on reports, "Five cows, four hens and one *chucho*," the child reader might try to count along with her. However, the pictures do not exactly fit her count, as they show three cows rather than five, with the other two being herded off the side of the page. Because the written text counts things that are leaving or disappearing from view, it draws attention to the ambiguity of counting something that is in the process of arriving or leaving. The visual also shows seven yellow chicks that are not mentioned in the written text at all; although a child reader might count them out loud, their presence is not documented on the page in a quantifiable way. Unlike classic counting books, then, where a child reader is guided to note every object shown in the illustration, this text plays with the process of selection, teaching readers about the ways that counting—or not counting—indicates the extent to which something matters. And because the narrative from the outset invites young readers to count, it normalizes (only to later critique) counting as the standard by which we determine whether someone matters.

The text also critiques counting by disrupting the reading process. For example, it does not always show the illustrations on the same page as the words that label them. Near the start of the story, the picture of hens and chicks (referred to above) has no accompanying words, and when we do read "four hens" on the next page, we can no longer see the pictured hens. We have to search for them by turning back the page and then returning to the words to see if the chicks have also been accounted for. This back-and-forth activity is part of what Sipe describes as our reflexive and recursive habit of reading picture books, where, because of the tension that results from our differing ways of reading pictures versus words, we "go backward and forward in order to relate . . . the text on one page to an illustration on a previous or successive page; or to understand new ways in which the combination of the text and picture on one page relate to preceding or succeeding pages" (101). This potential back-and-forth movement also shows how governed we are by our need to search for what has been documented and our need to ascertain what is missing from that documentation. It brings tension into the reading and cataloging process, disrupting its forward movement with the recognition that if someone exists in the shadows and thus cannot be counted, his or her official personhood vanishes.

The objects being counted are also given other attributes: the little girl notes "one little bored donkey," associating an emotion to the things being counted ("bored"). She then begins to count clouds but quickly moves to counting the shapes she sees in them, deciding that "they are swans. They are trees. They are rabbits." Later, upon arriving at the train tracks and seeing the tent city set up there, the little girl remarks, "When we travel, I count the people who live by the train tracks" but does not provide a number. To do so would be impossible, as despite her need to play a counting game, the figures by the train tracks cannot be understood in quantitative terms. Instead, the drawings' intricate details attract attention to the complex and varied experiences of migrant travel.

Toward the end of the story, counting becomes even more imprecise and problematic. The girl stares up at the night sky from the back of a truck and says, "Sometimes, when I'm not sleeping, I count the stars. There are thousands, like people. And I count the moon. It is alone. Sometimes I see soldiers but I don't count them anymore. There are about a hundred." Here, in each case, counting is qualified by a distinguishing marker. The stars, like people, are in the thousands, which to a child's mind makes them almost infinite and impossible to record precisely. The moon is not defined through its quantity (she does not say there is *one* moon) but through its isolated status ("alone"). And the soldiers, shown in the picture as sinister mountain formations that progress from soldiers holding rifles to soldiers aiming rifles, represent the violent surveillance and, possibly, actual memories of her past that cannot be controlled through counting but that instead become more frightening the more they are counted. Thus, by this point, the game has taught the child (protagonist/reader) that she is powerless. Rather than her being able to control and manage her environment by counting, her environment is attempting to control, manage, and quantify her.

In response to this surveillance, the story shows how the trauma of undocumented children also cannot be easily quantified or communicated. One of the story's main strategies for expressing this trauma is through its word-to-picture balance. The colored line drawings are intricately and realistically detailed, while throughout, there is very little written text. Several pages in fact contain only illustrations. The two narratives relate different messages: the drawings often show disheartening and troubling scenes, while the girl's voice, presumably in an attempt to manage those experiences, relates them with innocence and simplicity. This kind of "enhancing interaction," as Maria Nikolajeva and Carole Scott describe it, where the pictures and words amplify and expand one another, produces different information and thus a more "complex dynamic" ("Dynamics" 225). In *Two White Rabbits*, the distance between the written and visual narratives also exposes a gap in the story, as the former articulates a child-centered vision of migration removed from political and ideological biases, while the latter illustrates the realistic and punitive obstacles of the journey. Read together, the visual and written texts create an effective narrative strategy for highlighting not only the hard-to-access nature of trauma but also the unethical logic of the law. For example, the written text uses a young child's age-appropriate vocabulary of travel to describe her journey, such as *travel, wait, move* ("When we travel," "We wait on the highway," "We aren't traveling right now," "We are on the road"). This shifts her identity away from political labels such as *refugee* and *migrant* that would connote her unauthorized status; the ordinariness of her words suggests ordinary movement.

But at the same time, the visuals also undercut the written narrative's playfulness and simplicity. The first page ("When we travel, I count what I see") shows migration as a game: the girl rides happily on her father's shoulders, arms out as if in flight, with both figures moving from left to right to undertake a classic and successful picture book journey. As discussed in chapter 1, in examining the placement of pictures, Perry Nodelman refers several times to the English temporal movement of a story and the convention of moving left to right as we read text and look at pictures (22). The action usually moves from left to right (163), and characters traditionally voyage away from home to the right and return to the left. Any break with that convention suggests impeded progress (164). To this point, in the story the protagonists' environment becomes sinister if we note their shadow against a wall and the ground fading away beneath them, foreshadowing potential danger ahead and emphasizing the dislocation and uncertainty of the trip. Their journey is also not shown as originating from a specific home when we first meet them. They are, instead, always already in motion, and this ungrounding, together with the blank white background, further helps depict the reality of migration.

The narrative's artistic choices also call attention to the individual person-hood of migrants. In several of the illustrations, for example, we see many other migrant figures that appear several times over the story and thus function as secondary characters. Governmental quantification of migrants (as discussed above) not only categorizes individuals and ignores properties that do not apply to the group but also risks not telling a fuller story, leaving experiences and memories unacknowledged. In *Two White Rabbits*, however, there are several wordless pages that encourage readers to slow down their reading and therefore acknowledge and absorb such migrant experiences. According to Nodelman, the picture on a page invites readers to linger over a space, in contrast to the faster verbal pace of the story; a picture demands our attention and will not let us move forward (246). Sipe also argues that we tend to gaze on, contemplate, and dwell upon pictures because of their primarily spatial nature and our drive to form "unified atemporal structures" (100), while the written narrative's temporality drives us to keep on reading in a linear way (101).[6] In one instance of a wordless page in *Two White Rabbits*, for example, where the picture shows migrants crowded on the top of a train, the reader is compelled to remain inside the moment rather than move past it and to take in the realistically drawn landscape and the detailed facial expressions, body postures, gestures, and clothing of the migrants. The change of pace resists quick or easy categorization of the migrants depicted, encouraging readers to slow down and explore the art and thus take the time to recognize and wonder about the multitude of unspoken stories and experiences represented on the page.

The text's detailed illustrations also support the ethics of recognition and responsibility that frames the text (as directed by the book's opening information and by Aldana's note at the end). Overall, the story invites readers to feel immersed in the protagonist's experiences, particularly with its use of first person, but it is also concerned that those experiences not fall into a problematic narrative about individual, possibly unique, heroism and suffering. Full immersion takes place in various ways. First, the pages are entirely unframed, encouraging a total experience and unlimited view (for the reader) from "within" the action of the story. Second, on the wordless pages the reader does not need to reconcile two different mediums. When pictures are accompanied by words, the words remind readers that the story is mediated, because words (as visual marks rather than carriers of meaning) are depthless and flat compared to the depth and perspective of pictures.

Here, with fewer reminders that we are looking at an illusory representation, the experience of "reading" is more immersive. Consequently, if the picture depicts a harrowing experience, our immersion in its trauma is more complete and lacks relief or respite. And finally, unlike in many picture books, *Two White Rabbits* presents characters in realistic poses. Nodelman notes that in picture book illustrations, characters on the page usually form what stage directors call "stage pictures" (achieved on stage by blocking actors), where they take positions in relation to each other that create "a pleasing and informative visual image rather than mirror the ways in which people orient themselves to each other in reality" (156). Thus, he says, characters in picture books often converse with each other while standing with their bodies and faces at ninety-degree angles from each other (156), but here, in a text that urges readers to recognize the reality of what's being represented, visual accuracy is a priority.

At the same time, other artistic choices challenge the reader's normative expectations for "heroic" characterization and thus do not allow us to feel absolved by our empathy for this particular child. For example, several pages feature long-range shots, where the protagonists are hard to locate among many other migrant figures. The main characters are often placed off to the side of the page, signaling to the reader that our focus should be on the context and community around them. Nodelman notes that if a character is off to the side, we are supposed to be interested in what they see and look at, that is, the action rather than the character's response to it (133). In this respect the text asks us to question whether our interest in a particular protagonist is in itself ethically shortsighted, as this presents the protagonists' situation as an exception (and the protagonists themselves as exceptional heroic beings) and might minimize or erase the multitude of other untold stories of migratory crossing.

In addition, the visuals often pan out, encouraging readers to view the specific and broader details of a picture simultaneously and thus to understand the migrant experiences from various angles. For example, several pictures, such as the ones showing the daughter and father crossing the river, begin with what later turns out to be a small section of a larger scene, allowing us to absorb particular details: the herded cows, a man loading boxes from a crate, the father and girl meeting the coyote dog. The following pages then provide a wider view of those details: we are at the river's edge and then crossing it. In this way, we feel invested in the protagonists' situation and also in the broader context. The panning-out process means that even once we are looking at the larger picture, we still retain knowledge of the more intimate details. Similarly, the glance curve—the path of our visual habit of looking at pictures from the left foreground and then around the picture space to the right background—allows readers to identify with the father and daughter (left foreground) as they sit on top of the train, and then to follow the illustration along the path of the train top, toward the right background of the page, crowded with other migrants. We absorb both their situation and that of the wider population of migrants. Offering both intimacy and scope, then, the illustration thus presents a more fully imagined migrant identity, one that is contextualized by other migrant experiences rather than decontextualized into a singular heroic quest.

In mainstream culture, the border is frequently shown as a vulnerable and threatened space overwhelmed by the numbers of migrants that cross over it, and as white nationalism moves into the mainstream, its premise about U.S. borders being under siege becomes increasingly normalized (Siegler). For example, an April 2019 poll found that more than a third of Americans believe we have a border crisis, while 45 percent say that "illegal immigration" is a "serious problem" (Guskin and Nakamura). Moreover, the border is the line where undocumented personhood is established when an unauthorized crosser becomes part of the nation's criminal demographic. In response, *Two White Rabbits* depicts national borders as artificial constructs that, in order to be meaningful, have to continually announce themselves—and establish themselves in the nation's collective imagination—as markers of inclusion and exclusion. Both borders in the story are shown as impositions that have turned the natural landscape into a geopolitical space, which can now be reenvisioned. For example, the first national border is a river (presumably one that brings migrants into southern Mexico) that appears on a visual-only page. It is simply a natural feature that people cross by boat and car, and even though the sign "Frontera" identifies it as a border, that marker first appears as distant, on the horizon, situated alongside buildings, trees, and birds. For a preliterate child reader, in fact, the word "Frontera" functions only as a visual marker with no semantic meaning, and so the river remains just a river. On the next page, which shows the same scene close up, the implicit diagonal lines formed here by the bridge, the boats, and the lapping water indicate perspective, focus our attention, and guarantee that we pay attention to the "Frontera" sign. However, this border has been constructed (rather than appearing naturally), as it has formed gradually and secondarily to the river as a natural landscape feature. Furthermore, by introducing a framed word into the visual-only page, the text reminds us of its own mediated constructedness, and in turn, of a national border's constructedness. Thus, even though the river becomes a border, it does so in a resistant way.

In terms of the story's action, the river border does not function as a significant barrier because the girl and her father cross it easily and continue their travels. In contrast, the story's depiction of the United States–Mexico border on the last page shows how strongly entrenched it is in our collective imaginations as a symbol of exclusion. However, it too offers the possibility of reimagining boundaries through metaphor. The visual shows only a wooden fence in the empty desert, with two white rabbits running alongside it. Like the river, it is not militarized and is not an obvious point of conflict or danger. To a more knowledgeable reader, however (whether it is an adult reader or a child reader with first- or secondhand experience of crossing this border), the fence is an artificial and foreboding feature and is immediately recognizable, even without signage, as the United States–Mexico border.

The previous page shows the protagonists in a truck heading left, implying (according to classic readings of picture book visuals) a problem with the journey's culmination at the desired destination, and on the final page they have in fact vanished, indicating that they have moved into the anonymous category of "disappeared." As an ending to the book, of course, this move resists closure because there is no arrival at a destination, and readers also do not know what side of the border they are looking at. We are denied an ending, and even an attempt at border crossing, because the process of migrant travel is a continually unfolding reality. For every person who succeeds in crossing (and still faces borders and surveillance throughout the nation), there is another for whom the endeavor still looms ahead, and still another who is unsuccessful.

But in not showing us an attempted crossing, the story also avoids locating the border as a concrete site of conflict, and in this way, it perhaps encourages readers to reenvision the semantics of this particular landscape. In the case of *Two White Rabbits*, the reader's desire to read closure into the ending in itself allows the border landscape to be reimagined. Nodelman writes that picture book stories usually achieve a state of balance and resolution at the end by moving beyond the disruptions that constitute their plots

(126). Although there is no written narrative to provide resolution at the end of *Two White Rabbits*, visually the double-spread pages are symmetrical and balanced, and the rabbits, newly released from their box, could be interpreted as metaphors for the girl and her father. In fact, because the book's title is *Two White Rabbits* and the father and daughter are now nowhere in sight, the impulse might be to read the rabbits as their replacements, even though prior pages showed both the rabbits and the protagonists together. In one respect, this metaphorical transformation indicates the protagonists' vulnerability, innocence, and potential freedom and releases *migrant* as a semantic term from its negative cultural connotations. But at the same time, because any metaphorical process involves the elimination of something (as one thing is replaced by another), attempting resolution by seeing the rabbits as our protagonists might only reiterate the disappearance of the father and daughter. That is, as we turn the page and see only the rabbits, we witness (and possibly enable) the disappearance of the father and daughter at the border.

Whereas the rabbits may serve as a problematic metaphor for the protagonists, the border itself functions more as a metonym. Although less experienced readers might not interpret the fence as an obstacle or divide (like the "Frontera" sign earlier on, it is just a feature of the landscape), others will immediately discern its political significance. The United States–Mexico border, whose meaning is understood without words, is represented metonymically as a fence (a boundary) because it cannot be reimagined as anything else. There is no possibility of metaphorically eliminating the border and replacing it with something else. Even without any visible militarized surveillance, this "border" operates for knowledgeable readers as a political boundary between nations because its role has been so normalized. Yet insofar as both child and adult readers are the intended audience for picture books, *Two White Rabbits* speaks to both with this last visual, showing the ethical gap between what the border is (how adults know it) and what it could be (what children might see and imagine).[7] It reminds adult readers of what a child sees—the border is just a sign or a fence—and begins to teach children what adults already know: that the border is a barrier and a site of conflict, whose cultural significance and role in the national imagination and the geopolitical landscape are the continual enforcers of place-based and quantifiable definitions of personhood.

Migrant: The Journey of a Mexican Worker

Migrant: The Journey of a Mexican Worker, written by José Manuel Mateo and illustrated by Javier Martínez Pedro, tells a familiar story of Mexican migration to the United States in a distinctive new way.[8] The unnamed male narrator and protagonist retrospectively recounts his life in an unnamed Mexican village; the experience of travel and border crossing with his sister and mother in search of his father, who has left ahead of them; and their eventual arrival in L.A. The writing plainly communicates events to the reader, and there is relatively little dramatic or symbolic language. In fact, Serrato argues convincingly that its lack of depth problematically "[smooths] out" the difficulties of the migrant experience, thus failing to maximize "insight into and respect for" such experiences ("Visual Brilliance"). While I do a brief analysis of some of the written narrative's more nuanced implications, I see the words as a guide to the pictures rather than a story in themselves. The illustrations, however—about which, as Serrato notes, there is "much to say and do"—direct readers away from the sparse language and are powerful. As Mateo and Pedro explain in their note to readers at the end, the story is illustrated on *amate* paper (a vegetable-based canvas made from tree bark), following the tradition of Pedro's village of Xalitla in the Mexican state of Guerrero. Replicating the way that the peoples of Mesoamerica wrote stories, it uses the codex form, where stories are told in drawings or hieroglyphs and one long sheet of paper is gathered into an accordion fold, so that the story is read from the top of the art to the bottom as one unfolds the paper. For this reason, *Migrant* radically departs from traditional picture book conventions: in the basic act of engaging with the story, contemporary readers must learn a new way of reading by which, rather than turning pages, they unwrap and unfold a scroll. The black-and-white ink illustrations themselves are densely packed and filled with tiny details (showing throngs of people, plants, houses, mountains, animals, cars, fences, and highways) and require careful close viewing and time to comprehend.

Reviews of *Migrant* unanimously applaud the codex form (both the illustrations and its accordion fold) as central to the text's appeal: the way it unfolds is "aesthetically astonishing" (Review), and unlike the manageable pages and chapters of most printed stories, reflects the messiness of real life (Mallonee). Reviewers also remark on the art form's pedagogical value: its effectiveness in promoting empathy for the "all-too-real risks surrounding migrants" (Review) invites readers to learn more about contemporary migration. Like *Two White Rabbits*, then, *Migrant* takes (in Ramirez's words) a "borderlands ethical stance" that questions normative understandings of the nation as a bounded space. It does so mainly through its codex form, presenting a new strategy for documenting the presence of unauthorized migrants that appears to literally restructure mapped representations of the United States and Mexico. This experimental use of visual form shows how cartographic perspective—both artistic and ideological—can both express and challenge national narratives of surveillance and border control.

In challenging these narratives, *Migrant* also challenges the totalitarian impulse of the border area. Ramirez explains that "when governments envision themselves as complete and immune to change, this provides an impulse toward totalitarianism" but that regarding the "foreigner" as a constitutive and restructuring element of the nation, rather than a threat to it, creates new norms and new universal criteria by which to judge such norms (52). In *Migrant* that "disruptive foreignness" is represented by the allegiance to Mesoamerican codices as cultural storytelling practices that pictorially and historically evoke the land as one space (without the modern-day divisions of the United States and Mexico), as well as disrupting conventional representations of the Americas by depicting Mexico in the north (at the top of the page) and the United States in the south, at the bottom of the page. Thus, like *Two White Rabbits*, *Migrant*'s response to undocumented border crossers is to articulate an ethical rather than legalistic narrative of national belonging. It does so not only by giving a public voice and presence to the individual telling this story but also by resituating and legitimating that voice as a blend of "ancient" storytelling form (the historical Mesoamerican codex) and modern-day narrative (the verbal—i.e., spoken and written—part of the text).[9]

According to Linda Alcoff, using codices as a rhetorical and linguistic practice of the Americas in this way "poses new lessons for northern cultures that continue to fetishize pure lineages, clear boundaries, and secure borders" (xii), while for Damián Baca, they function as strategies of resistance, critiquing enduring power structures (2, 64). In analyzing the role of pictographic murals used by the Chicanx civil rights movement in the 1960s, for example, Baca notes that their Mesoamerican aesthetic strategies critiqued recent colonizing events "as they articulated a desire for social and political changes, instilled ethnic pride in Mesoamerican artistic roots, and raised cultural consciousness about prevailing economic injustice" (74–75). In its use of the codex, therefore, *Migrant* also embeds itself in the rhetorical practices of the Chicanx civil rights movement and reminds readers of the connection between aesthetics and social action.

As part of its ethical outlook, the text articulates migrant personhood in various ways. First, it explains the family's economic and personal reasons for migration and the dangers of their border crossing, and second, it uses the author and artist's note as a testimonial to contextualize and document child migration more broadly. Most important, it uses unconventional visuals to reposition the United States and Mexico and present them as borderless. The narrative begins by describing a young boy's innocent life playing on a farm in a village where there are no borders: "The animals roamed free, because in the village there were no pens, nor walls between the houses." The idyll continues with a description of the working conditions, and we learn that although the father works for a landowner sowing watermelons and papaya trees, "this doesn't matter, because we took care of it as if it were ours: the crops, the water." Here, the narrative presents economic injustice in order to advocate for a new ideological position, where land, already unbounded, is "owned" through one's physical and experiential connection to it—in this case, that of hard work and play. The story then shows how one shifts into the status of an economic refugee, explaining that all the men, including the narrator's father, left because "there was not enough money to continue planting." The story's central conflict—the disappearance of the father after his arrival in the United States—then provides the impetus for the family's own migration.

Some of the difficulties of the journey are conveyed as moments of antithesis to the earlier descriptions of play: jumping onto a moving train or hiding in a hole in the ground, for example, are "not fun" because "this time it was not a game." When it comes time to cross the United States–Mexico border, however, the text just describes it as a "very high wall" they must "jump" over. As such, the child protagonist does not recognize its ideological significance. Once the wall is scaled, the narrative moves immediately to the family's life in L.A., as if to imply that the challenging journey is over; the border was a site of play, or, at most, an inconvenient barrier. But although the border remains unnamed as a political and national boundary, the narrative also mentions the child's fear—"some police arrived and let their dogs loose . . . I was very scared"—using the ellipsis (an unusual strategy in picture books) to show how some aspects of this adventure fall into silence, beyond the child's storytelling and processing abilities. The text thus distinguishes between the physical border—which, as a high wall to be climbed, might well be part of a child's game—and the experience of being an unauthorized migrant at the border, indicating how the "border" operates as a site of disciplinary surveillance that potentially gives the child a criminal status. The effectiveness of that surveillance depends on the unpredictability of the state authority: after the dogs are let loose, for example, the police suddenly call the dogs back and the narrator ponders, "Who knows why . . . ," underscoring the fact that survival depends on random luck because no one can really understand or know why some are able or "allowed" to cross at any particular moment.

Both the economic impetus for the journey and the dangers of it are part of the broader humanitarian crisis described by the author and artist's note at the end of the story, which asks readers to remember the fifty thousand children who migrate to the United States each year (not all of whom make it) and urges that we demand their right to exist and tell the story to safeguard their memory. As with *Two White Rabbits*, the explanatory note contextualizes the story as a call to action. In some respects, *Migrant's* note also functions as an integral part of the main story because, unlike in most picture books, it appears on the same page (there is, after all, only one page) and in the same font and type size as the story. Thus, the book also defies the conventional separation of the author/artist's direct voices and the voice of the protagonist, breaking the frame that usually distinguishes fiction from factual explanations of the story's intent. In other words, in *Migrant*, the story cannot be separated from the reasons it was written and the broader narrative it represents; at no point can readers turn the page and believe that the crisis of migration exists only as fictional representation, because the facts (in the note) remain in sight all the time. The book—both the story and the note—thus works as a testimonial, creating a document that legitimates children's rights to cross into the United States on ethical rather than legal grounds.

The text's visuals also document ethical ways of understanding citizenship, first by positioning the protagonist as a collective rather than individual figure and second by reorienting conventions of gaze and perspective. The narrator's story is communicated as a collective experience told through an individual voice. Although the storyteller's voice relates his experiences in the first person, he remains unnamed throughout, as if to symbolize the lack of documentation mentioned in the author and artist's note at the end of the book. Moreover, his physical body is barely discernible in the illustrations, indicating a radical departure from conventional picture book representations of a central protagonist. Instead, the visual codex, all in black and white, depicts hundreds of characters who are virtually identical to one another, pressing in and around a busy landscape of desert features, farmland, mountains, and sea, as well as roads and train tracks. As in *Two White Rabbits*, the protagonist's experiences indicate a broader collective drama, although *Migrant* takes the role of protagonist as an everyday figure even further, as it never features him in any distinguishable way, not even on the front cover. While this visual anonymity provides realistic chaos, the accompanying first-person voice gives us clarification and linear chronology. Blending the modern written text with Mesoamerican aesthetics in this way creates a historical and literary borderlessness, one that necessitates reimagining stories of migration and belonging as collective testimonials that become a collective responsibility for those who bear witness to them.

This endorsement of collective responsibility is also borne out in the codex form's visuals, where the lack of perspective requires readers to shift their literal and ideological gazes. Perspective, traditionally, depicts solid objects on a two-dimensional surface to give the right impression of their height, width, depth, and position in relation to other objects when viewed from a particular point. According to Nodelman, our preference for viewing objects as three-dimensional and "real" in terms of density, texture, and coloring is a cultural one (16). He notes that such pictures—perspective drawings, detailed oil paintings, and photographs—in fact "depict the world as human beings never see it." They imply a way of seeing that is different from our usual one, and we believe them to be most "real" exactly because that way of seeing is so unlike our usual one: "in viewing the actual world we tend to glance at it from a series of different angles, to build up a picture out of a process of different perceptions that make us conscious of the ever-shifting process of the world and of our own place within it." Through the "gaze of the painter," however, the flux of phenomena is arrested (16–17). In other words, perspective pictures freeze the flux of movement and gather up disparate, shifting angles into one cohesive view. In not adhering to these rules of perspective, then, *Migrant*'s visuals refuse to impose order or stasis on the pictorial representation of migrant experiences, and with this refusal, they document the chaos and danger of the journey.

In particular, the lack of perspective in *Migrant*'s visuals breaks with linear conventions of space. The drawings do not proportion objects "realistically" in that they are not situated in the background or foreground but rather appear to be piled on top of one another. Generally, we spatialize objects in pictures according to our rules of perspective because culturally speaking, spatial location helps us understand what we are looking at. Without this spatialization, the painting presents the important things as simply larger, even if that makes them "unrealistically" large or small. For example, the people figured in the drawings are disproportionately large compared to the buses, the buildings, the wall dividing the nations, and other features in the environment, although the wall, trains, highways, and buildings in L.A. are themselves also large. We can deduce from this that the people, movement, and the restriction of movement are all important to the story; quite straightforwardly, they seek attention through their size.

In reading the visuals, then, we have to unlearn what we know about recognizing the essential elements of a story. The codex form, in fact, offers us several ways to engage with the physical text, all of which involve shifting our own literal perspective and, in turn, our ideological one. This suggests that the experience of "recognition" and the resulting knowledge that comes out of it is itself an unstable one that is ideologically determined. So, we can peruse the visuals with a close-up gaze, we can look at them from afar, or we can consciously interact with their playful and tangible form. The close-up gaze draws the reader deeper into the story's details but also places us in a position of surveillance. For example, although *Migrant* does not prominently feature its protagonist in the illustrations, most readers are habituated to look at (and look for, if necessary) a visual representation of the main character in a picture book. Close up, then, we become involved in a search process as we try to locate *Migrant*'s protagonist based on what he says he is doing in that moment. It *is* possible to find him, with his sister and mother, but just as easy to lose him again, as he seems to continually appear and disappear, moving away from us as our eyes are drawn to other intricate details in the illustrations. This game of appearance and disappearance, stepping in and out of sight, of course mimics the experience of living in the shadows that many migrants are forced into, and in this instance, because our interest forces us into a situation of surveillance, we are made to participate, symbolically, in the very system that the story critiques.

The view from afar, in contrast, makes readers reconsider the relationship between the space of the United States and its narratives of inclusion and exclusion in a more ethically responsible way. We have literally eliminated the need to turn pages; that is, the storytelling process is no longer broken up into segmented parts, and because the illustration appears on a continuous sheet of unfolded paper, the United States and Mexico are depicted as one continuous landmass. The border wall is not a significant boundary between the two nations: it is no larger or more prominent than other features such as the train, tracks, and highways, and the illustrations on either side of it are identically teeming with details, highlighting the energy of the transborder communities and families. From a distance, when the entire drawing is unfolded, displayed, and spread out, those features take on broader patterns: in literally stepping away from our search for the protagonist, we see a new visual shape, and a remapping of nations emerges. The train, tracks, and highways become diagonal slashes across the page that appear, as we might expect, to indicate movement (i.e., travel and migration) toward the bottom of the page, but the border wall itself also appears as a moving line, as if to defy its own regulation of movement. This kind of gaze resists the arresting of movement practiced by the state; pictorially and physically the nations have opened up to create a geographic borderlessness.

This respatialization of the spaces between and within the two nations also creates a temporal borderlessness. If we read the book from top to bottom rather than attempting to treat the folded pages as individual sheets, then the past, present, and future are visually continuous and blended into one another. The "past" is not passed or finished but remains at the top of the page, and similarly, the future is always visible. The reader's gaze, particularly from afar, will move up, down, and across the unfolded codex without attention to the passage of time that moves the written narrative forward. No aspect of the migrant experience is closed off from sight, and the past, present, and future are all able to coexist simultaneously. With this perspective, the act of reading also becomes highly tangible, interactive, and playful. Even opening and closing the book involves a greater degree of tangibility than a traditional book would and thus recalls the Mesoamerican sacredness of paper, as the reader has to untie and later retie the ribbons that hold the book closed, turning the book into a sort of gift and storytelling into the disclosure of a new, important secret that must be secured after it is told.[10] When the book is unfolded and spread out on a floor or hung on a wall, it encourages the reader to actively walk around it and view it from various angles and positions. In this way, the story takes up space and fills the room. And of course, the experience of "reading" (viewing) is potentially more communal; rather than inviting a solitary and silent experience, the text is a spectacle on display, urging multiple audiences to collectively confront and take responsibility for the story.

Reading the text from afar thus brings the borderlessness of the whole space into view and disrupts the surveillance of the close-up gaze. This perspective suggests the illogic of borders and implies that it is the process of surveillance, in part, that creates them. All these ways of reading challenge national criteria for belonging, as the text's representation of temporal, geographic, and historical borderlessness reimagines the sovereign nation-space as unbounded. It also documents a new vision where the story of nation and migration is tangible, historically and culturally complex, and collective, relocating itself in the reader's space and insisting on its own importance and impact. Furthermore, because of the circularity of the codex's temporal, national, and historical narratives, the story's end cannot provide closure: there is literally no last page. While *Two White Rabbits* refuses narrative closure, *Migrant*'s art form has no place for a last visual. The writing also resists complete closure. There is some hope at the end, as the family has found community and the promise of work, and the child's rhetoric about searching for his father is expressed as a touristic adventure in a new, exciting city: "Maybe we can even see the buildings or the neon signs or something we have heard about." But there is no resolution of events: he winds down the account by saying, "Well, I can't write any more because they are going to turn off the light. It is time to sleep." The turned-off lights prevent this story from being completed and evoke the unfinished nature of such stories, as well as symbolizing the child's own new status as an undocumented person who must now live in the shadows of the nation.

―――――――――

In his 2012 article "Latinos as the 'Living Dead,'" John D. Márquez (quoting Giorgio Agamben) remarks that it has been routine for the ruling elite of modern nation-states to manufacture "national emergencies" to reinforce their hegemonic influence over the masses, particularly at times when such influence appears to be waning (484). The restrictions on the movement of persons across frontiers have long been considered legitimate even by those who are critical of U.S. immigration and border-control policies, as the body politic imagines the United States–Mexico border as the bond that cements the nation's identity (Spener 14). However, under "emergency" conditions the sovereign state takes reinforcement further, deeming some nonmembers to be expendable or, in essence, killable (compared with legal citizens, whose lives are to be protected at all costs). Márquez cites a 1993 U.S. Immigration and Naturalization Service report that explains how by militarizing major ports of entry, border militarization has "aimed to push immigrants toward desolate terrain where they are more likely to die from conditions such as starvation or overexposure to extreme levels of heat and cold." As he notes, "This seems like a clear example that the state planned to not only let immigrants die, but to also encourage their death in large numbers as a means to secure the border from the transnational flow of laborers" (484). This means that the rule of law is suspended at the long-militarized border, and violence becomes not an event but an inherent structure of the nation.

This underlying structure of violence, as well as the immigration policies that perpetuate it, clearly have a dramatic impact on the social, political, and literary environment of the nation, and it is within this environment that books such as *Two White Rabbits* and *Migrant* intervene in important and necessary ways. Even though the violence they depict is modulated for a child audience—soldiers with guns appear as mountain and cloud formations in the sky, borders appear as peaceful fences, crossings become games of chase—the missing characters in the stories are never found, indicating their expendability. Through literary representation, however, the narratives of expendability and invisibility that structure the nation's border rhetoric can begin to be challenged with discourses about belonging and mattering, as they build resistance among readers who can identify with the material. As Norma Elia Cantú puts it, "now, our children can see themselves in books . . . [and have] the feeling that we belong, that we matter" (xx). In addition, in drawing attention to the difficulties of the migrant journey and to those who disappear during border crossings, the texts potentially turn all readers into a more "empathic, informed and critically thinking citizenry" (Aldama 13). Through their various critiques of state sovereignty, they highlight the broader collective crisis between legal and humanitarian understandings of migration, documenting ethical rather than legalistic narratives of belonging and personhood and compelling readers to read—and behave—in more ethically responsible ways.

Disappearance, Documentation, and Sovereignty in Alexandra Diaz's *The Only Road* and *The Crossroads*

As I outlined at the end of chapter 4, in his 2012 article "Latinos as the 'Living Dead,'" John D. Márquez, quoting Agamben's Foucauldian theory of sovereignty, remarks that it has been routine for the ruling elite of modern nation-states to manufacture "national emergencies" so as to reinforce their hegemonic influence over the masses, particularly at a time when such influence is waning due to growing frustrations (among the masses) about government corruption (484). Understanding, as Foucault did, that the ultimate expression of sovereignty resides in the nation's power to dictate who may live and who may die means rethinking the dynamic of violent lawlessness that operates at the United States–Mexico border (473). Without a doubt, since the 1990s both political parties in the United States have used border militarization as a political maneuver, in part because the body politic imagines the border as a bond that cements the social formation of the nation. In other words, the nation's concept of itself has to do with knowing the other and defining that other as not belonging or as foreign. Following Foucault's model of the sovereign state, some nonmembers are deemed to be expendable, or, in essence, killable, compared with full citizens whose lives are to be protected at all costs (477). This means that the state is designed to define and seek out those who do not necessarily need to be killed but who are "allowed or encouraged to 'let die' as a method of reinforcing the discursive and ideological ties that bind modern states together" (477). The rule of law is suspended at the border because systemic violence is not an event but rather an inherent structure of the nation. As explained in the previous chapter, in the 1993 U.S. Immigration and Naturalization Service report titled "National Strategy Report" that Márquez cites, details of the "battle plan" explain that by militarizing major ports of entry, border militarization has "aimed to push immigrants toward desolate terrain where they are more likely to die from conditions such as starvation or overexposure to extreme levels of heat and cold." As he notes, "This seems like a clear example that the state planned to not only let immigrants die, but to also encourage their death in large numbers as a means to secure the border from the transnational flow of laborers" (484).

This underlying structure of violence, as well as the immigration policies that perpetuate it, clearly have a dramatic impact on the social, political, and literary environment of the nation. My interest here is in how the nation's exclusionary practices of terror impact Latinx children's middle-grade literature in particular. In other words, how are violence and surveillance indicated in the texts? How is American citizenship and belonging rethought? These are pressing questions as we enter the third decade of the twenty-first century, at a time when, according to recent statistics, the Latinx population in the United States has grown at such an exponential rate that *all* children in the country will one day encounter some aspect of Latinx culture in their lives (Naidoo, "Magical Encounters" xi). How then do Alexandra Diaz's recent children's books *The Only Road* (2016) and its sequel *The Crossroads* (2018) negotiate these concerns? The first novel is a fictional account of Jaime (a skilled artist) and his cousin Ángela, two undocumented Guatemalan children who escape gang violence and journey north to the United States after the murder of their cousin and brother Miguel, while the sequel explores their new life in New Mexico. Rewriting traditional tropes of travel and movement, *The Only Road* presents the migrant journey as a narrative of terror, creating a continuum of "disappeared" migrant bodies (broadly defined as the dead, the missing, the overlooked, and the neglected) and exploring alternative forms of documentation to restore their visibility and personhood. The novel also interrogates sovereign practices of establishing national borders, deconstructing those borders in the same way that many Latinx children's picture books do. Near the Guatemala-Mexico border, for example, "the lush jungle foliage seemed to take over the landscape, including an abandoned immigration checkpoint" (53), and the trees, bushes, and grasses, analogously to migrants, are all "squeezed together, fighting one another for their right to live on a bit of earth" (58). But while appearing to deconstruct some of the state's practices of exclusion, both *The Only Road* and *The Crossroads* also validate certain principles of American sovereignty and belonging. Both assert and renegotiate Americanness by moving between two kinds of assimilation narratives: that of passing, and that of conversion or transformation. In this sense, they reassure their (probably) mostly American readership that these foreign others are, in fact, deserving of membership in the nation and that they are, in some kind of essentialist way, already American, even as they also come to embody a transnational identity in which foreignness is in fact necessary for reframing the nation as a borderland space.

The Only Road

Rewriting Quests

In *The Only Road*, one of the fundamental strategies for interrogating citizenship and national membership is its building on, and rewriting of, children's classic adventure or quest narratives. Traditionally, these narratives present a journey of hardship, endurance, and credible but exciting danger, featuring an identifiable protagonist who has a special asset or gift (Butts 70). Although most critical analysis of adventure writing focuses on early children's adventure narratives during the time of the British Empire, its salient point—that the literature stresses ideological assumptions about particular national assets and qualities—is apt here as well. Namely, a text such as *The Only Road* builds on and departs from a traditional odyssey trope with, as Caminero-Santangelo puts it, "new politically and historically specific meanings" (*Documenting* 60) that reflect and perpetuate the hierarchies of power and authority operating around the state's border rhetoric.

In one important departure from traditional stories, the story complicates tropes of movement that are generally celebrated in American literature.[1] Instead of celebration, it emphasizes the paradox of movement associated with the Beast (the train that takes migrants through Mexico), where the playful games that children normally associate with trains become shadowed with the reality of death. The story describes the train as alive, gobbling people up and spitting them back out, against the backdrop of play: "Jaime remembered playing trains with Miguel when they were younger. Miguel always liked to balance the passenger toy people on top of the train cars and see how fast he could roll the train before the plastic people fell off" (120–21). Rafa, another young traveler, assures them that "it'll be fun" to ride on top of the train, and Jaime thinks, "If their lives weren't at stake, riding a train cross-country would be fun—going through big cities and one-horse towns, getting the conductor in his striped hat to toot the horn, borrowing a piece of coal to draw it all" (122). The story reminds readers of the parallel life the children are not living (but should be), and retrospectively, those games become a dress rehearsal for this sinister game of survival. Through descriptions of people screaming, children crying, and general hysteria on the train (139–40), where "images of plastic men toppling off toy trains" are replaced with "faces of real boys" (159) and where a train can "bite off" arms and legs (196), the story creates synchronous narratives of their bygone childhood and their present-day childhood. It thus underlines the central paradox of the train: it is the thing that moves them north to safety, but it is also what can kill and "disappear" them. Movement, then, is difficult and dangerous, but it does also offer an unlikely (temporary) space of belonging for the stateless children. Once on top of the train, among the strange collectivity of a population brought together and defined through their movement, Jaime feels that "the top of the train [is] his home" (200).

In a further departure from traditional adventure narratives, the text shows how Jaime and Ángela's journey is framed by commercial enterprises—tourism and the border-crossing industry—that are also undercut by a collective narrative of terror and survival. After the first leg of the journey, during which the children cross the Guatemala-Mexico border hidden in the back of a truck, Jaime fills his lungs with fresh air and finds that his "sense of adventure" has taken over (38). Although "he should be nervous [and] scared," he is instead amazed to be in Mexico, "a different country, a new place, a strange town" (38). Several times in the novel, as the children traverse Mexico, the narrative turns to tropes of leisure travel, adopting an almost ethnographic tone as Jaime tries to capture various scenes (the sunrise, the changing landscapes of mountains and villages, and the open plains and farms) in his sketch pad. In Tapachula, where he and Ángela have a few hours to kill, they enter a beautiful church where "gringo" tourists are taking pictures and "babbling" across the pews (44). Jaime longs to stay there forever, and for the first time since his cousin Miguel's death, he feels at peace. These moments represent a respite from immediate danger, but they also remind readers of the way that sovereignty rests upon certain fundamental injustices. In this case, a mere accident of birthplace (some people are born in the United States, some in Guatemala) renders some documented citizens while forcing others into conditions of statelessness, and determines whether a space of beauty is navigated simply as an aesthetic experience or also as a space of survival.

Like all adventure heroes, Jaime and Ángela's need to journey is unavoidable; even the novel's title indicates the children's lack of choice, while each chapter heading is illustrated with the same small drawing of a boy marching ahead and a girl standing still, watching him, both wearing backpacks. There is no path drawn in for them, but their migration is both inevitable and uncertain, and as the author's note later attests, it is also ongoing beyond the pages of the story. But their journey is also part of a profitable industry. At the refugee camp in southern Mexico, for example, the coyote El Gordo tells the gathered crowd of migrants the cost of crossing, and continues, "That's right, only four thousand pesos. That's not very much for a guaranteed safe ride on the train, let me tell you. If you don't go through me, half of you won't make the train ride in one piece. Not with the immigration checkpoints, or the gangs that control the rail lines, ready to beat you up or throw you off the moving train" (113). In order to sell the migrants a passage north, the familiar inviting tone ("let me tell you") asks for permission to share insider information, while the rhetoric of bodily dismemberment and state surveillance persuades by preying on their fear and vulnerability.

In Juárez the border crossing industry is even more explicit: coyotes emerge from the buildings "like cockroaches. Young men with bulging muscles and red eyes, older men with barrel chests and untrustworthy smiles, all of them offering passage into El Norte, all promising they [are] the most efficient, reliable, and cheapest" (237). Critics point out that this industry of crossing is driven by the militarization of the border. Fernández-Kelly and Massey, for example, trace today's positioning of immigration as an issue of national security (rather than labor regulation) back to 1986, which saw rising capital mobility and growing U.S. investment south of the border together with repressive efforts to limit the cross-border movement of Mexicans (99). Such contradictory policies shape and are shaped by the political, humanitarian, and economic environments that we see in the novel, where many migrants (not only Jaime and Ángela) continue to cross, and the crossing industry continues to thrive, despite the pervasive narratives (and experiences) of terror that constitute the journey.

Narratives of Terror

These narratives of terror reinforce how the characters are subject to the violent lawlessness that structures life in Guatemala, the journey and border crossings north, and (should they make it) their shadowed lives in the United States as undocumented migrants. Critical interpretations of nationhood often focus on the geographical border as the main political demarcation of the nation-space, but here, because terror pervades the entire journey (not just the border itself), readers are encouraged to broaden their definitions of the border. In *The Only Road*, all Mexico is experienced as a border—that is, as a site of exclusion and death—but so is the protagonists' home village in Guatemala, which is terrorized by the violent Alpha gang. The narrative describes gang life in detail, establishing for its young readers the role played by drugs, poverty, and corruption and the closed system in which it operates: "Money meant more than morals and justice to the [police] force" (13).

The story opens with the gang's killing of Miguel, Jaime's older cousin, and the family's shock and grief at learning the news: Jaime hears a "piercing scream" from the kitchen, after which "the wailing only grew louder . . . *No, no, no, no, please no* . . . Dread twisted his stomach into knots. *It* had happened, something he'd feared for a long time" (2). Diaz emphasizes the physical impact of Jaime's fear in the same way that she later employs physical fear to describe the migrant journey: in thinking about Miguel's death, Jaime shakes and cannot swallow or breathe. Acting like a sovereign power, the Alphas practice surveillance ("Ángela could feel the Alphas' eyes on her too . . . The Alphas had been watching them" [16]), dictate who lives and who dies, and after Miguel's murder, try to recruit Jaime and Ángela to join them ("No one escaped the Alphas" [10]). Jaime knows that if he joins the gang, "his life of being in the shadows [will be] officially over" (18). The text's rhetoric here draws clear parallels between hiding from the gang and hiding from *la migra* (40): because both create sovereign spaces that negotiate the individual's status of membership and expendability through terror, one must live in the shadows to remain safe.

The story also demonstrates the structural violence through which a sovereign state establishes itself by examining narratives of "disappeared" migrant bodies. The protagonists are familiar with stories of how "*la migra* beat you up, sent you to prison, and then returned you to your country in pieces, if you were lucky" (59), and rhetoric about mortality and cadavers is common in this landscape of terror where one coyote insults the other, for example, by saying, "I hope your corpse rots in the desert" (241). These ingrained discursive practices speak to the way that, in Lázaro Lima's terms, some bodies are made to matter more than others, in a hierarchy that "privileges nationally 'belonging' bodies over those of 'extranationals'" (168–69). In the text, we see the process through which dismembered Latinx migrant bodies come to not matter, in that the journey itself turns the migrant body into something nonhuman, or something that we cannot recognize as human, thus both creating and justifying the body's expendability. In one part of the journey, as Jaime and Ángela walk to Huehuetoca, they come across a tennis shoe attached to a waterlogged body, "a brown-and-red mass with a pale rod protruding from inside the shoe" (186). The children hide and overhear two police officers discussing the body. The officers note that "*El tren se lo comío*" (the train consumed him), wonder whether to search for the rest of the "pieces," and decide not to because "stray dogs or birds will take care of him." They do "take a picture of the head to put up at the station, in case anyone comes looking for him" but add that "they never do, though" (186). In the moment the authorities state that no one will claim the body, they strip it of its personhood and reestablish its disappearance: notably, what they then photograph is a corpse's head rather than a person's face. Even in the moment of being found, then, the person remains disappeared. The text here shows how the body's unbelonging happens: no one can come looking because of the very conditions that killed the person in the first place, but because no one comes looking, the body confirms, for the state authorities, its own expendability and worthlessness. In other words, it isn't, and never was, a person; its history of personhood is erased.

This dismembered body is part of a broader continuum of disappeared bodies that the narrative draws attention to. But the disappeared are not just those who have lost their lives trying to cross. As Marta Caminero-Santangelo puts it, "they also include the overlooked, the unattended to, and the unrecognized" (*Documenting* 91). The dismembered body described above, which is no longer recognizable as a person, is placed on the same continuum as living migrants that the children encounter on the journey, foregrounding death as a possible outcome for them and also highlighting the "missing" personage of a cadaver. The state's suspended rule of law, which permits violence, essentially creates this continuum of disappeared, where the missing, the maimed, and the abused are not only interchangeable but also expendable. In one instance early on, Jaime, Ángela, and other migrants on a bus in southern Mexico watch as one woman, the victim of domestic abuse in El Salvador, is beaten by an immigration officer. He "whacked her across the head with his arm. She crumpled to the dirt, blood oozing from the side of her head . . . her screams echoed across the jungle until she was flung into one of several windowless white vans waiting a few meters away" (67). Later, the remaining passengers on the bus stare at the empty seat left behind "that a few minutes before had held a woman searching for a better life" (71). The windowless van essentially "disappears" the woman, but her empty seat on the bus functions as a kind of memorial, denoting an absent presence that problematizes the expendability of Latinx bodies writ large by the state authorities. Similarly, the text's attention to physical suffering, particularly noticeable given that this is a children's story, insists on narrating the violence of border crossing and its role in creating stateless—i.e., nonmember—bodies. One description notes that "some [migrants] were missing teeth or limbs. Some had gashes so deep or beatings so bad . . . One man had had all his clothes stolen hours before and sat naked . . . It was like being surrounded by the homeless, which Jaime supposed they were" (177).

As a response to the state's expendability of migrant bodies, the novel shows how narrative production can go some way toward restoring or memorializing personhood. Of course, the book's very existence represents an important speaking out that legitimates migrant experiences and allows voices—albeit fictional ones—to emerge from the shadows. And within the frame of the story, too, multiple narratives attempt to either locate or mourn "disappeared" bodies. From the outset, however, narrative production in the form of stories and drawings both constitute and damage the community. Stories provide knowledge (as the children consider how to ride *la bestia*, the Beast, we're told that "advice bounded around from the veteran train riders, and everyone else who liked to give an opinion" [118]) but also contribute to the ongoing anxious trauma that in itself pervades much of the community's reality.

In a fundamental way, recountings of the journey north are part of the cultural fabric of the nation, and the narrative of crossing is deeply familiar: "Everyone knew the stories. Gangs robbed you at every turn. Immigration officers beat you up before sending you back home" (21). These are not just "horror stories" but "events that happened to real people [Jaime] had met" (196). What Jaime knows about the crossing terrifies him even before he sets off, because of news reports that show immigration officers shooting anything that moves, packed detention centers, and "politicians [in the United States] who said all immigrants were rapists and criminals" (49). In addition, friends at school talk, and advertisements on television and on billboards warn of "the horrors" (50). Toward the end of the journey, as Jaime and Ángela finally face the United States–Mexico border itself, they remember what friends, family, and newscasters have said, and know that crossing will be harder than anything they have already gone through (236). The stories circulate and create a culture of testimonial and witnessing such that the line between firsthand experience and secondhand experience blurs. In addition, while producing a narrative might be healing, hearing it is traumatic and terrorizing, and as the narratives continually circulate, there is no absolute distinction between storyteller and listener. The job of storytelling and the experience of the journey seem to belong to everyone in the community, including those who have never left home, and because the traumatic event (the journey) is actually an ongoing experience, a collective group trauma develops. As Caminero-Santangelo points out, the transmission of stories makes individual trauma more collective, even though the trauma and narration also *make* community ("Lost Ones" 323).

In traditional adventure and quest stories, an integral part of the return home involves the protagonist's recounting of his experiences to solidify the experience of travel (Goodnow and Ruddell 246). In *The Only Road*, of course, there is no return to Guatemala at the end of the journey, but there are recountings *during* the journey, and because the quest is a communal rather than individual experience, the recount in this case is not that of the protagonist but Xavi, a friend they have met along the way. After Xavi is separated from Jaime and Ángela and then briefly reunited with them, he gives testimony to Ángela about riding on top of the Beast. Experiences of trauma are thus narrated while still in the environment of trauma rather than later in recollection, as Xavi describes the rape of one girl, the way gangs run the tracks and work with *la migra* officers, and how a boy failed to get on and was "gobbled up by the train" (179). Giving testimony is difficult: Xavi responds slowly to Ángela's questions "as if he wasn't sure he wanted to relive what happened" (180).

As in traditional stories, solidifying the journey into narrative helps create a community memory and history, but here, the open-endedness of the experiences (they all still face many miles of travel) means that the story is produced from a place of uncertainty and often a situation of danger. That is, bearing witness happens in a space of danger because as one character listens to another's recounting of a traumatic part of the journey, they all remain at risk of the same event. And along with its therapeutic effect, the story becomes part of the circulating narratives that heighten anxiety and establish trauma as a collective ongoing experience for the listener. Nevertheless, the compulsive need to narrate also suggests that even with the uncertainty of survival and the impossibility of return and closure, documentation has to take place. In fact, the act of documenting itself marks out the storytelling moment as a brief one of survival and closure. In traditional adventure tales, the hero's stature increases when he tells the tale; so too, here, the character establishes himself as a survivor, at least for now. Similarly, when the story is recounted, there is a brief moment of closure, as the experience becomes marked off into a narrative past.

Just as in traditional tales where the hero has a special asset or gift that helps him on his travels, Jaime's talent at drawing repeatedly helps him and Ángela out on the journey. His pencils and pad are tools for survival: among other things, he sells his drawings to tourists to raise money to cross the border, distracts an immigration officer with his pictures, and uses his sketch pad to draw maps of their journey. He draws for catharsis, to "make the trip bearable and to forget why they had to take it" (54). However, most of all he is able to document the experiences of the journey, to "freeze time" (68), to "capture the sensation of being there" (45), and to preserve memories: when their photographs are stolen, he thinks with relief that "at least the rest of his family were safely drawn in his sketchbook" (206). The text also explores the implications of documenting trauma during the moment of trauma itself, challenging traditional understandings of trauma and narrative which have tended to separate the two by arguing that narrative production can occur only after the traumatic experience is over, because trauma itself is inherently undialectical.

Because Jaime's trauma is an ongoing experience rather than a singular event, its narrative expression must occur from within moments of paralyzing fear. In one instance, to avoid detection during an immigration raid on the bus in southern Mexico, Ángela urges him to "keep drawing, keep drawing," and while he wonders, "How could he draw at a time like this?" he does so, with hands shaking, in order to pretend that he has nothing to be scared of and that he "belongs" (68). He realizes that drawing what he is actually going through would be too dangerous, so instead begins to sketch figures such as Snoopy, Batman, Mickey Mouse, and Teenage Mutant Ninja Turtles. Such classic icons would usually provide a playful and familiar reference point for U.S. readers, but in this context, the migrant trauma out of which they are produced casts a new shadow over them. The drawings avoid representing trauma directly but instead replace trauma (that cannot be recorded) with child-oriented cultural icons. In the unlikely relationship created between border violence and popular children's cartoons, those icons now become a metaphor for border violence. Because the genesis of the cartoons is fear, the meaning of the cartoons is altered for child readers as they become newly imbued with a haunting trauma that comes to belong to, and be the collective responsibility of, everyone in the nation.

The production of narrative art from within (rather than after) the experience of trauma also shows up when Jaime is crammed inside a train car among people screaming, children crying, and little oxygen. He sketches in semidarkness, deciding that it is "an experiment, a new stretch of his artistic abilities" (142). Because he cannot see what he is drawing, he produces abstract "blind sketches," documents of trauma in the moment. The drawing of people "huddled and trapped in a dark train car" (142) turns out "slightly distorted and creepy with elongated skulls and askew mouths half on the face, half floating in the air beside the person" (181). They are, in fact, reminiscent of his cousin Miguel's face in his coffin, "distorted and grotesque" (187), making the dead exist on the same continuum as the migrant body. In this moment of documenting the "disappeared"—the overlooked and unattended to—the text shows the process that transforms a person into an unrecognizable and nonhuman other: this documentation of the journey, produced by fear, records the loss of personhood.

As narratives of documentation, Jaime's drawings not only record experiences but also reorient definitions of selfhood and belonging, as they come to represent the absent legal documents that the children do not possess. Metonymically, then, his drawings stand in for the absent citizenship papers: legally he is stateless, but his drawings document his personhood, his experiences on the heroic journey, his history, and his identity. They are a form of speech that "[reinvests] the body with its individual personage" separately from his nonmembership in the nation, to the extent that when the pages are torn, it feels like a violation of his selfhood (Caminero-Santangelo, *Documenting* 189). When the sketchbook is roughly handled by an immigration officer, Jaime realizes that "he could live with this different, violated feeling, . . . just as long as he never lost the book completely. It was his life, or what remained of it" (71). Later, when the children wade across the Rio Grande into the United States, Jaime does momentarily lose the book and lunges into the water after it, justifying his actions (which could have delayed them dangerously) by saying, "It's not just a book. It's my life" (259). Ángela responds: "But this life—she poked him in the chest, hard—is the one that matters" (259). As Jaime has no chance to reply, the tension between the recorded life and the embodied life (and the question of which one is more valuable or worth saving) remains unresolved within the frame of the story. What is clear is that the children are often denied the privilege of being able to both exist in their bodies *and* to have a historical and recorded sense of that life. Personhood, of course, requires both, and Jaime's sketches are not only a documentation of his migrant journey but an insistence on a history of the self.

One of the most important functions of narrative within the frame of the story is its ability to preserve the memory of Miguel. Miguel's death at the hands of the Alpha gang at the start of the novel is somewhat redeemed over the course of Ángela and Jaime's journey north, as they frequently evoke his exceptionalism. Remembering Miguel inspires Jaime to be brave ("he'd have to be brave, like Miguel" [34], "time to be strong and brave. Like Miguel" [226]); to look at things logically as Miguel would have done ("*Un paso a la vez*. One step at a time" [74]); and to solve problems ("Miguel always knew what to do, how to solve problems" [136]). Miguel also functions as a deity figure that watches over them as they journey: "*Querido Miguel . . . Please help us to stay safe*" (136). But the death and memorialization of Miguel do not just inspire heroism during the journey. Miguel's cadaver lies at the center of the text's preoccupation with personhood, documentation, and trauma, particularly as it brings together migrant deaths (or disappearances) and Central American gang violence. Near the start of the story, Jaime looks at his cousin's body in the coffin and finds that "Miguel looked . . . not like Miguel" because the beatings he has received have left his face "distorted" (12). Here, the disappearing personage of a cadaver is further accentuated because of the lawless (but permitted) violence inflicted on it by the sovereign power of the gang. Although Jaime looks at the cadaver, when he draws the body in his sketch pad, he intentionally restores Miguel's personhood by redocumenting the "real" Miguel: for the face, "he drew the features he remembered . . . This was the real Miguel, not the beat-up body left behind. The real Miguel was the one on his way to Heaven" (13). In restoring the cadaver's personhood, Jaime resists the disappearance and expendability of the body that has been destroyed by gang violence and creates his rebirth as an exceptional hero. The drawing, as a representation of the body, is part of the body-that-does-not-die and that can survive independently of the cadaver; it is, effectively, a narrative of rebirth that emerges from trauma, violence, and disappearance.

Miguel's death thus functions in two ways: as a frightening metonymy for disappeared migrants (they could be dead like him; they are certainly absent like him), and at the same time, because of his rebirth, as a hopeful metonymy for them (he can watch over them all and protect them; if they are dead, they are still remembered). Brief allusions to migrant figures such as the "battered men" (58) that alight on the bus in southern Mexico are also reminders that Miguel is "missing" (14) because the men and their untold story also soon vanish (they "disappear" back into the bushes [58]), while descriptions of maimed bodies and desperation evoke Miguel-as-cadaver, as a nonperson. At one refugee camp, some people are barefoot, while "some sported raw bruises on their faces; some looked like their soul had left their body and all that was left was a corpse operated by memory" (84). When Jaime sees these migrants, then, Miguel's reborn personhood becomes, potentially, reerased.

Personhood is thus not easily restored in the text but rather moves back and forth. When it vanishes, the moment is more indicative of trauma: during the cramped train ride, for example, Jaime wishes Miguel were there to help but knows that "dead [is] dead" (140). But when personhood seems present, Jaime and Ángela's remembrances of Miguel as a hero redeem his death. Ultimately this contradiction—the metonymy's close association of a person's absence and presence—shows the instability of the metonymy and the uncertainty inherent in the status of "disappeared." In political terms, placing Miguel's dead-but-reborn body on the same continuum as the bodies of disappeared (overlooked, missing, mistreated) migrants also places the story's various sovereign powers—the Guatemalan Alpha gang, Mexico's immigration law enforcement, and the United States' *migra*—on the same continuum and calls attention to the ways in which such sovereignties operate through a broad-reaching expendability of Latinx bodies.

Americanness and Return

Despite the novel's critique of sovereign violence, both it and its sequel ultimately advocate for U.S. national belonging by presenting its Guatemalan protagonists as fundamentally American, perhaps to counter fears about "illegal aliens" popularized by mainstream rhetoric. Such rhetoric, according to Caminero-Santangelo, "ensures that the unauthorized migrant is seen as . . . *essentially*—rather than just incidentally or temporally—not belonging in the nation" (*Documenting* 9), suggesting a permanent foreignness that poses a threat to national security and integrity because it is inherently unassimilable. Under such terms migrants might attempt to fashion themselves as American but would never successfully be transformed into Americans. In *The Only Road*, however, Diaz's Guatemalan heroes are presented as essentially American, future child citizens that already embody a particularly American personhood. In this respect, the novel seems to imply that the expendability of Latinx bodies is morally wrong, in part, because of those bodies' inherent or potential Americanness.

To this end, the novel's characterization of Jaime and Ángela carefully situates their social and ideological membership in the United States in several ways. They are, for example, inherently law abiding and therefore dismayed at their own statelessness. Several times Jaime *wishes* that they were authorized: "If only he and Ángela had passports. And papers that said they could enter los Estados Unidos legally . . . If they had passports or papers, he and Ángela could sit up front" (28, 36). Their lack of documents makes them unauthorized in Mexico and the United States and also suggests a political, national, and even cultural estrangement from Guatemala that makes their connection to it accidental. Guatemala itself is often "disappeared" from the text not only within the frame of the story (when Jaime and Ángela frequently have to "pass" as Mexican) but also outside of it, for the reader.[2] In particular, the text references but disengages from Indigenous languages, either suggesting their incomprehensibility (one old lady on the bus whose words Jaime "couldn't have translated" "babbl[es]" in Mayan [55]) or conveying them only in Spanish (Abuela's "regional dialect" appears as "*Sentate*" [sit down]). In this context, Jaime and Ángela's statelessness is in fact a precondition for their future American belonging rather than a sign of their foreignness.

Even the barrier of their racial otherness referred to early in the story (the "black hair and square faces" inherited from their Mayan grandfather [36]) is resolved after the border crossing when their escape car is stopped by a uniformed man who is also Mayan. His "black hair is combed to one side, his eyes hidden in the shadow of his large nose, and his skin shone brown in the flashlight glow" and Jaime gasps when he realizes how "familiar" this official, who even shares their last name, Rivera, looks (265). While moments earlier Jaime had assumed that their blue-eyed car driver was "the only one who looked like she lived and belonged here" (265), he now hopes that his own brown skin not only grants him permission to belong but might also hold a certain authority. But in first assuming a stereotype of American racial belonging (the driver's white body) and then disarming it, the story also produces another stereotype of the United States as a savior nation for the child, where, as Jaime hopes, there might be "some room" left for him and his family despite the wall they are building "to keep us out" (81). The familiarity of the uncle-officer's face obfuscates the fact that he is still part of the nation's violent expression of sovereignty. His familiar brown face is part of the border's law enforcement and still represents the state's capacity to dictate who belongs; after all, to survive the moment of interrogation here, Jaime and Ángela must still "pass" as citizens.

Within the U.S.-centric vision of the novel, which does not address any historic causes or reasons for violence in Central America or the factors that have shaped the contemporary refugee crisis, the protagonists are also ideologically American. They exhibit courage, determination, resourcefulness, and an entrepreneurial spirit (setting up "shop" in Juárez and selling Jaime's drawings) that enables them to pay their own way across the border. Although they have never had a pet because animals "back home weren't companions," the dog they rescue on their journey, Vida, becomes a faithful friend and family member who on more than one occasion saves their lives or helps reunite them with friends (164). As Guatemalan children raised in a small village, they seem to have been educated in an American cultural context, learning about Abraham Lincoln and Mahatma Gandhi (51) and celebrating Disney characters (Papá, we learn, used to call the children Hugo, Paco, and Luis, after Donald Duck's nephews).[3] Jaime's brother Tomás, in fact, who has already moved to the United States legally before them, speaks perfect English because of his long obsession with Hollywood and American culture (23). In these various ways, then, their American legitimacy is established and their Guatemalan identity slowly erased.

In some respects, Jaime and Ángela's essential Americanness means that in making the journey to the United States, they are actually fulfilling the traditional patterns of the adventure narrative that ends with a return home. However, that "return" is also problematized as the narrative underlines the complexity of what it will mean to live in the shadows of the United States (something that is further explored in *The Crossroads*). The border crossing itself, for example, seems to anticipate this unresolved tension. Although they are crossing the border to be with Tomás (235), the family reunification that might legitimate their "return" to the United States (and refuse to relegate their bodies as abject "illegals" or criminals) is offset by the displacement and surveillance they feel (in Juárez, for example, they feel eyes glaring at them from the walls [242]). Similarly, although the crossing is depicted as a rightful and glorious return ("They'd done it. They were finally here. In the United States of America. The land of the free, where they would make their new home"), readers are also cautioned "they weren't safe yet" (261). Although the border itself is easily identifiable and the river crossing is momentous and climactic ("This was it. They were really going to cross. Into a new country, into the unknown. Everything that had happened in their journey . . . had led to this moment" [258]), the "crossing" in fact is not a singular event but multiple stages of journeying. Traversing the river and the chain-link fence, running, and escaping in a car all happen under heavy surveillance. Even temporary moments of relief, such as when they run through the grass and Jaime thinks, "This was it. Their last flight to freedom" (262), all take place within a broader framework of uncertainty where arrival and "freedom" are (and will be) continually delayed. In these ways, the descriptions of arrival in the United States simultaneously announce the completion and incompletion of the journey.

The border crossing and the children's first few hours in the United States thus show them negotiating the terms of their national identity as they become aware that there is no place that is definitively safe and no moment at which they are done journeying. The safe house where they wait for Tomás, for example, has a "nice backyard" where they can play as children, but also a "high fence that kept out peering neighbors who might report the suspicious number of 'cousins' [their host] always had at her house" (271). As soon as they cross the border, they begin to engage in acts of passing that enable a transformation of identity. They ride in the escape car "with music playing and headlights on, as if they were normal people in a normal car" (264), with Ángela sitting up front looking "pretty" in a silky shirt that makes it look like "she had come from a party" and with her hair brushed "as if she hadn't gone weeks without washing it" (266). When the officer questions her, she is not merely costumed as an American; in that moment her passing transforms her migrant body into an American one, eliminates the journey and the crossing, and situates her as someone "normal" who simply "lives here" (264, 266). But the same move that denotes the authorized body as "normal" of course renders the unauthorized ones (that they have left behind) as abnormal and deviant. As the chapter ends, Ángela further documents herself and Jaime as American, reporting that the officer "wanted to know if we live here, so I said yes. Which is true. We do. Now" (266). In conversation with the officer, she performs a speech act that legitimates their presence in the United States, and in repeating it to Jaime, she establishes it as a kind of truth that becomes self-fulfilling. Here, Ángela begins her transformation into an American teenager (fully fleshed out in the novel's sequel), correcting Jaime's English pronunciation and rejecting plain "blending-in colors" in favor of bright new clothes (269). Living in the shadows, it appears, will mean standing out as Americans.

Such discourse is a logical conclusion to the novel's desire to redeem the Guatemalan children's destiny by returning them to their true home (the United States), although the novel does briefly raise the question of why Jaime and Ángela survived the journey when so many did not. When Tomás asks them, "Do you two know how lucky you are?" (273), Jaime remembers the now disappeared migrants they encountered on their journey—the Salvadoran woman on the bus; the man under the bridge; their friends Xavi, Joaquín, Rafa—as well as the various people who "all seem to have been sent especially to help them" (274). Within the frame of the story, the children believe they are both lucky and protected (they glance up at the sky, "feeling eyes looking at them from above" [274]); outside the frame of the story, child readers are to understand that alongside their luck, these particular children, with their American values (plucky endurance, strong work ethic), must not be allowed to disappear. Furthermore, the narrative of Americanness also imagines a new and more compassionate America, as child readers are shown how migrant Americans can awaken the nation to its privilege and, consequently, instill in it a more collective ethics of care and responsibility. Jaime and Ángela's community-minded work ethic, for example, is frequently referenced: in the refugee center in Mexico, not only are they willing to help out, but they fully expect to (88); later, when they stay with a family in northern Mexico, they do jobs around the house, fix things, and care for the babies, appreciating that "it was nice feeling useful" because that way they are "worth something" (233). Potentially, then, they will contribute to the American marketplace, increasing their social value and becoming worthy of inheriting the American dream.

By the end the story has somewhat diluted the terrors of the journey. Miguel's death seems redeemed once the children are reunited with Tomás (who much resembles Miguel), and the disappeared (both cadavers and living migrants) of the journey fade into the margins of the story as the narrative sharpens its focus on the successful protagonists. The story ends, appropriately enough, with a description of Jaime's final picture on the last page of his sketchbook, as he looks out from the car at the sparse new landscape ("nothing like home" [276]) and considers a new set of worries about belonging (family, language, homesickness, and fears of deportation). In terms of an adventure narrative, the story refuses closure: we end on the road moving toward home but not yet at home, and in terms of recounting the experience, the described final drawing simply solidifies ongoing travel. As Jaime draws the car they are in, the perspective is from behind instead of facing forward. It is a group portrait of them all moving into the future; that is, a document of what has not yet happened. In this sense it is a recording of anticipation and hope rather than of their past, echoing early twentieth-century ideologies about European immigration in which new arrivals were supposed to face forward toward the new land without casting a glance back at their history. An important aspect of personhood is restored here, as Jaime's drawing shows the need for a person to have not just an embodied and recorded history but also a planned future. Here, he documents and asserts the right to—and the privilege of—having a future.

But the description of the drawing also represents what it will mean to live in the shadows of the United States, as it does not show the characters' faces or expressions but only their hair flying in the wind. As such, they have become symbols of a "normal" family going home and, at the same time, of migrants on the move. This paradox demonstrates unauthorized belonging in the United States: although they are essentially American in terms of their values and they are able to perform and pass as "normal" (legal), they must also remain turned away and hidden. The novel's desire to nurture a compassionate child reader into feeling empathy for the relatable child migrants probably also reassures a conservative readership that the Guatemalan characters are thoroughly American, inside and out. The bond that cements the cultural character of the nation remains intact. But, perhaps in memory of the disappeared of the journey, or to indicate their own potential status as disappeared, as the characters move toward and face their future, they do not face the reader. Thus, the novel's ending is shadowed with fear. What appears to be a happy ending also contains an ambiguous message about how to narrate Latinx presence in the United States. Even a novel that deconstructs the ongoing violence that structures systems of national belonging, and undoes the perception of Latinxs as a foreign threat to U.S. sovereignty, unwittingly transforms Latinx personhood into Americanness, making it palatable to the point of disappearance.

The Crossroads

The Crossroads, Diaz's sequel to *The Only Road*, examines Jaime and Ángela's experiences in the United States as unauthorized migrants living on a ranch in New Mexico. In this text, which picks up the story where *The Only Road* left off, the novel's main concern is the reframing of U.S. national identity as both children struggle with acts of passing and assimilation. The disappeared characters from *The Only Road* (such as Xavi and Joaquín) who were so central to the protagonists' lives are referenced infrequently. Xavi's disappearance is treated by both children as a death: Jaime believes that rather than flirting with her new American friends, Ángela should be in "mourning" for Xavi and show "grief" (61); Ángela herself insists on forgetting the past because "Xavi's dead" (111), he is "gone," and their dog Vida is "all they [have] left of those friends they made along their journey" (20). The disappeared, however, never completely recede but instead represent the residual trauma of the journey and continue to occupy the liminal spaces of the novel. After learning of Abuela's death, for example, the children share reminiscences about her, during which Tomás learns that his former girlfriend Marcela disappeared a few years ago trying to cross Mexico (99). The stories about Abuela are funny and embarrassing "instead of ones that focused on the loss and grief" (99), but the dead and disappeared intersect: the singular traumatic event (of Abuela's death at the hands of violent gang members in Guatemala) is inevitably embedded in the broader ongoing trauma of the community's attempts to journey and cross into the United States (exemplified here by Marcela).

As a sequel to a story about the disappearances that take place crossing the United States–Mexico border, *The Crossroads* presents the state of being unauthorized in the United States as a kind of disappearance in itself, and the protagonists' navigation of their new lives in the United States as a process of slowly coming into view. As the sovereign nation tries to make them simultaneously invisible and hypervisible, they move into a more audible center, where they (their personhood; their stories and experiences) can be heard and seen.[4] In this part of the chapter, I explore how *The Crossroads* attempts to challenge normative sovereignty. Rather than advocating nationalism as something bound by anxieties about borders and the workings of biopower, the novel presents foreignness—the very foreignness that the nation fears—as necessary for reframing the nation as a borderland space. The story demonstrates how migrants connect to the community through acts of passing as American and also shows how the power of passing is limited because it does not foreground any new testimonials or experiences. Passing hides (or tries to hide) otherness and does not explicitly restructure the nation's narratives of normativity. Instead, *The Crossroads* shows how those narratives can be restructured through the migrants' connections to the land and through the formation of nonbiological kinships that disrupt ideas of belonging based on birthplace or legal documentation. And despite its challenge to sovereign norms, the novel also advocates for documented belonging in the form of multimodal testimonials that recognize the presence, worth, and value of migrant children.

Sovereignty and the Expendable Migrant

A central concern of the text, then, is how sovereignty wields power and the ways in which any unauthorized presence poses a threat to those practices of power. Mae Ngai argues that nationalism's ultimate defense is sovereignty, which she defines as the nation's self-proclaimed, absolute right to determine its own membership, a right believed to inhere in the nation-state's very existence, in its "right of self-preservation," which has historically meant treating migrants as proxies for foreign troops (11). As I outlined in the introduction, Jonathan Xavier Inda explains how biopower, as a "regulatory power whose highest function is to thoroughly invest life in order to produce a healthy and vigorous population," is also a means to routinely do away with certain lives "in order to preserve [the nation]." Under the rationale of biopower, "contemporary U.S. repudiation of the immigrant, particularly of the undocumented Mexican immigrant, can be situated on the underside of biopower" (135). While immigration is part of the American nation-state's formation, sovereignty is central in determining immigration policy, so that "the law conditions people to regard membership in the nation as intended for some and less so, or not at all, for others" (Gerber 16).[5]

Given these discourses, it is important to consider how Latinx personhood—both as an embodied thing and also more abstractly—is read by the nation and dealt with in the novel. In describing the reality of Jaime and Ángela's presence in the United States in the context of Donald Trump's presidency, for example, Tomás says, "There's talk of a massive wall and deporting all of us." Even with his legal papers, Tomás would be at risk because "officials capture first and let lawyers answer later. *If* you can afford a lawyer, and we can't" (16). Here the rhetoric of immigration policy, which the characters have fearfully internalized, gives the nation the authority to wage war on migrants (they "capture" first). Modern power thus manages life by protecting the social body but also excludes migrant and immigrant life and renders it expendable, creating what Ngai terms "impossible subjects, persons whose presence is a social reality yet a legal impossibility" (xxiv).[6]

As every society distinguishes between those lives that purportedly deserve to be lived and those that do not, the exclusion of undocumented immigrants is seen as necessary for the survival of the nation. It is specifically cultural differences that threaten the integrity of the nation, which is, for Inda, "conceived as founded on a bounded and distinct community which mobilizes a shared sense of belonging and loyalty predicated on a common language, cultural traditions, and beliefs" (140). Racialized nativist discourses construct undocumented immigrants as enemies who threaten the overall well-being of the nation, figuring them as "hostile foreign bodies, as dangerous beings who only bring malaise to the nation" (Inda 140), a sentiment we see unfold even in the local New Mexican community depicted in *The Crossroads*, which is majority Latinx. One of Jaime's classmates, Diego, vehemently denies speaking Spanish, as if it would be a shameful thing (51), and when Jaime accidentally touches one of his playing cards, Diego says to his friends, "Can you believe it? Now I've got grease marks on my cards" (51). Such discourse contributes to the broader immunity rhetoric of the nation, where the state tells people that by putting certain measures into place (such as the border wall, or the pop-up checkpoints we see in the story), it is helping to "protect" the population and build immunity against the perceived threat of foreigners.

Reading *The Crossroads* through the framework of sovereign biopower allows us to contextualize Jaime's and Ángela's bodies (as well as those of other undocumented migrants) as ones that the state generally defines as fearful, expendable, and unrepresentable in the polity.[7] For example, research shows that the Latinx immigrant population in the United States is predominantly composed of Indigenous peoples from rural areas but that this fact is often hidden or unknown (Machado-Casas 535). While Guatemala itself remains somewhat present in the story as the threat of its gangs extends into the United States—Jaime feels that "they still weren't safe" [from the Alphas] (35)—the characters' Indigenous Guatemalan identities, which began to be erased in *The Only Road*, become, in *The Crossroads*, completely unrepresented. The logic of biopower also accounts for the undercurrents of fear that the protagonists feel about their own existential disappearance or nonpresence in the United States because of their unauthorized status. The term "illegal alien" denotes a frightening "ineligibility to personhood" (J. Pérez 27), and in fact at one point when Tomás calls Jaime "illegal," he demonstrates how the rhetoric of the state has become internalized even within the immigrant community. Jaime "[catches] the word 'illegal' like a stab to his heart" as he wonders "How could his brother say that?" (144–45). The violence of the image shows how acts of discourse continually threaten both the embodied and abstract markings of personhood. Jaime, however, reminds himself that he is "no different than any other human" (145), separating the illegal act from the person and thus beginning to validate his physical and social presence in the United States.

American Core / American Masks

To legitimate migrant presence, the narrative humanizes political issues, builds understanding, and implicitly uses "empathic outreach" (Rodriguez and Braden 46). Such empathy can "enable cultural healing and facilitate community building" (Cummins, "Border Crossings" 60); Philip Nel notes that literature that "cultivates an empathic imagination" and shows how the refugee "embodies our shared humanity" can expose the "immorality of basing human rights on nationhood." Such texts are especially crucial at this time, as "we are now witnessing the highest level of displacement on record" (358). However, the need to produce empathic (identifying) readers can create a narrative arc that seems at times to advocate assimilation and passing rather than to challenge sovereignty's fundamental aversion to otherness and foreignness. In the same way that *The Only Journey* emphasized Jaime's and Ángela's inner "American" core or essence (their hardworking determination and entrepreneurial spirit, their familiarity with American cultural products, et cetera), *The Crossroads* similarly centers U.S. ideologies in its efforts to have readers relate to the protagonists. When the novel presents the protagonists' familiarity with these cultural products, it is not just acknowledging American globalization but also implying that they are, fundamentally, American. It also makes otherness more palatable: according to David Gerber, America "sort[s] people out by ascribed characteristics that predict whether they will possess or lack an essence that is somehow American. . . . Such a tendency has been present throughout the American experience of immigration, especially when significant cultural and racial differences are perceived" (102–3).

As with *The Only Road*, this text's references to Jaime and Ángela's Guatemalan childhood echo an American childhood: Jaime recalls "coin-operated horse[s]" (56), Western movies (19), *Star Wars* (58), art supplies, comic books (50), email (although no personal computer or fast internet), and Pokémon cards (50). When Doña Cici, who lives next door with Vicente (the ranch hand), gives the children their first Sunday breakfast in El Norte (the North), she realizes that her spicy Mexican food is too strong for their Guatemalan palates and decides that next time she will use the mild green chiles that she keeps in the freezer "for when the [American] grandkids visit" (75). But in implicitly reassuring American-centered readers of the familiarity and safety of foreigners, in denying difference as a vital part of a nation, is the novel building its own immunity rhetoric? In some respects, such characterization of Jaime and Ángela is part of what Arlene Dávila refers to as the "Latino spin," where sanitized and marketable Latinx representations "advance a vision of Latinas/os" that embodies "quintessentially American values and behaviors" (2). The media creates and re-creates an "unaccented," "sanitized," and "whitewashed" Latinx identity simultaneously to dominant political and popular images of Latinxs as threatening and invading contaminants (Flores-Gonzales 16). The "Latino spin" is then a form of immunity against the negative stereotypes that invoke fear, but it also needs and thus sustains those fears to validate the truth of its own reassurances.

The text's desire to counter (or immunize itself against) negative stereotypes is particularly noticeable in its handling of transnational child-parent relationships, where, within the framework of the story and from the perspective of its Guatemalan characters, American definitions of parental love are presented as normative. For much of the story, Jaime (and, we find out later, Ángela as well) is convinced that his parents have permanently "given him up." He feels displaced and orphaned and wonders how they "had allowed [him and Ángela] to risk their lives going through unknown terrain, be at the mercy of gangs that could have killed them for sport or abused Ángela" (65). Diego, Jaime's schoolmate, remarks, "It sucks when your mom doesn't like you enough to pack you a lunch" (122), and later clarifies his point even further: "Parents that love you don't send you away" (157). Although Jaime tries to convince himself that this isn't true ("They did it to keep him safe, because they loved him" [156]), Diego's words gnaw at him. Later Jaime decides, "If his family really loved him, they would have done more to keep him and Ángela safe . . . Their parents knew of the dangers, which meant their parents could have sent them to their death. And what parent who loved their child would do that?" (157).

The narrative explores the issue of the parents' decision as if to anticipate an American reader's question about what sort of parents would abandon them (so to speak) in this way. It allows, for much of the story, an American-centered understanding of parental love, as if parental love is something that, according to Marta Caminero-Santangelo, "looks the same across places and situations" (*Documenting* 47). A Guatemalan child would presumably question his parents' decision but would also be familiar with—as Jaime was in the first book—the structural conditions in Guatemala that frequently force parents to send children north and separate families. It rings false that a Guatemalan child who has grown up with the fear of deadly gangs and lived through his cousin's murder would repeatedly articulate the fear that his parents do not love him, but the American-oriented perspective allows an American reader to empathize with Jaime on their own American terms.

The American-centric fear also, obviously, contributes to the story's presentation of its protagonists as essentially American. Within the story there is a satisfying narrative closure to this fear when, near the end, Tomás shows the children a letter from their parents that explains how parental love manifests itself differently in different circumstances and confirms their love and understanding of the risk they took. They write, "We are desperate. Parents without another choice. Parents who love their children so much we have to let them go . . . We love you all so much, we'd rather not be together than lose anyone else" (271, 272). The letter's didactic explanation is geared toward an

American child and implies that there is not a universal parenting standard, but of course, Jaime's and Ángela's pedagogical reactions to the letter also firmly place them in the same space as an American child. Here, the child protagonist has seemingly forgotten his own history and cultural context. The readerly intimacy and empathy that the novel encourages, then, comes with the risk of eliminating historical and cultural contexts. Caminero-Santangelo argues that this kind of empathic response to a seemingly universal category or situation "without historically and situationally specific manifestations, need not consider specific differences of class or privilege that might produce different forms of loving parenting" (*Documenting* 49). Consequently, it stops short of eliciting an ethical response to suffering or difference.

Another way that the novel's privileging of American normative values is both demonstrated and problematized is through the characters' passing strategies. It is perhaps not surprising that one of the main protagonists, Ángela, is excited to navigate her new environment through various acts of passing, while Jaime's older brother, Tomás, seems not so much to be passing as already transformed: he already goes by "Tom" and likes to "show off" his near-perfect English (4). Historically, of course, critics have explored strategies of passing as they play out in literature about race (and often slavery) to examine how dominant U.S. race discourse is based on the transgression of legal and cultural boundaries. Elaine Ginsberg notes that those who passed out of slavery engaged in a movement that "interrogated and thus threatened the system of racial categories and hierarchies" (2), but passing's fundamental attempt to challenge assumptions about the inherent and unalterable nature of identity categories can obviously be applied to notions of ethnicity and national belonging as well (4). The demographic of the novel's New Mexican setting is largely Latinx, allowing Jaime and Ángela to easily blend in in terms of racial belonging: at any moment, whether they successfully pass (and evade the authorities) is arbitrary and dependent on acts of specific cultural belonging, such as fluency in English. Jaime notes that at school "lots of kids passed him who looked like they might speak Spanish—at least they didn't look too different from kids who had gone to school with him back home" (44). In the hallways, he is "camouflaged in the crowd of kids with no one noticing him" (13). But when he speaks out in class, he is mocked for his accent (he says his age is "telv" and asks to "go bat-rume" [7, 8]), clarifying how his name and brown skin allow for a silent passing as American but his accented and limited English as well as his acute awareness of his own unauthorized status display his foreignness.

For Catherine Rottenberg, the important question is whether passing serves to reinforce hegemonic norms or whether it functions as a viable survival strategy "which has the potential to disrupt" and perhaps ultimately enable a more democratic notion of Americanness (33–34). In the novel we see some acknowledgment of this disruptive power of passing. For example, Jaime's first encounter with the Pledge of Allegiance at school makes no sense to him: when the children "all stood and put their hands over their hearts like in sports with the national anthem," he expects a song, but instead of singing, "they recited some kind of poem in bored voices" (45). He is able to easily mimic the American children by standing with them and adopting "the same bored look." While the children in his class may be uncertain of his exact legal status, readers are not, and thus outside the frame of the story, his brief moment of passing (reciting the pledge as if he is American) demonstrates a more inclusive, or at least permeable, understanding of American belonging.

But while passing involves the reproduction and regulation of U.S. cultural norms, "the attempt to embody a norm is always incomplete" because "norms are *ideals* that can never be embodied or accomplished once and for all" (Rottenberg 11). If attempts at emulation are only partially successful, then the deception is at once visible and hidden. Ginsberg points out that "passing is about specularity: the visible and the invisible, the seen and the unseen" (2); to pass successfully as an American means that ethnicity can be enacted and can reveal the disguise of nationhood. Taken further, in its deception passing can destabilize and interrogate the essentialism at the root of identity politics: Kobena Mercer notes that identity only becomes an issue "when it is in crisis, when something assumed to be fixed, coherent and stable is displaced by the experience of doubt and uncertainty" (43). If the immigrant reveals national identity to be a construct or performance and at the same time disappears seamlessly into that performance, then passing also arouses suspicions that a foreigner might always be openly hiding in plain sight—a frustrating situation that can never be entirely proved or disproved. In this respect, passing is perhaps a radical gesture.

The physical documents that the characters possess are also part of the dynamic of passing and play an important role in establishing open/ occluded social citizenship and belonging. The protagonists are unauthorized but not actually undocumented: Jaime learns on his first day of school that "all the paperwork had been filled out already" (3), although the narrative is vague about what exactly this means. When he fills out a form to receive a free lunch—amazed that anyone "in this country that hated immigrants and jailed them for no reason" would give him a free lunch (123)—he notes that there is nothing on the form about his immigration status. Not only does Jaime have school paperwork, but Ángela has a driver's permit and Cici has a license; their existence on paper presents them as on a path to citizenship, as they exist (and want to exist even more) in the legitimate way that a sovereign nation expects them to. The book thus advocates for their valid status as near citizens or potential citizens, although it also underlines the inherent contradictions of social belonging versus legal unbelonging, as Jaime notes that Ángela's permit "doesn't require legal status but still allows legal driving" (262). Echoing Ngai's statement about the creation of impossible subjects—Ángela both can and cannot be present—the permit, as a document, enables continual small acts of passing and suggests that Ángela is already part of the community while at the same time maintaining the existential strangeness of "illegal" unbelonging. In this respect Ángela occupies a space of liminal legality, where, as de la Torre and Germano put it, a migrant is simultaneously extended some kinds of legal protections and social benefits and some forms of sociocultural inclusion (for example, the right to a primary education and a typically equal treatment in classrooms and within groups of peers) while being excluded from formal citizenship and other forms of belonging (253). Such "unauthorized enactment of social citizenship," explains Adelaida Del Castillo, questions the "fixity of political communities" (92) and, as a strategy of passing, "reveals an outside presence within the state that . . . disrupts normative practices of membership" (93).

In the novel the act of openly hiding or passing can also be theorized as a way of inhabiting a sanctuary space. Some of the novel's physical settings obviously function as actual sanctuary spaces: the school as a legal one; the ranch, because of its remote location, as an informal one. But if we understand acts of passing as performances that transform the immigrant from a foreign other into an apparent member of the nation, then successful passing—which I define as both deceiving the observer and revealing the constructedness of national identity—also allows the immigrant's own body to function as a sanctuary space. In passing, that is, the immigrant continually creates and inhabits a safe space of performance, albeit a space of performance that can at any moment be broken. Understanding passing as a kind of ongoing sanctuary "space" that the immigrant carries with them allows us to see the body's potential as a platform from which the immigrant can (safely) challenge the nation's normative attitudes to foreigners. Such challenges would manifest as moments of passing that also display their own incompleteness, where deception—and thus difference—are allowed to be briefly visible. Like sanctuary spaces, acts of passing temporarily permit the presence of unauthorized foreigners, but they also feed into xenophobic fears about the fact that the nation cannot always identify and detect its others. This ambiguity (or doubt), of course, becomes an asset that the state exploits as well, as it justifies right-wing rhetoric about ongoing and hidden dangers in plain sight.

Some of these issues play out through Jaime's feelings about his presence in school. From the beginning he never feels completely protected there, noting that if he tells the truth about where he is from, "they might guess he didn't have any papers" (6). Later in the story, his fears grow as he wonders, "What would prevent immigration officers from stopping his school bus? Or even coming into the school building?" Although he knows "he couldn't be the only undocumented kid at school" (119), the very nature of passing and inhabiting a sanctuary space depends on maintaining a collective silence. In a moment that becomes doubly pedagogical, Jaime (and the reader) learns from Ángela that schools and churches are in fact "sanctuary spaces" (119), but the threat of detection remains constant even within this supposedly safe space: later in the novel, Diego, who bullies Jaime and destroys his sketchbook, warns him, "You can't say anything to anyone about it or I'll have you deported" (185). Here, the state (represented by Diego) attempts to silence and discipline Jaime by exploiting the ambiguity of the sanctuary space (and of an act of passing): it is precisely the contradictions at the center of this identity (it can be here safely, but it also cannot; it appears to belong, but at times it also appears not to) that make it so disruptive and also so vulnerable.

The novel's presentation of sanctuary spaces and schools is, appropriately enough, explored through a pedagogical angle as within the frame of the story the characters debate and learn about immigration. In Jaime's class, the children learn to distinguish between terms such as *immigrant, refugee, migrant,* and *pioneer* (153), and the teacher asks him whether he is interested in "sharing a little bit about [his] immigration story" during social studies (151). He is initially frightened of doing so, having already "relived the horrors too many times in his head" (153). Unlike sharing with Vicente and Cici, who know the hardships themselves, Jaime believes "his classmates would never understand" and "might even think he'd made things up just for the attention" (153). The novel thus raises questions about whether the sanctuary space can in fact offer an appropriate platform from which Jaime can speak out about his experiences and be heard. But while he initially anticipates a lack of empathy and understanding, learning the term *refugee* suddenly releases him from the shame attached to his unauthorized status. He realizes that "coming here hadn't been his choice or even his parents' choice. The choice to leave had been made for him. Had he stayed, he would have died. A weight seemed to lift from his shoulders and was replaced with self-assurance" (154).

This new self-assurance makes him determined to speak out because "some people thought he and others like him were all criminals. If he didn't speak up, no one would know the truth" (155). Although the suddenness of his confidence comes across as somewhat contrived, especially given his great levels of fear up until this point, it allows Diaz to make her point about the necessity of speaking out. More important, the teacher's words to him— "whether you're here legally or not is none of my business" (152)—restore the safety of the sanctuary space and also allow it to become a place from which he can, after all, begin to challenge negative stereotypes of immigrants by offering up his testimonial. And although his storytelling is not polished—he feels the limitations of both his English and the singularity of the experiences—it is effective, and the students listen. The question of illegality is lifted, and ambiguity is set aside, leaving space only for stories. Ideally, this is the productive purpose of the sanctuary space: it offers a place for the "illegal" label to be nullified.

For Ángela, exploring the possibilities of performance serves the similarly productive purpose of nullifying (or setting aside) her unauthorized status, even if only temporarily. Almost immediately upon arriving, she is enthusiastic about the limitless opportunities of the United States, for instance relishing the opportunity to be in a school play. She tells Jaime, "You know how I've always wanted to do more acting than the nativity play" (17). The play offers a legitimate way to costume oneself and practice alternate personas, but in the context of the story, it also becomes a model for Ángela's broader performance of national identity. Multiple scenes show her participating in American rituals with apparent ease: on the bus, she "smile[s], wave[s] and in an instant... [is] swallowed by the mob [of teenagers]" (43). She laughs along with them "as if she understood everything they did" (44), and Jaime worries that she will end up becoming like them (63). Her eagerness to improve her English is based on her awareness of its global power ("being able to speak English can open so many doors" [80]), as is her eagerness to perform as an American. From Jaime's perspective (which is also the reader's perspective), Ángela's passing appears such a natural extension of herself that it seems either to suggest a complete transformation or to be evidence of an inner American essence that was there all along.

However, the story's eventual revelations about Ángela's passing strategy imply an act of costuming rather than transformation. Americanness is something she has clothed herself in that allows her to convincingly (but sometimes unhappily) perform a role. For much of the story Ángela's various acts of assimilation (her eager fluency in English, her vanishing into a crowd of friends, her new popularity, her alienation and retreating from Jaime, and his inability to recognize her) make her seem lost to Jaime or are evidence of her desire to forget the past ("maybe she hadn't wanted to remember it" [76]). When Jaime tries to get Ángela excited about the fact that one of their fellow travelers, Joaquín, has recently been in touch with him, he hopes that she will "smile again and return to her normal self" because if she does not, "he knew there would be no hope of finding his cousin again" (242). In other words, her passing is a form of disappearance and a denial of her history.[8]

For all its radical possibilities, then, passing is also limited. The text questions how effective it is as a strategy for challenging and redefining the workings of sovereignty, given that it operates as a temporary measure. Like a sanctuary space, which unauthorized migrant schoolchildren must leave behind at the end of each school day, it is helpful as a platform for communicating only when the subject remains inside its boundaries. How groundbreaking is it, therefore, to give testimony to an audience that is either already sympathetic to or familiar with your story, or that will not realize the performativity of your passing? Passing and sanctuary spaces go some way toward building social belonging, but once the costume falls away, how does the unauthorized migrant step into and function in a nonsanctuary space? More important, how do they begin to move toward reframing the sovereign nation through a more clearly visible transnational personhood?

Land and Kinship

The text posits that shifts in normative understandings of national identity begin when we recognize how powerful connections to the land can provide legitimate membership in the nation, outside of any legal documentation that would authorize that membership. Young readers are given a brief history lesson about the changing United States–Mexico border through Vicente's and Cici's personal stories to Jaime and Ángela, and learn that border security itself is relatively new and that the United States originally encouraged migrant workers from Mexico. Vicente recalls that "back then [when he came to the United States] there wasn't much enforcement in the desert . . . guys came to my town in Chihuahua . . . Said there was work in California on a farm and anyone who wanted to come was welcome" (77). Similarly, Cici relates simply crossing over as a child with her parents ("it wasn't hard to cross" [81]) and taking a job with Mr. George's mother, as "no one worried if you had papers, just as long as they didn't have to pay you as much as a gringo" (81). Jaime instinctively understands that "only those desperate or without other options took these jobs" (78) and models what the child reader's response should be: the realization that, like asylum seekers, economic migrants have no other choice.

The narrative contextualizes these personal accounts, too, broadening their significance. Describing the economic need for migrants, Vicente explains that a hundred thousand undocumented workers in New Mexico work "on the farms and ranches out here, and in the cities we work in construction or restaurants or clean houses. If we're all taken, the state wouldn't be able to survive" (82). He adds, "Everyone knows we're here, but as long as we don't get into trouble, they're happy with us doing the work they don't want to do" (83). This systemic creation of impossible subjects is demonstrated by Ngai, who writes that undocumented immigrants are "at once welcome and unwelcome: they are woven into the economic fabric of the nation, but as labor that is cheap and disposable" and are "situated outside the boundaries of formal membership and social legitimacy" (2). It is particularly appropriate, too, that the novel is set in the Southwest, where the modern political economy has long been based on commercial agriculture, migratory farm labor, and the exclusion of Mexican migrants and Mexican Americans from the mainstream of American society (Ngai 128).

But in *The Crossroads*, Vicente's and Cici's meaningful connections to the ranch and to Mr. George's family make their presence in the United States necessary not just for the economy but for the civic and emotional health of the nation. These connections have also, over time, left them with no apparent need to formalize or legitimate their membership. Although they are unauthorized in the eyes of the state, their permanence on the land counters notions of a Mexican agricultural population that is migratory and transient. Vicente's longevity on the ranch also destabilizes the nation's measures for determining eligibility, in part because Vicente does not know his exact age or the date he came to the United States. In one instance Jaime finds an old newspaper photograph of Vicente and searches for the date but finds that "whoever cut it out of the newspaper hadn't preserved the year" (83). In not being able to measure his presence in the United States through a linear and numerical concept of time but nevertheless successfully building a productive connection to his community, Vicente shows how exact linearity comes to not matter. Indeed, such nonlinearity interrupts the sovereign state's need for documents and other records as measures of membership eligibility, as well as its efforts to construct and narrate the time of the nation in a normative way. In showing a gap in that linearity, Vicente also destabilizes the border because the lack of dates suggests that he has always belonged here. That is, because there is no start date for his arrival, there is also no time when he did *not* belong: he has, they say, been here "forever" (117).

Vicente's long-standing connection to the ranch and the land centers on kinships built from chosen families, which according to Alex E. Chávez are an example of the individual and the community's "resilience strategy," which reclaims the human intimacy often severed by immigration policies (53). Because border management makes migrants "illegible illegals" with no social means to reproduce their original social structures, new family connections can reshape and reinvigorate personhood transnationally (A. Chávez 58). For example, the text illustrates certain rituals of meaning-making that create a strong sense of home: positioning Cici as a nurturing *abuela* figure (148), new personal relationships (Tomás's budding romance with Jaime's gringa teacher; Jaime's relationship with Vicente), and worker-employee kinship ties (between Mr. George and Vicente) that are "crucial in establishing support systems" (A. Chávez 60). In an impassioned and heartwarming message for both Jaime and child readers, Vicente says, "I had Mr. George riding with me before he could walk; I remember his two sisters being born. . . . His whole family are my kids, and quite a lot of people in the community as well. Mexicans, gringos, Indians. Family knows no race and they're all my kids, a part of me" (59). Photographs of Vicente appear framed on Mr. George's wall, along with photographs of Mr. George's parents, children, and grandchildren (82). In fact, according to Vicente, his original impulse to come to the United States was based on not an economic drive but an unfulfilled need for family: "I left México because I had no one. I didn't think of it at the time, but I came looking for a family and found it in the people I met" (91). In retrospectively positioning the United States as a sort of fated destination that fulfills a necessary (albeit unrecognized) desire for family, the text appeals to readers' traditional understandings of (American) family values, and it also problematizes the nation's underprivileging of undocumented migrants by challenging the "fundamental belief that [undocumented migrants] do not deserve intimacy, or can serve the state better, that is, be better laborers, without it" (A. Chávez 69).

The established and emerging kinships we see in the story create a social foundation that disturbs, in Alex E. Chávez's terms, the "racial project" (69) of the American dream and family because in it, the worker is neither expendable nor replaceable. Early on, Jaime learns that despite Mr. George's wealth, he is a "strict but fair man" who pays Tomás an "honest wage" and lets him drive his old truck and live rent-free in one of the trailers (19). After Vicente's arrest by border authorities, he initially seems replaceable (Mr. George says, "I have to find two replacements for Don Vicente, immediately. Preferably guys with papers" [130]), and even his praise of Vicente's work ethic—"he did the work of two men" (146)—foregrounds Vicente's status as a laborer. But the long-standing intimacy layered into this economic relationship soon makes Mr. George realize that Vicente belongs on the ranch: "This is the man's home and he deserves to be here. His arrest has made me realize how much he's needed" (214). In addition, what's emphasized about the new ranch hands is not their legality (they have been in New Mexico for generations) but their irreplaceable skill at ranching. In the world of the story, then, even a laborer with documents is valued not for those documents (although we recognize their bureaucratic necessity) but for the way their talent forges a real belonging to the land. Neither they nor Vicente are replaceable: their ranching work has "incredible" artistry, and Mr. George becomes determined to keep them on permanently even after Vicente returns (213).

The New Mexican setting is also significant in legitimating Vicente's presence, as he transforms it into a place of spiritual and geographic belonging that transcends political borders. The land stretches "to infinity," as Vicente tells Jaime: "From here, you can see anything, talk to anyone" (92). Jaime looks south and imagines "he can see beyond the cacti and juniper bushes, past the Río Bravo and through México . . . into Guatemala and into the house where Abuela lives" (93). Vicente's connection to the land makes that land transnational, as it shrinks geographic distances and renders political boundaries null and void.⁹ Vicente's attachment is not to American land per se but to a way of living (the ranch) that exists (or has appeared to exist for many years) independently of the sovereign nation's laws. His sudden arrest at a pop-up border patrol checkpoint later in the story reinstates that space as a political entity, but until then, his belonging is measured through connections and experiences rather than dates and documentation.

Through Vicente, the text thus renegotiates what is meant by an American "essence": his "real home" (121) is on this New Mexican ranch. However, he also rejects—or at least remains separate from—various American cultural practices. Vicente has never learned English, claiming that "here, so close to the border, there's always people that understand me," while his job is with horses and cattle that "don't care about my native tongue" (80). In a broader sense, his rejection of American materialism also represents an important reorienting of national values. Mr. George, defending Vicente in court, later says, "It's true he never earned enough to file taxes, but that's only because he's never accepted much pay. So I pay him in other ways. When he admires a mare, I buy him her foal. If his wife says her back hurts, I get them a new bed. . . . There isn't anything in the world I wouldn't give him, but he's not into material things." In response, Vicente says, "For what do I need money when I have everything I desire?" (286). Classic narratives of the American dream that define success through monetary acquisition might read this kind of relationship as exploitative because the employer manages and controls his employee's personal life. But in the context of the text's exploration of kinship, this is a rejection of the wage-labor relationship (where the worker is expendable) and an example of a new value system whereby the employee's full personhood and worth is measured in nonmonetary ways. Their relationship is based not on transaction but on friendship, which is ultimately the biggest challenge to the sovereign state's (and capitalism's) desire to keep undocumented (and even documented) migrants and laborers outside the realm of intimacy and kinship.

While Vicente's attachments to land and kin legitimate his presence in the United States, immigration law structures his presence on the land as a violation of sovereign space. That is, Vicente may interpret the ranch as his borderland home, but the law interprets that same space as part of the sovereign state. When Tomás arrives home and announces that Vicente is in a detention center and may be deported, he begins to cry. The power of sovereignty overwhelms even Tomás, with his "big cowboy muscles" (114). As the story plays out, Vicente turns out to be just as vulnerable as the more recent arrivals, Jaime and Ángela: his capture marks and criminalizes him as a racialized and illegitimate other. Meanwhile, the pop-up checkpoints where immigration control has blocked the entire highway shift the New Mexican landscape and all it has connoted—its seamless transnational connection to Guatemala, its borderless status, its remoteness, and its feeling of sanctuary—into a political state. The pop-up immigration checkpoint, of course, is part of the nation's protective security theater, which appears to build immunity against the perceived threat of foreigners, and it also (intentionally) has the effect of maintaining a state of fear, as it circulates anxieties about a nation under attack. But hearing Tomás's account of Vicente's arrest and of his own interrogation by officers (who are "convinced" that Tomás's papers are fake [118]) also triggers Jaime's own traumatic memories of checkpoints that he and Ángela encountered in the southern state of Chiapas in Mexico, where "men with rifles assert[ed] their power and scar[ed] everyone in their path" (117). In the text, then, actual threat originates not with unauthorized migrants but with the state's violent assertion of surveillance and racial profiling and the memories such violence evokes.

Multimodal Communication

While the state's rhetoric about the dangers of migrants encourages citizens to practice caution and be on high alert to any infiltration across the border, *The Crossroads* depicts migrants themselves as sometimes paralyzed by fear. As one might expect, Jaime's past traumatic experiences cause him to be almost constantly overprepared for danger. For example, when he first sees Mr. George, he believes him to be an immigration officer and freezes in fear (130), and he later panics when his friend Sean is not on the afternoon bus one day, wondering, "What happened? Sean was alive this morning" (164). For much of the story, his residual trauma remains unspoken, emerging only as heightened panic, so when his teacher asks him to share his immigration story in class, he starts to shake and becomes convinced that she has a secret life as a *migra* officer who has "been sent to schools to find out exactly how

immigrants continued to infiltrate the country despite all the border surveillance and guards" (151–52). The text shows how such undialectical memories must be expressed both to heal and to communicate with and educate
others. In earlier sections of this chapter, I established how acts of passing in
the story can reveal, at times, the constructedness of American identity and
how forming attachments to the land and to nonbiological kin legitimates
social connections and belonging in the nation. Even though the policies
and laws of the state can step in at any moment and turn the landscape into
a political space, the attachments remain in place as strong foundations,
providing the possibility for more ethical approaches to migration. In this
last section, I show how the text presents multimodal communication as an
especially productive way for testimonials to be articulated and heard. In this
multimodal communication, the narrative centralizes characters' bodies in
various ways to counter the logic of biopower, which has represented those
bodies as unworthy.

To address the worthiness of migrant bodies, the text explores how those
on the margins of society communicate despite their inability to do so nor-
matively, and how that communication makes a real difference. Vicente, for
example, cannot read or write, so after his arrest, to prove that he is "an important and valued member of the community" (173), Jaime decides to tell
Vicente's life story in immigration court by drawing scenes from it. Drawing
Vicente's oral testimonies about those whose lives he has touched over the
years turns Jaime's art into a legal document, as Vicente's oral stories become
part of the permanent record of the court system. *The Only Road* already
introduced readers to the power of visual communication with Jaime's art,
which in *The Crossroads* evolves even further into a necessary way of documenting one's life. His sketchbook is a "safety blanket" (96), a tangible place-
holder for experiences and memories, until it is "massacred" by Diego when
he urinates on it at school (184), but his new drawings, based on the tales he
is told by Vicente's old friends after Vicente's arrest, become a platform for
recording and speaking out about the value and worth of the unauthorized
migrant's connection to the community. Deciding that he will use his drawings at Vicente's trial, Jaime gathers stories from many people who value
the strength of their kinship with Vicente. One of Vicente's oldest friends,
Sani, relates how Vicente "found a home with that gringo [Mr. George] and
came to visit us, his other family, every weekend" (267) while Jaime listens
and sketches Sani's words "with quick lines and artistic notes that he would

develop later into full drawings" (267). Jaime's art builds a document that illustrates Vicente's long history in New Mexico and that, in its visual form, can transcend national borders and languages.

Readers are clearly expected to recognize the radical nature of Jaime's documentation strategy. When Jaime enters the detention center for Vicente's hearing, he is not asked for an ID and appears to pass safely inside, but the metal device does beep and flash "an angry red light" (279) as if triggered by the sketchbook, itself a witness that inside the courtroom will reframe how the nation "reads" its unauthorized migrants. Ultimately, after reviewing the case and "*experiencing* such captivating drawings" (290, my italics), the judge decides to release Vicente on bond (which Mr. George will pay): the art, it seems, is so vivid that the viewer (the judge) felt she was immersed in the events. In other words, the judge does not only see the drawings visually but experiences them in a multisensory way. In validating multimodality, the story not only allows for a new way of understanding immigrant life in the United States but also reframes what might be possible inside a courtroom. The testimony of belonging that Jaime presents to the judge, which is based on evidence of Vicente's connection to the community, gives Vicente a documented history in the United States that, because of the judge's stamp of approval, turns social and emotional belonging into legal membership.

However, it is also important to recognize how the text presents other unauthorized migrants who, unlike Vicente (and eventually Jaime and Ángela), are not able to legalize their status in the nation. At his hearing, Vicente is just one of a dozen men in orange jumpsuits, none of whom have a successful trial because they are represented by an ineffective (presumably free) lawyer, unlike the expensive one paid for by Mr. George. The public defender's paperwork is "all disorganized," and she frequently responds "I don't know" (283) to the judge's questions. When her client Juan García is asked to stand up, two men do so, and she doesn't know which one is hers. Unlike the beloved protagonists of the story, these look-alike undocumented persons do not even have their own distinct names, let alone the support of a community. They also do not have a child hero whose skill translates their testimonies into moving humanitarian stories. We know that they must have a story, but we also see how there is no platform from which they can tell it. In showing these marginalized figures, the story acknowledges that not everyone can be rescued or as lucky as Vicente and thus tempers its own impulse to provide a fully celebratory ending. In then also marginalizing those characters (they are quickly forgotten within the frame of the story), the text also demonstrates the necessary move by which the sovereign state expends some lives to save others.

On its own terms, the system does not fail but continues to function exactly as it should, to allow the nation to determine who its members are. The other men in the jumpsuits are simply unlucky (and, it follows, Vicente, Jaime, and Ángela are lucky), but the narrative arc of the story also implies that our heroes are deserving and therefore, perhaps, that the other migrants are undeserving. That is, even an unsympathetic reader would be hard pressed to argue that Vicente, with his long (unmeasured) history in the United States, should be deported or that Ángela's flourishing American "essence" does not make her "worthy" of membership. Jaime himself, although more resistant to performing as an American, earns our admiration as a child hero who has willingly risked his safety by going to the detention center and openly approaching the judge. He understands this as a sacrifice he must make because unlike with his cousin Miguel, it is not too late to make a difference: "with Don Vicente, he still had a chance. He could make things right" (273). On a personal level he can now alleviate his guilt about the disappeared figures in his family. In fact, if the status of being unauthorized functions as a kind of disappearance, then "rescuing" Vicente—authorizing him—brings him into view. On a broader level, though, Jaime's ethical act also restores the nation's biopolitical immigration policy where some must remain ineligible for personhood in order for others to become citizens who are worthy of protection.

In addressing the worthiness of marginalized figures, the novel also validates Jaime's friend Sean. For a long time, Jaime (and the reader) is unaware that Sean is hearing impaired; indeed, what Jaime likes best about Sean is that although they "never talked," they "understood each other without speaking" (163, 164). Jaime does not find it unusual that Sean "talks with his hands" (164) because most of his family "used their hands in addition to verbal communication. The more passionate the topic, the bigger the gestures. He never thought Sean's signs were actual words" (164). They bond together to create a comic strip (Jaime draws and Sean writes) featuring a creature with four arms, four stalk eyes, a human body, sharp teeth, and wheels like an army tank instead of legs (136). Their collaboration works well: the abnormal creature is an empowered other that through its very embodiment represents the borderlands inhabited by the undocumented, or in Gloria Anzaldúa's words, "the prohibited and forbidden" (*Borderlands* 25). When Sean teaches Jaime sign language, he signs the images and words that Jaime has drawn (168). In this way, Sean validates alternative forms of communication. The children's expansion of literacy also allows for a potential restructuring of the nation because as the art is physically and tangibly spelled out for Jaime, the body's presence is foregrounded. In this process the migrant/marginalized figure insists on its own presence—its stories, its experiences, its personhood—rather than being forgotten or disappeared.

The narrative clearly presents sign language as multimodal: the interpreter (Mr. Mike) who signs for Sean during a class presentation "moved his hands and made facial expressions as if he were acting or dancing" (175). The alternative literacies at work here—the body's gestures and signs—also tap into normative fears of the other: Diego, for example, who earlier feared contagion when Jaime touched his playing cards, says of Sean, "I don't want him touching me. What if deafness is contagious?" (176). But in modeling how listeners can listen differently (listening to the body's movements, for example), the text also hopes that new practices of listening can lead to new social behaviors and understanding. Inviting in such "foreignness" potentially reframes the nation as a borderland space, bound not by sovereign anxiety about borders, nationalism, and immunity rhetoric but by ethics. After all, "without the prospect of an outside, an enemy, sovereign politics fails" (Edkins 133). The "disruption" of multimodal communication—gestures, bodily movements—can perhaps, in Ramirez's words, create new norms and new criteria by which to judge such norms (52). Rather than seeing Jaime's limited English, Sean's sign language, and Vicente's illiteracy as obstacles, the story treats them as opportunities for new avenues of communication. That is, Jaime's art, Sean's signs, and Vicente's abilities as a rancher are enduring contributions to the community as they exemplify alternate ways of belonging to the place. Early on, Sean and Jaime decide that they are "not normal" (68), but in the world of the story, it is precisely that lack of "normalcy" (a lack of documents or of hearing) that enables them to produce such important testimonials.

======

Ultimately, Diaz's novels identify and exemplify a tension between assimilationist narratives of passing, where unauthorized migrants display normative behaviors to imply their American "essence," and more transparent performances of foreignness, where migrants display their transnationality. This aligns with the logic of biopower that structures the nation: migrants' experiences are "a contradiction of simultaneous surveillance and invisibility" (Machado-Casas 545), suggesting that at times they can (and wish to) disguise (or deny) their otherness, while at other times they wield it openly and powerfully enough to reframe national norms. Displays of passing and displays of foreignness both interrupt the fixity of national identity: in the first, nationality is a performance and a construct; in the second, it is fluidly interwoven with alternate cultural practices. In this respect, the text's message is not contradictory: Ángela's and Jaime's different strategies (passing / refusing to pass) both end up revealing and creating gaps in the ways that U.S. sovereignty determines identities. In fact, by the end the narrative establishes that Ángela's performances are not a denial of her Guatemalan self but expressions of personhood beyond national identity: "She was Ángela, and apparently that meant something different every minute" (300).

Beyond this, the text introduces children to the idea that documented citizenship has limited bearing upon one's personhood. Citizenship obviously provides security: at the end of the story, future legal channels are opened up that will keep Tomás, Jaime, and Ángela safe in the United States, as Mr. George decides to sponsor Tomás's green card application and apply for Special Immigrant Juvenile status for the children (217). Narratively speaking, however, there cannot be closure until Jaime makes peace with his hybrid identity. Jaime wants to "stay Guatemalan" (222) and fears that staying in the United States legally means "I have to give up who I am and become like everyone else" (222). In collapsing cultural identity with legal belonging, he here mimics the assimilationist rhetoric of the sovereign state, where American behavior is reassurance of American citizenship, and American citizenship is the foundation for American behavior. Of course, the reality is more complex. When Tomás explains that "citizenship doesn't change who you are. It's just a piece of paper" (222), he breaks the inherent connection between documented citizenship and cultural citizenship that the sovereign state depends on for its narratives of belonging, suggesting that even with documented belonging, one can still resist the assimilationist tendencies of normative American culture.

Although Tomás's words imply that there is space for such resistance— that one can have political membership that imparts civil, political, and social rights to its bearers while one's "cultural" self can remain somehow authentically foreign—outside the frame of the story, cultural membership, according to Flores-Gonzales, is often based on "cultural homogeneity (manifested in shared values and ideals) such that assimilation is required in order to belong" (10). Ángela's desire to pass and to make a home in the United States implies that she is aware that without that display of homogeneity, she might become an "alien citizen" who remains "forever foreign" (Flores-Gonzales 11). At the end of *The Crossroads*, she asks Jaime, "It's not too bad here, is it?" (298), pushing for an acceptance of their life in the United States. His response is one of guarded acquiescence: "It's okay, for now," as the horses they ride climb a hill into an open landscape where "they could almost see all the way back home. To both of them" (298). The sovereign state may deny that difference is a vital part of the nation, but here the novel concludes with a vision of both Guatemala and New Mexico (or the United States) as home "for now." Through the idealistic but important eyes of the child protagonists, then, the United States is both a temporary haven and a permanent home, continually restructured and re-formed by both its passing and its nonpassing citizens.

CHAPTER 6

The Dreamer Brand

Immigration, Storytelling, and Commodification in Alberto Ledesma's
*Diary of a Reluctant Dreamer: Undocumented Vignettes from a Pre-
American Life* and Maria Andreu's *The Secret Side of Empty*

On June 22, 2022, the daily talk show *Charlotte Talks*, on NPR's local radio station WFAE, hosted a discussion about DACA and the future of immigration in North Carolina. Invited guests fielded questions about the establishment of DACA: its effect on immigrant lives, its positive impact on the economy, and possible repercussions if the DACA program was overturned by the Fifth Circuit Court of Appeals.[1] They also pointed to the complex intersections between policy, politicians' interests, popular opinion, and institutional failures in the immigration system. Toward the end of the hour, a local immigration attorney commented that Dreamers and the DACA population have become the "political football" representing a larger issue, which is "our broken immigration system." In other words, the Dreamer movement has turned the at times abstract figure of the immigrant into real-life people with real American lives. Of course, as a carefully curated set of immigrants who are presented as sympathetic and guilt-free, the Dreamers are not a real microcosm of the larger body of immigrants but a nonrepresentative sample that often overlooks those who do not fit within its parameters. This seems an apt entry point for this final chapter's exploration of two young adult narratives that explicitly and implicitly address the role of the Dreamer movement in American culture, because the movement's shaping of political discourse since 2001 has transformed national belonging, membership, and citizenship into highly commodified American brands. In this chapter I look at how Alberto Ledesma's *Diary of a Reluctant Dreamer* (2017) and Maria Andreu's *The Secret Side of Empty* (2014) reflect and build on Dreamer narratives, with new scripts that question what it means to articulate one's identity through a brand. Ledesma's graphic memoir interrogates what the political and personal function of the Dreamer brand has meant for undocumented youths, while Andreu's novel tackles the consequences of living without the Dreamer brand, and the ultimately inevitable need for the collective identity and political opportunities it offers.

Both texts show how the sovereign state's immigration policies intersect with lived reality, that is, how social and cultural membership unfolds at the experiential level while one's legal status also determines one's existence. As Cecilia Menjívar points out, "political decisions embodied in immigration law constrain and enable human action" (1001) and immigration law produces "suspended lives" (1015), creating and recreating "an excluded population" and ensuring "its vulnerability and precariousness by blurring the boundaries of legality and illegality to create gray areas of incertitude" (1002). Immigration laws do not just establish boundaries for inclusion and exclusion but also transform normal activities "into illicit acts" and thus "shape the terrain on which immigrants carry out their daily lives, . . . [curtailing] undocumented migrants' ability to pursue the normal activities of everyday life" (R. Gonzales, *Lives* 216). For example, undocumented children may initially be somewhat protected by more inclusive institutional practices and are thus allowed (temporary) integration, but they eventually *learn* to be "illegal" as they mature into young adults, when "laws promoting their personhood conflict with those that delimit their rights as noncitizens" (R. Gonzales, *Lives* 225).

Prior to the 1980s, when Ledesma and his family came to the United States, undocumented Mexicans in the United States were mostly seasonal labor migrants whose families remained back home, but since the 1990s, increased militarization and border enforcement has made the repeated act of crossing much more difficult, costly, and dangerous (R. Gonzales, *Lives* 20). Immigration reform became a key agenda item for the federal government, and both chambers of Congress signaled a willingness to pass significant immigration legislation, including the DREAM Act proposal (R. Gonzales, *Lives* 209). Joanna B. Pérez explains that to get support for the passage of the DREAM Act, "leading immigrant rights associations created the public figure of the Dreamer [by] investing considerable cultural and symbolic capital" (30). The organizational infrastructure (national organizations, together with online networks such as blogs, Facebook, and Twitter) provided a "safe and supportive environment for individuals to come out and talk about their status with others like themselves" (Nicholls 5), and leading associations provided training sessions that helped youth activists develop a Dreamer discourse and transform themselves into a political group (Nicholls 49). Thus, in the early 2000s, the development of a specific Dreamer identity emerged from public immigration policy, which has long constructed undocumented immigrants as "undeserving outsiders" with "illegitimate claims of belonging to the nation" (L. Chávez, "'Illegality' Across Generations" 85). As Pedro de la Torre and Roy Germano point out, the process of Dreamer identity formation has given young immigrants a new category to inhabit: "One could be an undocumented student and a student in the 1980s, for instance but one could not be a Dreamer until roughly two decades later" (452). The Dreamer's political assertions "contrasted sharply with the situation of undocumented youths ten years earlier when, as a political group, undocumented youths did not exist. There were no arguments, messages, or rhetoric to represent undocumented youths and their cause in the public sphere. There were no organizations to sustain their campaigns and interventions in public life. And there were few if any networks that allowed individual youths to connect to one another and create a sense of themselves as political beings" (Nicholls 2).

After the September 11, 2001, attacks, of course, immigration was repackaged as a security issue, and statistics on deportations were "touted as evidence that the United States was making itself safe from terrorists" (Caminero-Santangelo, *Documenting* 231). In the face of unwavering conservative hostility, between 2005 and 2007 a string of immigration reforms failed (Nicholls 41). By 2010, then, how had the Dreamers entered the national political stage so successfully, with an explosion of open, public, and assertive demonstrations across the country? Walter Nicholls argues that the Dreamers did not emerge in a vacuum but were part of a longer-standing movement conceived by immigrant rights associations as a way to "push the general struggle for immigrant rights forward in a context where few political opportunities existed" (7). Within the generally hostile environment, there existed niche openings for some groups' "illegality" to be considered ambiguous: those with "strategic legal, economic and cultural attributes," such as students, children, youths, and workers in certain sectors (agriculture, hospitality, and construction), made demands for exceptions (11, 10). In this space a legitimate public voice was produced for this group: "creating such a voice . . . was the product of a long, complicated process . . . [that] required making arguments for why their group deserved basic rights, gaining the support of many different allies, and asserting a certain degree of unity and discipline within their ranks" (9–10). Dreamers were able to argue that they were not a foreign threat; that they contributed civically, morally, and economically to the nation; and that they had a right to live out the American dream (5).

Specifically, the ongoing creation of the Dreamer collective confounds and inverts negative stereotypes, turning a stigmatized status into a more powerful identity, and although the DREAM Act has repeatedly failed to pass, the movement has shaped U.S. political discourse since 2001, catalyzing a new youth movement that "asserts its members' rights to legal, civil and social citizenship" (de la Torre and Germano 450). According to Caminero-Santangelo, the undocumented are generally understood to be a "non-nation" "outside of history," without a space for public hearing and thus without the possibility for public subjecthood (*Documenting* 222–23). In other words, one's status is the very thing that creates the impetus for the story that needs to be told and that also renders the storyteller's presence as illegitimate and their voice as invalid. The stories also emerge from an ongoing legacy of concealment because of the speaker's need to hide in the shadows and silence their experiences. Narratives such as Ledesma's and Andreu's, then, draw the undocumented speaker into the nation and into history by creating a testimonial space where the combination of public illegitimacy, obscurity, and subjecthood have become integral parts of the Dreamer's brand narrative.

Insofar as personhood is partly tied to the ability to assert one's subjecthood in a public setting, speaking out becomes a way to restore personhood. In the case of the Dreamer's narratives, however, that personhood is intentionally crafted as a collective group identity, and self-assertion is in fact "group assertion" (Caminero-Santangelo, *Documenting* 228). That is, the stories build on core national values such as a strong work ethic, a love of family, and civic engagement with a shared repertoire of metaphors, critiques, and life-story plots and common themes such as "innocence, worthy character, and achievements, in opposition to the criminality tropes of anti-immigrant rhetoric" (229). According to Nicholls, the Dreamer movement has blended a generic narrative with a life history that stresses repeated tropes, such as hardships faced by children, the ability to overcome difficulties, striving for the American dream, and the burdens imposed by an unjust immigration system (63). The life histories, too, all use a "master-frame narrative" that highlights American symbols and values, exceptional exemplary students, and innocent children (51). Such stories "resonat[e] well with the moral and humanitarian sentiments of the media, politicians, and the general public" (42) and, in addition, are a strategic act of documentation that brings the rhetoric of deserving innocence into the national discourse on immigration. In this discourse, a specific public persona that is both collectively and politically motivated becomes continually produced and reproduced for public consumption.

Alberto Ledesma's *Diary of a Reluctant Dreamer: Undocumented Vignettes from a Pre-American Life*

Commodification, Branding, and the Undocumented Laboring Body

In his cartoon memoir *Diary of a Reluctant Dreamer* (2017), Alberto Ledesma explores how to tell his story—the story of a formerly undocumented child—in a political and cultural climate that has come to expect prescribed narratives about undocumented immigrant children. Such narratives increase awareness, sympathy, and activism but also seem to perpetuate a system that fetishizes citizenship and maintains fixed categories of legal and "illegal" membership in the nation. Ledesma's memoir highlights the problematic power of those stories, showing not only how Dreamer narratives are commodified but also how that commodification rests on the shoulders of, and is directly connected to, a history of commodified migrant laborers. His text attempts to resist such commodification by refusing to present a single story, instead delivering complex experiences and nonlinear stories through multiple artistic styles. By complicating the Dreamer narrative, *Diary of a Reluctant Dreamer* gives voice to those who are marginalized by its central archetypal message and shows Dreamer identities as continuously unfolding and under formation rather than fixed. In this way, it becomes in itself part of that new Dreamer narrative.

In particular, Ledesma talks about listening to the new voices of Dreamer youths after decades of silence about his former (but still taboo) undocumented status, before the term *Dreamer* was familiarized. The core of the memoir's existence feels at times like an act of defiance, as "even privately acknowledging one's lack of papers broke a cultural taboo held by many insiders in Ledesma's undocumented community." The silencing "reached inside the very walls of his family home, where the fear of detection and deportation hung like a black cloud over their daily existence" (Weaver). And as Ledesma states repeatedly in his *Diary*, the fear of being hunted persisted long after he and his family acquired amnesty and then legal citizenship through the 1986 Immigration Reform and Control Act: "though we were now 'legal,' those twelve years of conditioning did not disappear" (4). As we see in the memoir, this legacy and habit of silence and trauma insinuate themselves into one's personhood, revealing the ways in which state power is "exercised, understood, and sometimes resisted" at the level of lived experience (R. Gonzales, *Lives* 30).

Ledesma's intervention in the Dreamer narrative highlights some of its problematic rhetorical strategies, which have created a narrative of exceptionalism by trying to "strike a balance between a discourse that is . . . compelling to a hostile and conservative public" and that also stresses "the need for recognition as complex human beings" (Nicholls 141). Scholars, however, have also shown how the silencing of "undeserving" youths *within* Dreamer narratives has further stigmatized them. Ledesma critiques the Dreamer's narrative of exceptionalism, which presents obstacles as opportunities that can be overcome through hard work. He writes, "It is because of this ideal that Dreamers are expected to be flawless academics and emotionally impervious workers. That is precisely—so the story goes—the reason why they deserve to be protected against deportation, because we don't want to lose their exceptional talent as a nation" (*Diary* 111). To gain public sympathy, Roberto Gonzales argues, DREAM-eligible youths have also been depicted as innocent, clean-cut, college-bound youngsters, depictions that "also deepened divisions not only between 'innocent' youth and their 'lawbreaking' parents but also between high-achieving students and the more general population of undocumented youth unable to go to college" (*Lives* 27). Nicholls adds that the Dreamers' talking points and emotional stories also "stress the most strategic qualities of the group, silencing those other aspects that may distort their central message" (11). In other words, the Dreamers' *own* experiences are not all fully disclosed either. Ultimately, Gonzales notes that the scripted narrative does not address the "deeper and more far-reaching consequences of being undocumented," such as "navigating a world of exclusions while constantly looking over your shoulder, and living in fear of deportation" (*Lives* 212).

To this point, Ledesma's entries in his *Diary* often focus on the "undeserving" migrants left out of the Dreamer story and the silenced parts of the Dreamers' experiences, especially the ways they are prevented from feeling American. In one of Ledesma's cartoons, an undocumented girl recounts working really hard and obtaining a PhD only to now feel that "nothing I have is really mine" (26). The accolades and achievements belong not to her but to a version of self that passes as legally belonging; thus, there is a feeling of illegitimacy beneath every achievement. Nicholls notes that placing complex national loyalties, sexualities, and conduct onto the public stage would complicate the Dreamers' core message and imperil the cause, because when Dreamers *do* deviate from the script and assert a more accurate portrait of their lives and struggles, the media loses interest and pushes them back into the public and front-stage persona (54, 59). Ledesma feels marginalized and worn down by the neoliberal conformity of that persona, writing, "Unlike them, it seems that I am always on the cusp, always so close to running out of money or not doing well in my courses. The truth is that I am a founding member of 'The Bad Dreamers Club'" (*Diary* 51).

In the memoir Ledesma thus extends the Dreamer identity narrative by speaking out about the shame of having been undocumented in the 1980s and by exposing similar experiences of shame in contemporary Dreamer stories. This intersection of Ledesma's own experiences with those of the new generation presents a more complicated narrative history of undocumented personhood. Rather than presenting his Americanness, as a Dreamer might, as the single core value of his identity (although he does not disqualify his Americanness either, as I discuss below), the memoir repeatedly emphasizes the traumatic impact of having been undocumented and asks what kind of story can be produced out of such habitual silence, even after citizenship: "What happens to all the tragic, heroic, and often funny accounts of close calls and challenges overcome?" (*Diary* 5).[2] The genesis of the memoir and of his own subjecthood lies in the isolating nature of his very presence in the United States, so as an adult first encountering the emboldened Dreamers, he feels terror and shame in sharing vulnerable secrets: "It was all too much. It was all too sudden" (55). His text, then, explores how his "undocumented epistemology" determined everything and was the "critical essence" of who he "really was in private" (104), a private self that is now reluctantly deter-mined to publicize his personhood.

The narrative of *Diary*, both in its visual and written forms, is often non-linear: it documents events chronologically and then interrupts that chronol-ogy to demonstrate the contradictory nature of undocumented identity. But Ledesma's chapters also clearly use elements of the Dreamer master-frame narrative to give cohesion to his memories. In chapter 1 he situates his arrival in the United States with his family as an innocent event, explaining that initially he thought they were just visiting for the summer. He then acknowl-edges that spending twelve years as an undocumented child in East Oakland "conditioned [him] in a profound way" (4) and, Dreamer-like, establishes his eventual success: his hardships "deeply affected how I behaved as a stu-dent, an academic, and now, as a Berkeley staff member" (4). He reassures readers that his family were "good" Americans living in fear that any misstep could endanger the whole family; they worked hard at school, and his father "always figured out honest ways to provide food and shelter even when he was between jobs" (4). He repeatedly states that "being undocumented is just another kind of American experience" (4, 7, 105), implying that despite feeling ashamed of his presence in the United States, he is not a stranger in the nation. His undocumented experience is thus (for now) a normative narrative of American innocence, strong work ethic, and determination.

The memoir's opening also demonstrates a Dreamer-like desire to be-long and a belief that such belonging is fated and inevitable. Ledesma notes, "More than fifteen years before the immigration judge had asked me to raise my right hand to swear my allegiance to the United States . . . I had already decided that I would become 'un Americano'" (*Diary* 1). Here his citizenship is both destiny and a matter of choice, something that happens because it is desired and because it is meant to be. In addition, the moment of taking citizenship is an oath of allegiance, in which commitment to the nation is phrased as a promise of loyalty. In the language used to describe the mo-ment where one becomes American, one promises to protect the nation. Implicitly, this is part of the nation's rhetoric of immunity, because such a promise of loyalty must imagine a foreign enemy or threat (when that loyalty might be tested). In recalling this rhetoric, Ledesma lets readers know that his Americanness is rooted in choice and destiny and that such membership protects *him* from foreigners and thus from any anti-immigrant rhetoric that would define him as criminal or foreigner.

In working through how his own experiences intersect with the Dreamers' experiences, Ledesma traces a generational shift where previously silenced stories are transformed into branded commodities, and where the Dreamers themselves become commodified. Students now feel pressure to "confess who they were via ever-increasingly gut-wrenching stories" (*Diary* 53) that they tell, essentially, in exchange for sympathy and support: "As financial services and access to other support services become available, a validation of these resources was increasingly accompanied by testimonials of appreciation by students who had already survived and transcended what seemed like a ubiquitous pattern of hellish experiences" (53). Ledesma writes that Dreamers are suddenly a "new kind of model minority" who need to not only confess but also provide "a pre-packaged ode to their own talents for survival" (53). Although they can now speak their own stories, they do not fully own their stories, and they have built a brand (or had it built for them) that places its value on certain expectations: that the act of storytelling is always an act of danger and that they satisfy the criteria for a particularly American story. Broadly construed, the Dreamers have evolved into a brand that the public wants to possess; the stories are circulated in exchange for sympathy, and the public that listens to the stories (and perhaps eventually engages in social justice and activism) is willing to engage in the Dreamers' story because it brands them (the listeners) as patriotic Americans. Nicholls explains that the Dreamers' formation into a "self-conscious" and "internally bounded group" made it possible "to gain support from broad swaths of the public and mitigate the risks of detention and deportation" even in the "most hostile states like Arizona" where protesting Dreamers became "undeportable" (6). Ledesma notes that as we "requir[e] them to tell their story, in writing or in an oral presentation, as a condition for receiving support" (*Diary* 55), the storytelling is no longer merely educational, cathartic, or healing but also confirms that the only kind of "foreignness" that is palatable and legitimate is one that brands itself as American.

In part, this commodification is problematic because it is reminiscent of the commodification of the undocumented laborer's body, which Ledesma describes as a legacy handed down to undocumented youths by their parents. The laborer's body, rendered expendable by the state, is frequently referred to in the text (visually and verbally) as a cyborg with both human and machine components to convey dominant interpellations of said body as not fully human. In one visual, readers see a human skeleton clothed with a jacket and hat, with metal body parts (*Diary* 27). In contrast, an earlier sketch showing the "Anatomy of a Dream Act Kid" (19) shows a torso and head with labeled organs (the heart, brain, stomach) and descriptions of their function. All the organs' functions combine the struggle of being undocumented with an American perseverance to overcome that struggle, proving that the Dreamer is physiologically American. The organs create an American child: the heart "is the organ that gives you the courage to persist in school" and is also "your source of hope," while the brain, as a resource to help you "figure out how you are going to eat from one day to the next" (19), helps with survival. In other words, the Dreamer child's American traits and ideals are somatic and inherent.

While the American anatomy belongs to the child or youth, the skeleton body belongs to Ledesma's father. With its machine components, it lacks personhood and humanness, so that the laboring body (representing the Dreamer's parents' generation) becomes foreign and other, in the sense of nonhuman. In the words accompanying the skeleton image, Ledesma writes, "I used to think my father was a cyborg bracero when I was a kid. He always worked and never seemed to take a sick day off for any reason" (*Diary* 27). As a child, Ledesma himself saw his father as an invincible laboring machine and only "found out" that he was "human after all" when he was injured by a machine on the job. He knew his father only in the context of his labor; his father's humanness became recognizable only in the moment of injury and vulnerability. In other words, the father's physical strength rendered him machinelike, while his humanness was understood through weakness. As a laborer, then, his human self is defined through weakness and pain rather than, for example, a strong work ethic, determination, or perseverance. The passage ends with a reiteration of the workforce's treatment of laborers as expendable: after paying the father's hospital costs, the company "laid him off and hired another cyborg bracero" (27), implying that as a human, he has no place in that workplace and that the company never needs to face or acknowledge his personhood.

Ledesma's memoir explicitly connects the parents' laboring bodies and their Dreamer children's laboring bodies. The undocumented parents working in certain economic sectors inhabit a niche category that maintains the ambiguity of their "illegal" status; as nonhuman cyborgs, furthermore, their personhood and national identity are nullified. As machines, they have no national affiliation or attachment. Meanwhile, the Dreamers, in their own niche category of exceptional "American," inherit a legacy in which the un-documented body is rendered human only by enduring pain or by being (or appearing to be) *more* than human, that is, superhuman. Specifically, the Dreamer's body (or former Dreamer's body) experiences pain through hyperdocumentation, which comes about because undocumented students are driven to excel academically, accumulating many degrees and awards to "show that we are more than our legal status" and to "compensate for having been undocumented" (*Diary* 4, 35). One visual depicts a farmworker bent over in the field, with a caption that reads "I want you to get an education so that you don't have to break your back, like me" (37), seeming to differentiate—and correctly so—the two forms of labor. Hyperdocumentation is weighty, however, and like manual labor, the accumulation of accolades is backbreaking. Another image shows a youth in a cap and gown dragging a filing cabinet that is bursting open with awards and papers (35). This exhausted student bends over from the physical toll, with his head lowered and face invisible, symbolizing how the undocumented silence, isolation, and shame that are now rebranded into the Dreamer identity are borne as continuing physical, as well as metaphysical, loads.

In the memoir the Dreamer's superhuman branding is illustrated through Ledesma's images of Superman and Batman, where both iconic figures are reframed as undocumented. The reframing, in fact, turns out to be appropriate, as it highlights both the complexity of the superhuman character and his natural kinship with the undocumented condition. When the superhuman inhabits an undocumented body, or conversely, when the undocumented youth costumes himself in a superhuman outfit, they all endure the pressure of high expectations and the work of continually passing (as human and ordinary, and as superhuman). Superman's story, of course, is the Dreamer's story: he was brought to Earth (the United States) as a baby through no fault of his own, it is the only home he has ever known, and (perhaps consequently) he overperforms his Americanness. Ledesma writes, "It is a contradiction, really, the necessity of having to be brilliant and invisible at the same time" (*Diary* 46), and visually highlights the unexpected (although appropriate) coexistence of superstrength and farmwork. He draws himself in a Superman costume holding a crate filled with kryptonite rather than fruits and vegetables (46), suggesting that he (Superman, the Dreamer) is often defined by the very thing that has the potential to destroy him. While the Dreamer gains strength from speaking out publicly, his self-exposure increases his vulnerability. Meanwhile, Ledesma's Batman is shown reading Ralph Ellison's *Invisible Man*, and the bat on his shirt has the word *undocumented* printed on it. The written narrative states, "I was not passive or afraid. I was brave and cautious, a master of survival, learning to operate under the radar to move ahead, if only incrementally" (38). Batman, then, echoes the Dreamer's way of passing through the world unnoticed and anxiously masked, while at the same time motivated to correct injustices for the larger collective even though that motivation to act increases his vulnerability.

Storytelling Strategies: Distancing and Protest Art

Although Ledesma critiques the commodification of the Dreamers, he also recognizes the important role that such publicly accessible storytelling has played in visibly highlighting injustices in the American immigration system.[3] While at first glance the Dreamer narrative seems to maintain fixed categories of "legality" and "illegality," some critics believe that the Dreamer identity subverts them. Caminero-Santangelo notes that the "emergence from the underground is profoundly tied to the notion of telling one's story— both as a marker of belonging with a group identity ('undocumented') and as a *constitutive* action that participates in the building of a subaltern counterpublic (undocumented activist youth)" (*Documenting* 251). The stories are meant to be political: "they are clearly intended to have an impact on public discourse and on the shaping of national politics and immigration legislation" (229), and such intentional politicization, as a process and activity, in turn creates spaces for additional subversive narratives such as Ledesma's.

How then does the self-referring "Bad Dreamer" deliver his story in a way that critiques, dismantles, and reshapes the Dreamer brand into a more honest expression of undocumented personhood? In his early academic research on the representation of undocumented immigrants in Mexican American novels, Ledesma found that they were "chronicled as part of the setting . . . they were the aunts and uncles, the long-lost cousins, the nameless faces of passersby" (*Diary* 42), even though they had been part of the community for most of the last hundred years. By the time Ledesma comes to write his memoir, of course, immigrant rights groups have already selected a few of those background characters as exceptional American Dreamers; his cartoon memoir, then, builds on normative Dreamer stories by drawing (often literally) more of those background characters into the forefront, challenging the expectation for exceptionalism, and thus disrupting the nation's categories of membership and belonging. Ledesma now chronicles some of the remaining difficult narratives through various strategies, namely, by distancing, by presenting visuals as protest art, and by using metafictional techniques.

Ledesma admits that being undocumented is "a condition no one really understands" but that it is always better to share "those ambiguous moments of truth" (*Diary* 72) so that immigrants will not "continue to be regarded solely as cheap rental equipment, machinery devoid of spiritual or intellectual worth" (44). Repeatedly, he strategizes the storytelling as both necessary ("safety is no longer contingent on remaining silent and invisible" [47]) and something he must distance himself from, even going so far as to create a separate persona for it. In one chapter, he describes attending a Latino writers' conference and listening to another attendee, Jim (a third- or fourth-generation Mexican American), verbally attacking undocumented migrants. During the conversation Ledesma finally speaks up, and while Jim becomes quieter, Ledesma's voice seems to gain in strength: "the fainter his voice became, the louder my words sounded in the empty bar, until all that I could hear was the echo of an unknown voice emanating from my lips" (43). This perfectly captures the dynamic of undocumented speech: although Ledesma's voice seems strong, it is not his own voice but an "unknown voice" coming from his lips. One could interpret this as a strategy of disassociation, with Ledesma distancing himself from the "repugnant" demographic (43), but it is also an example of the reluctant Dreamer adopting a new public persona through which he can ventriloquize his position, after which he can return to his more familiar state of silence. Potentially, this is a moment where self-assertion could turn into group assertion, although it is worth noting that the bar is empty and that his listeners are not receptive to his speech (the bartender is "apparently disgusted," while the other two writers present "said nothing" [43]). Ledesma has effectively borrowed another voice, but his listeners seem reluctant to bear witness. By the end, Jim appears to feel ashamed (he looks guilty), but we can only speculate about the real efficacy of the exchange.

Ledesma adopts a similar strategy of distancing when he recounts his own border-crossing narrative to his readers, where he also demonstrates how one can reveal a secret and at the same time maintain its status of secrecy. We never get the exact chronicle of the journey because the memoir's interest is the experience of being in the United States, and for this, the ("criminal") act of crossing must recede. But in one section, he describes telling his daughter the story of the crossing as if he, together with the reader, is listening to someone else's experience: "I hear myself recounting only a few of the key events that happened when we crossed. All she hears is how María, Silvia and I were smuggled . . . I am not really explaining how I felt, how terrified I was about what we were doing" (*Diary* 65). The emotional truth of the experience is hard to convey. Furthermore, in this moment the readers of the memoir are not in the first layer of listeners (his daughter is), so we are further separated from the experience. Ledesma's own move is to emphasize his listening role as well as his storytelling role (he "hears himself recounting"), a move that seems to remove Ledesma from the original experience and maintains some of the experience's secrecy, as readers seem to be eavesdropping on his confession to someone else. In a Dreamer narrative, the Dreamer must disassociate from the border crossing (they are innocent and somewhat inactive in the "crime" of crossing) even while acknowledging that it centrally defines them. Ledesma exactly captures this contradictory dynamic: his story of the border crossing is spoken of indirectly and overheard, and thus kept simultaneously hidden and revealed.

Early on Ledesma refers to his book as a "chronicle" of all that he did, as he transitioned from "a nervous undocumented immigrant kid to, a few decades later, a university professor and administrator" (*Diary* 1). Although this sounds like the start of a classic life-story Dreamer plot (a modified rags-to-riches Horatio Alger "chronicle"), Ledesma's memoir builds on the conventional definition of a chronicle (a factual written account, presenting important or historical events in chronological order) in several important ways that attest to the contradictions of speaking out while conserving an element of secrecy, and coming out while remaining somehow invisible. In particular, his storytelling is visual, metafictional, and subversive in its reframing of undocumentation as an American experience. As one reviewer puts it, Ledesma "at times . . . uses a simple cartoony art technique that pokes fun and satirizes the situation in which he finds himself or his community. . . . At other times, Ledesma's art is serious, somber, or inspirational" (C. González 5).

Like the various strategies in his written text, Ledesma's multiple artistic styles allow him to express the past and ongoing trauma of being undocumented while at the same time demonstrating the difficulty, guilt, and anxiety inherent in expressing it. In his article "Doodling as Activism" (about the process of writing *Diary*), Ledesma notes that "cartooning is an effective form of communication: it allows for better mental digestion of complex ideas; engages multiple intelligences; and, it allows viewers . . . [the ability] to understand a story from multiple lenses. It is because of this that cartooning has allowed me to communicate the fears I felt when I was undocumented much more effectively than my writing ever could." The cartoons in *Diary*, then, depict undocumented figures variously contemplating many broader issues, such as the task of getting to college, the hard-to-access mental health services, and the debatable role of advocates (researchers, activists, educational advocates) working on "behalf" of these students, as well as his personal experiences (such as the gender dynamic between his parents, the story of his *abuela*, and the multiple personas that he adopted to survive). Such an eclectic, interrupted, and plural narrative is an especially effective way to tell a story that needs to be spoken and to remain hidden.

His art also works as a form of protest that provides an important counternarrative of undocumented immigrants in the United States, responding to negative visual representations of "illegals" as criminals. This protest art—or, as Joanna B. Pérez puts it, "undocuartivism"—can play an "essential role in dispelling myths of undocumented immigrants while also providing spaces of resistance and empowerment" (23). More precisely, undocuartivism "expands the value of protest art used in the streets and online in order to reach and gain support from the masses," and in the process it "begins to construct a series of decolonial and counterhegemonic archives that challenge historical and contemporary notions of illegality" (42). As protest art, *Diary of a Reluctant Dreamer* democratizes the reading process by comfortably blurring the line between artist and viewer. Ledesma comments about the cartooning, "[it] was . . . effective because of its flexible narrative form . . . In my cartoons the fourth narrative wall was pliable; I could as easily be an overeducated omniscient narrator as I could be a vulnerable first-person witness to the same story without jarring the viewer" ("Doodling"). In the memoir he writes that cartoons "are flexible in the way they shift our perspective" (7), meaning that we can occupy multiple angles of surveillance at the same time and take on new perspectives, both literal and, presumably, ideological ones, that give us new ways of seeing and hearing the stories of Dreamers.

Surveillance, of course, is how the state recognizes members of the population in a particular way (as criminal or as illegitimate, for example) and then imposes silence on them and maintains it. In his memoir Ledesma shows how he has moved from self-censorship and policing his own speech (even after becoming a citizen) to subverting and exploiting the surveillance apparatus. For the state's surveillance to be effective, we have to believe that everything is visible and that our "crime" has no place to hide. But now, in the Dreamers' narratives (including Ledesma's protest art), "crime" actually flaunts its own visibility, taking control of the contours of its story; the undocumented migrant is still being watched, but the habit of surveillance has shifted. Now, the undocumented person *needs* to be watched and invites the surveillance, even seeking it out, in order to manage the perspectives of the story and produce an effective resistance. Surveillance is thus no longer about silencing but about the spectacle of coming out. The situation on the ground is perhaps the same (one might still be undocumented), but now, with a story that insists on one's personhood, being undocumented can mean many things, including—most important for the Dreamers and for Ledesma—the idea that being undocumented is an American experience that must be displayed.

Protest cartooning is thus a form of resistance to the surveillance of the undocumented population because it reframes the way that surveillance operates. Another reframing of the state's power structure takes place through Ledesma's use of doodles, which he explains "represent a sort of therapy that helped me grapple with my shifting identities" (*Diary* 1). Quite apart from the important cathartic effect of the artistic process (he also describes the doodles as "nourish[ing] his growth" [11]), what we might normally dismiss as irrelevant art is here considered more seriously.[4] Ledesma's doodles emerged from the ground up, as he began sketching different aspects of an undocumented student's daily struggle to teach students at Berkeley about the DREAM Act (7). He calls it an art that developed "haphazardly" and was "crafted around used packages of ketchup and balled-up brown napkins" during his lunchtime (11). Doodles originate as something idle, absent minded, impulsive, and disconnected that sometimes turns into a coherent message but sometimes does not. In *Diary*, both are important. In other words, as a symbol for the Dreamers, the doodles permit both the production of a finished master-frame narrative about success and assimilation and the raw unfinished stories of "illegality." Ledesma's entire book validates the doodle, presenting the authentic and direct sketches he produced over a long period of time as worthy conduits of the experiences they articulate. And, as even the title of chapter 1 makes clear ("Doodling as Activism"), neither the marginalized doodle nor the marginalized migrant that it depicts should be dismissed, because they are both capable of strong acts of resistance even from—and especially from—their position on the sidelines. In fact, as Christopher González explains, the art is "more than doodles to the objective reader. Rather, [it] capture[s] the evanescent nature of uncertainty and transience that dominates the existence of the undocumented" (5).

In a similar move, Ledesma describes the written parts of his text as "musings" whose goal is to motivate social justice and activism. With them, he hopes to "help those who are still undocumented" and "afflicted" about the "profound ambivalence of our Americanness" and hopes that the reader too will "learn" from the musings (*Diary* 1). As with the doodle, he intentionally downplays the importance of his narrative form and pretends its informality, littleness, and nonsignificance, even as it exerts such a bold presence on the page. The musings are personable, intimately drawing the reader in with their confessional and frank tone. We immediately trust the speakerly voice that addresses us so directly, just as we feel invited to gaze long and hard at the doodles, which, whether in black and white or color, are eye-catching and attention seeking. The text, then, redefines musings and doodles as significant or, rather, implies that nothing is insignificant: there is no artistic production or voice, in this context, that does not matter. As the genesis of the text, the musings' power lies in the very display of their rawness and brokenness.

The text does not simply center the marginalized, however, because by definition the Dreamers continue to dwell in the shadows (of an "illegal" status and all that it implies) even after they have publicly delivered their stories (Ledesma calls himself a "shadowed scholar" [*Diary* 6] despite his documentation). The narrative coherence of those stories gives them a certain acceptable status, while their perceived authenticity and directness gives the experiences legitimate validity—a point Ledesma makes several times when he reiterates that being undocumented is just another kind of American experience. But without actual legislation, there can be no real movement to the center, and as is clear from Ledesma's depictions of the forgotten characters in the undocumented story, the appearance of narrative coherence is also often artificial or temporary. In contrast to the carefully constructed Dreamer narratives, then, Ledesma's stories are more suitably expressed through the stop-and-start nature, and overlooked power of, musings and doodles.

With his powerful visuals, Ledesma also subversively reframes undocumented experiences as American ones by subverting certain cultural norms. In chapter 7, "The Undocumented Alphabet," bold full-page visuals illustrate giant alphabetic letters in the style of traditional primers or alphabet books and offer an outspoken manifesto on how literacy, children's education, and national identity intersect. The visuals are particularly striking because of the mix of color and black-and-white drawings, some of which are cartoonish, with quick casual lines, and some of which are detailed and appear three dimensional, almost photographic in their precision and their attention to texture. The letters and their definitions are in bold black or various colors; the only other color is the background to the drawings, which often fades as the eye moves down toward the illustration. Prefacing the chapter is Ledesma's own rendition of the iconic immigrant crossing sign, which usually shows a man, woman, and child running or crossing, black figures against a deep-yellow background. Although the original design of these caution signs was intended to advocate for safety, the design has been critiqued as dehumanizing, and conservatives see it as confirmation of what they perceive to be the "Latinx threat," which is used "to construct an image of Latinos as a physical, cultural, and economic threat to the 'American' social landscape" (J. Pérez 25).

In Ledesma's version of the immigrant crossing sign, the child's silhouette grasps a giant *ABC* that trails behind them, foregrounding the role of schools in the immigration process and reiterating the fact that the American education of migrant children is (and has long been) a crucial component of the nation's process of cultural belonging, one that steadily continues even as immigration policy enforces border security and increases deportations. It also somewhat humanizes the otherwise anonymous figures, softening the supposed "threat" of Latinx arrivals with the innocent, childlike *ABC* letters, which in themselves foreground the innocence of the child. In other words, it sharply brings into focus the Dreamers' essential argument: while politicians, the media, and the public debate their Americanness, Dreamers live out their Americanness every day through the cultural and social membership instigated by and inherent in the schools they attend.

Certainly, Ledesma's reimagined immigrant crossing sign implies that no image is apolitical, and consequently, that even the most innocent teaching of alphabetic letters is ideological. Indeed, Cynthia Rostankowski writes that alphabet books are usually the earliest form of literature that children read, and that they are especially intended to be talked about and reflected on (117). Lissa Paul explains how letters, sounds, and images transform into "symphonies" of cultural associations: "Every time we say that 'A' is 'for' something, we attribute to the letter a meaning beyond a phonetic sound. Each letter stands metonymically for a world and when the word is associated with an image, a little cultural narrative is created, saturating the lessons on learning to read with lessons on learning to read culture" (128–29). In Ledesma's case, a new cultural narrative is created each time he reintroduces the letters, as a way to elicit discussion and activism.

The subversive nature of Ledesma's alphabet can be clearly seen by juxtaposing it to Lynne Cheney's 2002 alphabet book, *America: A Patriotic Primer*. Cheney's book enjoyed popular acclaim from book reviewers and critics for its perceived celebration of diversity in America, but several scholars have interpreted it as neoconservatively deepening the racial, economic, and social injustices of the nation, in part because of how it co-opts liberal discourses of multiculturalism and tolerance.[5] The book ostensibly educates readers in American history (as well as teaching them the alphabet), but Clare Bradford, for example, takes issue with its attempts to reassure post-9/11 readers of America's glorious history and future, its shameless promotion of nationalism, and its presentation of Native Americans (*N* for Native Americans) as yet another group of new arrivals. The occlusion of colonization, displacement, conflict, and loss distorts and limits readers' views of history and instructs us *how* to read America, positioning young readers as admiring and patriotic Americans (Bradford 1–3). Even more problematically, as Anastasia Ulanowicz points out, the book's erasure of American collective memory tries to produce docile "infantile citizens" whose "naïve patriotism inhibits their participation in present collective action" (343).[6] Child citizens are informed of their nation's history in a limited way, and citizenship is reiterated as a sentimental, patriotic, and private matter (360).

While Ledesma does not directly reference Cheney's work, his alphabet chapter exposes the damaging effects of what Ulanowicz calls the "cheerfully aggressive insistence on American greatness" in Cheney's book and the troubling erasures that take place under the guise of such pacifying pedagogical literacy (346). Ledesma's own practice of civic literacy intentionally unveils the lived cultural and political ambiguities and difficulties, even traumas, of being undocumented and forces readers to face and examine the underbelly of the nation's immigration policies. Although his topic is more specific and pointed than Cheney's, the lesson is broadly relevant: as a nation, partly because of narratives such as Cheney's, we have already gone too long without acknowledging the shadowed lives on the nation's margins, instead congratulating ourselves on our embrace of successful narratives of American assimilation, which too often "disappear" the shadowed narratives. In fact, Ulanowicz's critique of "tolerance" in neoconservative circles (such as Cheney's) could also work as a critique of the way that the public embraces (tolerates) the Dreamers' collective identity: tolerance, despite appearing to celebrate difference and diversity, actually "reaffirms the notion of a normative American identity that merely 'suffers' those marginal groups that have not yet adopted that normativity" (353).

The two texts are visually very dissimilar (Cheney's pages are busy with verbal and visual overload, and the art is heavily detailed and pastel colored; Ledesma's art is starkly bold in color and varying in detail), but what is especially striking is the difference in the visual presentation of the alphabet letters themselves. In Cheney, each letter is contained in its own framed and ornamental box, which is intricately decorated with things such as stars or bows. The frame around each letter is also presented as a replica of something else—a traditional picture frame, or a theater stage (for *D*), the Lincoln Memorial (for *C*), or a circle-like wreath of hands holding one another. The overall effect is one of ornate pageantry, which implies that these letters can and do stand on their own. They are worthy of portraiture, they are grandiose, and they do not need to stand for (represent) anything else. They are not referential but self-contained; their meaning is thus fixed and permanent.

In contrast, Ledesma's letters appear more informally as large plain letters with quotation marks around them: rather than lingering on each letter, the reader is clearly supposed to move on in order to read what it stands for (e.g., *S* is for "the SILENCE of undocumented workers . . . the sign of how thoroughly oppression works" [*Diary* 91]). These letters are highly referential; rather than being fixed in meaning, they open up the new possibilities of language, creating a space in it (both in terms of literacy and cultural belonging) for expressing fundamental undocumented experiences. Some of these experiences fit into the now classic master-frame narrative of Dreamer stories; thus, *A* is for "ABUELITOS left back in Mexico," *B* is for "the BACK PAY that was withheld from your father's paycheck those few years when he worked as a bracero," *C* is for "the COYOTE who almost got your father killed when he crossed the border in Arizona," and *D* is for deportation (76–78). Some, however, convey the psychological damage of being both undocumented and in the public light as a Dreamer advocate (*F* is for the "fetishization" of the overachiever Dreamer stereotype [80]). The entry for the letter *I* explicitly states that a single letter cannot be or encompass just one thing, in effect deconstructing even Ledesma's own alphabetical representations of undocumented life. Quite unlike the letters in a traditional alphabet book, *I* instructs us that letters are infinitely representational. What *I* (or any other letter) "is" can and does change, and being told one thing simply implies that there are many others that have been left untold. Ledesma writes, *I* "could stand for so many things: immigration, injustice, intolerance, invisibility, ignorance, insecurity ... etc." (81), and he adds that "*here*, 'I' stands for ILLEGAL, a term so well designed to dehumanize, that as soon as it is invoked, all empathy for the suffering that compels immigrants to brave a dangerous border goes out the window" (81, my emphasis). Normally, fixing meaning in this way might erase other meanings, but readers are supposed to also recognize the value of establishing meaning, at times, so that it can be specific and attentive to the context. The letter has infinite possibilities and also "stands for" something important that must be clearly articulated.

The use of quotation marks around each letter also magnifies Ledesma's deconstructive move, insofar as quotation marks signal the presence of dialogue, speech, and another's voice. They also call the word (or, in this case, the letter) into question, disrupting its authority. Although anti-immigrant rhetoric wields enough power to appear to have given certain terms a fixed meaning, Ledesma implies that no single authority can establish sole meaning, as his memoir goes some way toward dismantling that fixed rhetoric. Using quotation marks is also a sign that the language may belong to someone else—to anyone else, in fact—and as the letters become orally inflected, they move into speech and reveal gaps and opportunities for mimicry. In this context, therefore, the letters no longer belong to Cheney's America and to its idealized erasures of history but to Ledesma's. In this text language is never fully owned by any one community but is always part of an exchange and interaction, context dependent, and focused on specific experiential knowledge. The letter *K* states this explicitly: it stands for the "undocumented knowing" of a particular class of people who are denied basic dignities as members of a "disposable" community (83).

One of Ledesma's main goals throughout the memoir is to open up this undocumented epistemology to a broader readership, and to this end, he also uses the deconstructed alphabet to illustrate the expendability of the un-documented laborer. He writes that *M* is for "machine, the inevitable result of an immigrant worker's metamorphosis from human being to mechanical instrument" and adds that "in an effort to survive within the system, these workers must function as part of a cold, metallic organism . . . becoming . . . an iron tool so dedicated to its labor" (*Diary* 85). The machine-laborer trope that Ledesma frequently visits in the memoir is central to understanding how personhood is continually denied. The visual for *M* shows a laborer with his back to the reader, marked off with lines that ordinarily would show the dimensions of machine components (for example, the length of a part), but here the lines are labeled with the terms "depression," "monotony," "stress," and "chronic disease" rather than with numbers (85). The picture thus pushes back against the body-as-machine stereotype as it measures the psychic and physical diseases that account for real suffering, even as it also treats the body as machinery. It thus simultaneously demonstrates the problem (the expendability of the worker) while resisting it. In a system that "only values papers and stamps and hides the fact that only our limbs are allowed to be present in this economy, that only our arms are valued for the labor they can exert" (93), the text's foregrounding of the endlessly labor-ing body and the inhumanity of systemic migrant labor practices is crucial. And *O*, for "obfuscation—the art of creating narrative confusion through the rapid use of non sequiturs and references to irrelevant topics" in order to avoid "being found out" (87)—describes Ledesma's own narrative of un-documented epistemology, particularly when compared to the polished and scripted Dreamer narrative.

Ultimately, Ledesma's undocumented alphabet serves multiple pedagog-ical functions. The various entries (of what each letter "stands for") are il-lustrative interpretations of various undocumented situations, representing the experiential realities of a formerly (and in some cases, ongoing) silenced group. They describe the familial hurt, pain, and injustices of undocumented life in both humorous and sobering terms and offer up new associations and connotations for language. They are, of course, framed by letters of the al-phabet that themselves undo the hegemony of language by displaying them-selves as referential and oral. Although this chapter (like the entire text) does give voice to the unvoiced experiences of undocumented migrants, it is not a hopeful or celebratory alphabet because it does not pretend to resolve the issues simply by raising them. Often there is just despair (*Y* for yearning—

you yearn for a better life but sometimes that's just "an illusion" [*Diary* 97]). Because of this, Ledesma's text only begins to repair the potential damage of a text like Cheney's—namely, its desire to produce docile child citizens. Unlike Cheney's text, Ledesma's clearly invites participation in collective action: each letter has a story, a statement, or a speech that educates, explores, and describes, frequently with heartbreaking details and images that are troubling not only in their content but also in their lack of closure.

Metafiction and the Labor of Writing

One of the most important ways in which Ledesma's visual memoir builds on classic Dreamer narratives is by displaying the work involved in its own production. The text is full of metafictional images (both sketches and more substantial illustrations) of Ledesma himself hard at work writing and drawing, and his frequent references to the efficacy of cartooning contribute to the reader's awareness of the book as a product of labor. In foregrounding the process of writing, he disrupts any notion of stories as finished products that appear spontaneously: instead, creativity is part of a longer psychological, economic, and societal process. In fact, in one section he analyzes the journals he kept as a child, understanding them to be a mixture of wish fulfilment, catharsis, and escapism. Such documentation of documents, the writing about writing, draws attention to this writing as historically loaded and as having existed in multiple versions prior to the one we are reading. What lies behind his complex story are more stories, and that complexity seems fully revealed. Compared to the Dreamer script, this is (or appears to be) a more honest revelation of the parts that go into telling the uncomfortable story of his undocumented legacy. He describes his cartoon doodles as unsophisticated, for example, and attests to his own lack of experience as a writer but also states that he is "representing the real drama I had experienced as an undocumented kid as best as I could" (*Diary* 19). Acknowledging his lack of sophistication and experience makes him seem to deliver a more authentic product. Furthermore, the reminders that writing and artistry require effort turn them into more American experiences, insofar as they become evidence of a strong work ethic, while the physical perseverance and endurance of writing, also illustrated throughout, are evidence of his (American) perseverance.

Finally, in making the production of his writing and art so visible, he renders them vital and material rather than abstract and inaccessible. There is no doubt that throughout the memoir, writing is seen as physically weighty and the writing body as, at times, machinelike. Ledesma thus shows the continuing legacy of labor and commodification that takes place with the production of the Dreamer archetype, which itself never reveals its own production process. Instead, with their presentation of polished and finished testimony that appears spontaneous and authentic, the Dreamer stories produce young Americans that appear birthed by America rather than by their foreign parents. In contrast, Ledesma's work of writing is a legacy of the work his parents' generation did: both involve essential, physical tasks, and both exert an at times unbearable burden on the body. In fact, such validation of his own (writing) work also validates the work of the migrant laborer, and reaffirms his connection to, rather than his separation from, his laboring parents, a generation that is otherwise often silenced or criminalized in Dreamer narratives of success.

Of course, Ledesma is not arguing that the work of a writer and cartoonist is identical to that of a laborer, but in showing how the legacy of machine work bears down upon the newer generation's work of producing testimony in exchange for sympathy and (possibly) action, he shows how practices of commodification continue. Through this, however, the writer must find a way to keep recording the epistemological realities of being undocumented, and Ledesma is in part propelled to continue with his work by his young daughter's innocent ambition to one day publish her own book. He says, "If my work continues to inspire her, I will keep writing forever, though I may never publish another word" (*Diary* 73). Writing, but not necessarily publication, will heal and temper the trauma of his past; that is, it is work that validates the process rather than a final product (or commodity) tailored for public consumption.

Toward the end of the memoir, Ledesma depicts a detailed cartoon drawing of a giant fountain pen, in color, entitled "My Fountain Pen" (*Diary* 103). He explains that he began writing with fountain pens to "trick" himself out of his writer's block, hoping that the financial expense of the pen would compel him to write every day (103). The illustration seems to acknowledge the legacy of machine-bodies and shows how to separate from (but still acknowledge) that legacy. The drawing shows several tiny Ledesma-figures engaging playfully with the pen, holding and handling it, touching and embracing it, climbing on it, and positioning it in place so it is ready to write. Unlike images of the machine body elsewhere in the text, where the machine and body parts blend together, here the pen—the machinery and technology of writing—and the person's body interact but are also distinguishable from one another. The writer is not held hostage by the pen, and his physical self is not entirely subsumed by the instrument (and task) of writing.

This implies, in turn, that the story need not always be commodified and that the storyteller's personhood can be separated from his laboring body. This image represents the text's larger hope, which is that despite the commodification of the Dreamers and the gaps in their narrative, in coming out of the shadows, they have provided both a master-frame narrative and a platform for experiences that were, prior to this, ignored. And of course, they have left open doors that allow someone like Ledesma, a "reluctant" speaker, to interrupt and intervene in the mastery of their narratives. Thus, he is able to borrow from their collective story in order to build his own testimony of other troubling and difficult undocumented epistemologies, and in so doing, he amplifies and extends the conversation and maintains its urgency.

Maria Andreu's *The Secret Side of Empty*

Much like Ledesma during his childhood and young adolescence, Maria Andreu's protagonist M.T. (Monserrat Thalia) in the 2014 young adult novel *The Secret Side of Empty* is also an undocumented youth without access to (or apparent awareness of) the Dreamer movement.[7] As I discuss above, Ledesma's memoir explores what it meant to grow up without that group identity and what it means to have carried that isolation into the Dreamer-infused present, and his narrative thus engages with how today's brand offers support and opportunity to youths in exchange for their public storytelling. In foregrounding the Dreamer movement as a central part of the U.S. immigration narrative, he addresses the intersection of the movement's politics with the personal consequences of his own secret undocumented history. Andreu's novel, a fictional exploration of an undocumented teen's experiences during her senior year of high school, also explores what happens when normative adolescent activities enter a "grey zone of incertitude" (Menjívar 1002) and there is no viable future to move into. M.T.'s life becomes suspended as friendships, education, familial relationships, and her social and cultural sense of place and belonging all begin to unravel. Because of its genre, of course, the novel is able to vastly expand on the ideas usually introduced in Dreamer speeches; as Marta Caminero-Santangelo notes, "the life narratives that DREAMers had disseminated leading up to DACA's implementation in 2012 . . . [had] been told in soundbites (short prose narratives) rather than fully fleshed-out stories of a complicated life" ("Making a Place" 168). But where Ledesma directly addresses the discomfort and opportunities offered by the commodified Dreamer identity, Andreu's story exists in a political vacuum: although it takes place in 2012, there is no reference to the Dreamer movement until the very last page, when M.T. comes across President Obama's announcement of the DACA initiative on television.

The effect of the story's political vacuum needs to be considered because it represents such a departure from the highly politicized presence of Dreamers in the first decades of the 2000s.[8] As Eileen Truax argues, attempts to resolve the status of undocumented immigrants has turned them into "political pawns" who are "the political currency of private negotiations between Democrats and Republicans, legislators and government agencies, and in campaigns for office" (1). It would be hard to miss the enormous influence of the Dreamer movement, particularly with social media's role in the organization. In his now well-known coming-out story in *Time* magazine in 2012, undocumented journalist Jose Antonio Vargas describes how online, "most see the value of connecting with others and sharing experiences—by liking the page of United We Dream on Facebook, for example, or watching the Undocumented and Awkward video series on YouTube." But although Andreu's novel makes references to M.T. using Facebook socially and, at one point, to using the internet to research immigration options, the community of Dreamers remains invisible to her.

The novel thus emphasizes individual and family identity rather than a politicized collective identity, intimately conveying the emotional severity of undocumented life and foregrounding the personal impact of immigration policy. This intimate tone draws the reader in: critical acclaim for *The Secret Side of Empty* calls it "among the best books for high school readership in personalizing the hardships of living with 'the nine-digit problem' of lacking a valid social security number," and it is the winner of the National Indie Excellence Award as well as being a Junior Library Guild selection, one of *School Library Journal*'s top ten Latino books of the year, and a finalist for the International Latino Book Award in the category of Best Young Adult Fiction (Cummins, "Refugees" 27). Perhaps accounting for its popularity, the novel echoes the same Dreamer master-frame narrative that Ledesma interrogates and that critics have identified, with a protagonist who is academically exceptional, entrepreneurial, and culturally American. For Andreu to use Dreamer tropes and characteristics without referencing the group shows us how pervasive and adaptive that narrative is and how embedded it is in the fabric of American understandings of immigrant identity.[9] Even without access to the classic Dreamer label, M.T.'s story is still heavily structured by it. Most important, readers see how necessary it is to have a collective brand identity in American immigration policy. Not having the brand greatly isolates M.T., as each of her Dreamer experiences is underscored by her dangerous separation from society and community, which gradually develops into suicidal depressive thoughts that almost destroy her. The implication, then, is that the Dreamer brand is perhaps necessary for an undocumented youth's survival and, perhaps, for broader immigration reform.

Within the story itself, too, M.T. never understands her experiences and feelings as valuable or worthy because they are never shared as public (or even private) testimonial and never commodified or exchanged for empathy and support. Discussing the role of diversity discourse in universities, Gabrielle Cabrera notes that undocumented students' diversity is used "as a commodity" and that the neoliberal structure of universities (or, we might add, of American society) "commodifies the experiences and identities of undocumented students." Under such neoliberal regimes, "undocumented students must mobilize their lived experiences (which may include narratives of suffering and trauma) to make political claims" (67). Although storytelling grants agency and allows youths to make political claims, in the process they must "self-commodify or market histories of trauma and violence and identify with state-ascribed (and self-ascribed) identities like the DREAMer because of its mobility and appeal to the liberal savior trope" (81). Undocumented people "are expected to indulge readers with a story about the lack of educational opportunities and violence that we face in our country of origin, while stating that the United States is a land of inclusion, democracy, and opportunity" (77). To this end, during the story M.T. does have small "disclosure moments" (Cummins, "Dreamers" 95) where she reveals her status to various individuals, but her most coherent sense of undocumented identity comes only at the end of the story, when she sees the Dreamers on television. The Dreamers, she seems to realize in that moment, offer a particular brand of normative market citizenship based on storytelling as exchange that is exclusive to the Dreamer community and thus to her.

Although Andreu explores M.T.'s personal and emotional experiences to convey the effect of the nation's immigration policy on undocumented youths, the text shows how without the branding opportunity, her undocumented experiences cannot be categorized or understood as legitimate and thus cannot be valued as markers of citizenship and belonging. Dreamers "mark themselves as deserving of residency and citizenship" (Sati 36), but M.T., without that community voice, feels deeply undeserving of her place in the United States. For example, she uses the term *illegal* unquestioningly throughout the story to refer to herself and her family and seems to have internalized its pejorative connotations to such an extent that the narrative itself uses the term uncritically: "I wonder how many interloper alarms would go off if illegal little me snuck into the country club" (152).[10] Without the Dreamer's brand rhetoric, she is not able to critique or reject the term *illegal* because inside the world of the story, there is no other label. Admittedly, the process of branding one's national identity is one of cutting corners and details, of boxing in and cementing personhood, and of creating a shortcut that often silences, excludes, and obscures the complex ambiguity of living as an American without American citizenship. But with its collective voice and visibility and its recognizable script, the Dreamer brand also offers a place for youths that—against all odds—can safely repackage many of those ambiguities into a coherent identity and present opportunities for moving forward into an American future.

The Master-Frame Narrative: Adaptations and Departures

As a Dreamer, one's otherness is intentionally fashioned as an asset because of how otherness becomes synonymous with exceptionalism. Cabrera argues that people with "marked identities are . . . incorporated into institutions as 'value-added'" and that "despite being marked as Other because of their lack of citizenship status, undocumented youth and students are . . . constructed as productive, highly educated, and almost-American by the mainstream media" (80). After emerging from the shadows, a Dreamer must continue to mark themselves—and be marked by the public eye—as desirable to legitimate themselves as a "meritorious, deserving immigrant" (Caminero-Santangelo, "Making a Place" 166) who has worked hard in ways that are valued in society. This reflects the influence of market citizenship, notes Gabriela Monico, which "rewards human potential and economic contributions with belonging and citizenship" (88) and recognizes worth based on economic output. These ideas are not new: arguments that support reforming immigration legislation have always commodified immigrants and have a long historical precedent. With Dreamers, however, branding rests not only on merit and hard work but also on going public about a history of concealment and suffering, and on following an "enlightenment trajectory" (Caminero-Santangelo, *Documenting* 229). In effect, these youths grow up exclusively in the United States, but their Americanization is most fully realized in their moments of public confession, which they must sometimes repeatedly declare.

For M.T. in *The Secret Side of Empty*, there is no public testimonial, but there is merit and academic excellence. M.T. herself states, "I can pass most tests without a lot of effort. I sit in class when it's taught and then I just kind of know it for the test. I read fast. And I know what teachers want" (32), and characters repeatedly refer to her innate intelligence: one acquaintance remarks, "I mean, you're like . . . a genius, right?" (9). Her principal even tells M.T.'s mother that M.T. is "one of our brightest students," so it is "unacceptable not to send her to school" (144), inviting the question (which the novel avoids asking) of whether it would therefore be acceptable to allow a less bright student to be left on the sidelines and not attend school.[11] In the model of market citizenship, where worth is measured by one's contributions to the market, M.T.'s potential earns her a kind of belonging (and within the school's boundaries, a form of citizenship), but a less meritorious individual would be marked as less worthy. Furthermore, in a Dreamer market, one's own selfhood (comprising merit, hard work, and bravery for giving testimonial) can also become situated as a market commodity, but because M.T. is not yet part of this market, she believes more in her own criminality and fraudulence than in her worth. In contrast, if she were a "Dreamer" (even one who proclaimed her status as a "Dreamer" to only a few people), her acts of passing and pretense would be transformed from markers of deceit into valuable markers of her brand, making them legitimate, understood, and necessary.

In addition to M.T.'s academic excellence, she has several other classic Dreamer traits that appeal to the narrative pattern of the "good immigrant" that Caminero-Santangelo refers to ("Making a Place" 168). For example, both in the world of the story and outside of it, M.T. passes as a monolingual American. With both old and new acquaintances, she is silent about her background, about where she has lived, and about her ability to speak

Spanish, at times actively denying her roots (101). On an extratextual level, too, there is a notable lack of Spanish in the writing: there is no experiential evidence of her inhabiting a Spanish-speaking household, as dialogue among family members that presumably takes place in Spanish appears only in English. Even more widely known Spanish phrases and words (which presumably would not alienate monolingual English speakers, such as *mamá*, *papá*, *mi hija*, et cetera), often found in predominantly English-language Latinx literature, are absent. Similarly, M.T. lacks—and in fact, strongly opposes—any personal connection to Argentina (her birthplace), and in this respect the narrative is more typical of earlier rather than more recent Dreamer narratives. Caminero-Santangelo notes that the life stories of undocumented youths that started to emerge in the media in the first decade of the 2000s focused on the United States as the only home—"the nation of memory, experience, culture, and deep loyalty" ("Making a Place" 166)—even at the expense of discussing transnational ties or affinities with a culture of origin, while newer life narratives present a less bounded experience of belonging (169). Certainly M.T.'s "singular emplacement" (Caminero-Santangelo, "Making a Place" 168) in the United States seems static, as she repeatedly rejects her parents' attempts to make her feel connected to their homeland. Every time Argentina is referred to as home, she asserts that America is her home (Andreu 52). Although Argentina is full of family she has never met but is "supposed to love" (113), imagining a return there "feels like being buried alive . . . going to a country where I've never lived and in which, by my parents' descriptions, I don't particularly want to be" (106–7).

In an important sense, of course, the family's emplacement in the United States *is* a complex experience: quite apart from their undocumented status (which renders life in the United States precarious), the parents' connection to Argentina by default creates a network of links to a place beyond the borders of the United States, which turns the United States itself into a more nuanced space. M.T., however, firmly rejects this nuance, in part because of her rejection of her parents. For many Dreamers, the binary setup whereby they are innocent victims of their parents' "criminal" act of border crossing is an uncomfortable but vital part of the narrative. In a journalistic account of the Dreamer movement's development, Laura Wides-Muñoz relates how Marie Gonzalez, an early Dreamer activist from Missouri, describes the complex dynamics of this parent-child relationship: "The older advocates kept emphasizing that she and the others had come to the United States through no fault of their own. But that clearly laid the blame on someone else: her parents. . . . It was true: she wouldn't even be in Missouri if it weren't for them, wouldn't have her friends, wouldn't have lived in the small brick house on the leafy street that always seemed to her out of a picture book. How could she fault them or even insinuate they were guilty of some crime? She could because that was what was needed to win reprieve from deportation. She was a 'Show Me State' girl, and she wanted to remain one" (36). In a nutshell, the Dreamer child-parent relationship is one of contradiction, where the parents "criminally" provide their child with a safe, idyllic American life. The Dreamer's job is then to establish that the child in question is American and thus deserving of this life.

In Andreu's novel, M.T.'s relationship with and portrayal of her parents clearly indicates her Americanness, strongly falling in line with the images of parenthood usually seen in Anglo young adult literature and discussed in chapter 3. That is, M.T.'s parents do not appear to understand their adolescent daughter, and her rejection of their parenting leads her to make her own decisions. As Jiménez García explains, the cultural bias that expects adolescents to separate from their parents in order to grow does not account for the emphasis on strong family relationships and parent-child interdependence in Latinx literature, where adults are often not empowered in the traditional sense ("En(countering) YA" 235). But in the novel, the family's shared undocumented status is a cause of tension and violence rather than connection. M.T.'s recognition of her mother's helplessness and lack of authority (in the household, as well as outside of it) is filtered through an Anglo-centered lens, so that rather than feeling empathy and solidarity for her, M.T. turns her mother into a foreign other whose presence is both abject and discomforting. Just seeing her mother in the kitchen "looking all drained, as usual . . . like a dishrag washed too many times" makes M.T. "mad" (19). When her mother takes a job as a cleaning lady at M.T.'s school (to offset the increased tuition), M.T. shamefully refuses to acknowledge her presence, averting her eyes from her mother's laboring body and hoping that no one will connect them: "She's carrying a big bucket in her left hand, [which] holds a lot of heavy water . . . my mother is leaning left while carrying it. . . . I wonder if they're going to see a family resemblance between my mother and me, and ask me how I'm related to this cleaning woman. I wonder if I can shield them from seeing her by making myself taller, wider" (150). Building on the classic Dreamer trope where the innocent youth must separate from the criminal parent (who Americans must be "shielded" from), here the youth, as academic achiever, must separate herself from her laborer parent.

Jiménez García also notes that while Anglo-driven young adult literature thrives on rebellious youth figures, Latinx young adult literature does not always present the parents as the traditional agents of repression against which teenagers must rebel to acquire an identity ("Side-by-Side" 119). In the novel, however, external agents of repression that Dreamer narratives usually address head on (such as ICE, deportation threats, and immigration restrictions) form only an implicit backdrop, while M.T.'s father is the story's explicit agent of repression because of his domestic physical and verbal abuse. M.T., then, is an innocent victim of her undocumented status and of domestic abuse, both of which seem to be caused by her parents (her mother is a helpless bystander to and victim of her husband's abuse). The novel thus departs from the Dreamer script because, as I discuss later in this chapter, the political vacuum of M.T.'s world amplifies the domestic abuse while diminishing the structurally abusive role played by national immigration policy.

Exclusion, Inclusion, and Passing in the Nation

The Secret Side of Empty shows M.T. moving between moments of belonging and unbelonging in various spaces, as she alternates between connecting to and separating herself from her environment. In so doing, the novel explores what it means to live in an undocumented immigrant's "grey area of incertitude" (Menjívar 1002), but without the collective support of the Dreamer community. Generally, undocumented narratives show that young people do sustain a "sense of belonging in community even as they are excluded from opportunities to step into adult roles, and denied many privileges and rights" (R. Gonzales, *Lives* 7–8). All the relevant questions about M.T.'s relationship with her environment—how she claims it and is alienated from it, how she navigates being an outside observer, how she manages a life of concealment without kinship connections, how her outcast status suggests a divergent identity—are compounded by the fact of her American adolescence, a period when (like many adolescents) she wishes to separate from her home space and reattach herself to places and people beyond it.

In part, M.T.'s sense of America as a temporary home (despite her cultural and social connections to it) is exacerbated by her parents' continuous narratives of Argentina as their real promised land. Her mother's nostalgic memories of it ("it's like she's telling me the story of some fairyland she visited in her dreams a long time ago" [71–72]) combine with her father's continuous threats (for the past fifteen years) that they will return there imminently. He tells her, "You love Argentina, right? You can't wait to go back?" and adds "We're only here temporarily" (48), asserting, "This isn't home . . . we're illegal here, so you can't stay anyway, even if we wanted to, which we don't" (48, 49). Her father's anti-immigrant rhetoric (he says "we're illegal" rather than "our presence here is undocumented" or "we lack papers") makes M.T. internalize her presence in the United States as illegitimate and moves her even further away from believing—as many Dreamers try to—that she does belong in the United States. As such, she is less able and likely to take on an individual or even collective stance against immigration policy.

M.T.'s temporal and locational limbo thus makes for an unsteady foundation from which to move into American adulthood and is further underscored by her lack of documents. Near the end of the story, M.T. acquires her first passport (an Argentine one), and even though it is not from the country she wants it to be from, she is happy to be "officially an adult" (307) because "this passport is the only thing I have that says I'm me. The truth of me, that I'm here" (310). The passport recognizes her existence, but it does not speak to her American cultural allegiances, experiences, or identity. For most of the story, she is paperless and increasingly aware of how limited her options are. At one point she considers applying for a driver's license, only to learn that she has none of the "points" she needs: "I don't have any of them. Social Security card. Passport. Birth certificate" (83). Perversely, the process of listing and naming the documents she lacks only highlights her tenuous connection to the nation, because (to her) the absent documents seem to nullify her cultural and social ties to the United States and erase evidence of her history and experiences in the community.

M.T.'s cultural ties to the United States, however, exemplify part of the Dreamer narrative's attempts (by writers, scholars, and institutions) to present undocumented people as "able to conform to normative citizenship" (Cabrera 76). In the novel, M.T. defines normative citizenship based on the higher socioeconomic status she sees in her friends' lives. Such status seems to come with material wealth, opportunity, and privilege; a long history in the place; a functional family; and a particular physical appearance. All these intersect and guarantee (she imagines) a certain ease of belonging. She frequently compares herself to her best friend, Chelsea, noting Chelsea's new bracelet, which "her dad got her the other day, just because" (6), and her "thin fingers, delicate, pale, long" and wonders "if generation after generation of living in big houses and having everything makes people prettier somehow, maybe a good nutrition, superior genes thing" (6). Ancestry connects to geography, community, and nation: Chelsea's mother and grandmother grew up in Willow Falls, the setting of the story, leading M.T. to think about "what it must feel like to have a sturdy string of history tethering you to a place, giving you a right to be there" (28).

Repeatedly in the story, wealth and opportunity are paired with beauty, while poverty and ugliness intersect. For example, walking through a college campus on a visit with Chelsea, M.T. "aches more than ever to know I won't be able to go" (93), in part because of the beauty of the surroundings. The architectural details of the buildings symbolize the way that being denied this education will also deny her the experiential joy of living with beauty. Meanwhile, when her family is unable to pay the electric bill, they use a kerosene camping lantern that fills the apartment with a "gloomy glow" (70), and they feel a hopeless inability to move forward (her mother stands and wipes the stove "in slow motion" [70]) or grow into prosperous and happy Americans. And her own family's dysfunction seems to work as a counterpoint to the healthier dynamic of her boyfriend Nate's family. Observing their beautiful house with a "TV whose sound fills an entire cavernous family room like you're in a movie theater," she understands "how nice everyone can be to each other when they are happy where they are" (157).

The precariousness and "permanent anxiety" (Orner 9) that M.T. feels, though, is often also masked by her ability to participate in the mores of her peers' idealized life. To an extent she is able to echo the Dreamer script whereby the children are thoroughly American; in her case, she even physically passes as stereotypically American: "I don't look like what most people think of when they think of Spanish . . . I'm pale white and I've got blondish hair, which I sometimes help along with a little lemon juice," and she passively practices a form of symbolic ethnicity where her immigrant origins appear fluid and selectively European: "I am like the blot test of heritage. Ukrainians see Ukrainian. Poles see Polish. Italians invariably see Italian" (8). Related to this, M.T. also actively rejects any allegiance to a Latinx collective, shying away from correcting others about her origins because she doesn't "care enough to start something over it. I'm not proud enough of the whole 'Spanish' thing to take up the rights of 'my' people. I kind of hate it, actually" (9). With no kinship to the Latinx community and an illegitimate American identity, her sense of belonging in the community and the nation is based on moments of masquerade and passing, leaving her, essentially, with no land: "I will always be a stranger everywhere. With my parents, I am too American. With Americans, I am a spectator" (98).

Because of M.T.'s acts of passing (as American, as documented), the various spheres of her life do not easily intersect: imagining Chelsea visiting in her family's apartment, for example, is like imagining "the princess at the city dump. It's just not done" (70), and she knows that Nate "belongs in one world, but this [her apartment] is another world. I know that the two could never be one" (176). Nevertheless, she also sometimes enjoys the trick of passing in that "other world" (157); to her "it is delicious to know" that Nate has not yet realized that she does not "deserve" him, that in her mind she is not legitimately entitled to the contentment of a materially comfortable life or a romantic relationship (158). On the college tour, she imagines sniffing the walls and inhaling them "to make [this place] live in my lungs" for "when I get found out for the imposter I am and get escorted off the premises, out of the state, and out of the country" (95). The unattainability of college marks her as an outsider, much as a national border heightens someone's citizenship status, but in this moment, she also attempts to infuse her abject "illegal" body with molecules of this American landscape so she can later sustain herself and breathe, for a while, as an American.

But her acts of passing are also the moments when she feels the contours of her otherness most acutely. At times she "aches" to tell Chelsea or Nate about her status but cannot because her life sounds "so impossible next to the lives they're living" (236). Without the Dreamer script, there is no narrative with which to explain her "impossible" existence, and because of how the story subsumes national identity within domestic identity, her national deviance is often personally inflected. In imagining coming out to her friends, she asks herself, "How do you explain to someone that you are so horrible and useless that your own father despises you? . . . I am so ashamed. I don't want them to know because I know they'll figure out what that means about me. The dirty, ugly outcast I really am" (236). Her internalized shame about being the victim of abuse both at home and at the hands of the state means that the task of passing as an American citizen also becomes a task of passing as a human being.

As a young adult novel, *The Secret Side of Empty* also uses important adolescent rites of passage (school trips abroad, romance, driver's license acquisition) to illustrate the dynamic of inclusion and exclusion that an un-documented teenager experiences. Here too, M.T. continually slides between belonging and unbelonging. When she first meets Nate during a "crazy teen-age mating ritual" (17) in which her girlfriends banter with a group of boys on a suburban street, a neighbor woman almost calls the police because she isn't sure if the girls are in danger. M.T., with a pounding heart, thinks, "Cops. I can't do the cop thing" (16). Her normative teenage moment trans-forms, in this instant, into a moment of fear overdetermined by her secret. Increasingly, her relaxed time with Nate becomes marked and interrupted by her secret, for example when Nate asks about college plans and reminds her, unbeknownst to him, of her absent future: "I have no future . . . this whole 'illegal' problem makes my future and his future very different" (165).

The novel's romance plot does provide a brief period of stability in M.T.'s otherwise unstable life (she and Nate are "building an us" [157]) and shows how in some respects social connections and cultural emplacement unfold for M.T. just as they do for many teenagers. But it also demonstrates the limitations of her interpersonal relationships. Because rites of passage are about stepping into the future (they are a "passage" into it), they fold the future into the intensity of the present moment. In other words, the present (rite of passage) is keenly determined by and anticipatory of the future. For M.T., whose future seems indistinct, the present is always determined by this lens of future loss and thus itself becomes slowly eroded too. With Nate, she increasingly feels that although "he's sitting right next to me . . . a part of me hurts like he's already gone" (165), and she interprets ordinary departures or absences in substantially catastrophic and permanent terms. When Nate leaves for the summer, for example, she says that he will be "already gone like I always knew he would be" (229); rehearsing and anticipating the di-saster of abandonment allows her (she imagines) a modicum of control and preparation.

Increasingly M.T. starts to detach from her environment because of how her erased future ("nothing but empty space where my grown-up life should be" [257]) seems to render her present existence meaningless. This is partic-ularly apparent at school, whose "oasis nature" (Cummins, "Dreamers" 83) has enabled inclusion but also, as she progresses through her senior year, has made her unable to plan beyond it. Gonzales notes that the legal integration of undocumented children into K–12 schools "allows them a more stable point of entry into American society" and "provides positive messages about belonging," temporarily suspending exclusion from American life. Young undocumented immigrants are able to "leave the liminal space" and cross over "socially and culturally although still not legally" (9–10). Indeed, M.T.'s long and successful history at her school legitimates her presence there. Even though school has been the site of M.T.'s most rigorous passing, it has also been instrumental in forming her personhood and has served as a sanctuary space from both the abusive space of home and her undocumented status. Gradually, however, she starts to feel "the utter pointlessness of continuing to try in school when there is no hope of any more school in my future . . . Passing school is *not* real life when you are going to go on to a life where what you think and what you know don't matter" (171). Rather than offering a space of citizenship, school is now the place where her undocumented status feels most pronounced, and a gateway to the adulthood she cannot have.[12] For example, when she is unable to join the National Honor Society's trip abroad, she feels that this is "the beginning of the end. Of how things will always be from now on" (119). As she feels less and less able to claim the school's familiar landscape or define herself within it, she actively retreats, gradually peeling away the layers of accolades and academic achievements to reveal what she believes is the real self at the center of her passing: an abject other. Instead of concealing her otherness, that is, she starts to flaunt it, skipping classes, withdrawing from various extracurricular activities, and quitting her tutoring job (223). In M.T.'s mind, replacing her former hyperdocumented self with an unraveled academic self more fittingly represents her undocumented personhood.

Shame, Abuse, and the Rhetoric of Mental Health in the Nation

While school is the site of M.T.'s most intense passing as an American, home is where that passing is most stripped away. In the apartment she is openly undocumented and openly abused, and it is consequently where she learns and internalizes the notion that being undocumented renders one without value, worth, or personhood. Her father "carries his mood around him like an angry cloud" (21), and as with most instigators of domestic abuse, the only predictable thing about his behavior is that he is unpredictable: "Eye contact is bad. But not talking is bad, too" (21). Her home is a temporary migratory space: she sleeps on a futon that she can potentially fold up and take "somewhere better" (132), while her bedroom, shared with her little brother, "doesn't feel mine much, maybe because it's the fourth bedroom I've had in as many years" (47). M.T. is thus alienated in her own apartment and rendered an observer in her friends' houses; every place, for her, is defined through concealment, fear, and discomfort, and at some level confirms her illegitimate presence in the nation.

Clearly, given the political vacuum of the novel, it is M.T.'s father rather than the nation-state that is highlighted as the story's explicit antagonist. The failure of the immigration system lies very much in the backdrop of the story, while it is the father's abuse (up front, tangible, and immediate) that helps readers process the lived experiential effect of existing with daily fear. The nation's systemic failure to legalize its undocumented youths, however, also intersects with and enables the personal abuse at home because of how M.T.'s father acts with impunity and uses the family's status to wield control over them and guarantee their silence. He frequently reiterates, for example, that the nation is their enemy: "These people in this country are not your friends" (278). This intersection of national and personal abuse, and the way that the political abuse of a class of people is funneled through domestic abuse, construes (at an extratextual level) Congress's repeated failure to pass the DREAM Act as a form of abuse. Both the father's and the nation's abuses establish structural impasses that are about the absence of opportunity and the fear that underscores every ordinary aspect of daily life.

To this end, the rhetoric used to describe M.T.'s relationship with her father sounds like the language of national warfare. After her father takes all her savings, she vows to hide any future money she earns from tutoring, saying, "I will sabotage and I will carry out stealth actions. When you don't have armies, you go to guerrilla warfare" (57). Her double vulnerability as an undocumented person and as an abused child echo one another, making descriptions of surviving them interchangeable: "I am done, so sick of trying so hard to get the formula that makes it stop, but never finding it. Not silence. Not defiance. Not truth. Not lies" (308). Here, in describing her father's beating, she also articulates the state of being undocumented: the lack of solutions despite repeated attempts to find any, the ineffectiveness of both speaking out and remaining silent, and the impossibility of speaking either the truth or lies. She captures the exact helplessness of living in the shadow of an abusive parent/state, where self-perception, self-esteem, and self-worth are all worn away.

In the story, the concurrent verbal and physical abuses that M.T. endures at the hands of her father function as attacks on her psyche and body. Continually being told by her father that there is something wrong with her thoughts, character, and personality, that she is "good for nothing" (234) and that "in this country you're dirt, you're nothing!" (56), while being violently slammed around signals to her that her body has no value and does not deserve a home, which is of course also the nation's message to its undocumented denizens. Rather than believing that the nation *constructs* her as unworthy (as in more resistant Dreamer rhetoric), she learns that her unworthiness is innate, often evoking it when thinking about her physical appearance and her relationship with Nate. Thus, she decides that her lips are "inadequate" (124), that Nate is "ashamed" of her (226), that she does not "deserve him" (158), and that their relationship will not last (193). She conflates this with not belonging with her peers or in the nation, the city, the school, and every single place she has known: "No wonder Nate wants to go away and not be near me. No wonder I don't belong here" (233). Her political "illegality" and the abuse inextricably associated with it are also shameful: as a young child she becomes aware that she and her family are "fugitives from the law" (26) without understanding what they have done wrong but quickly acquiesces to and internalizes this criminal status. Later, when the police do eventually show up at her house (because she has been identified, by a schoolfriend, as being at risk for harming herself), the adolescent M.T. immediately imagines them putting her name "into some system" and it spitting out "that I don't belong here" (268), and her brother (who is U.S. born) "thinking I am some sort of criminal, that I did something wrong" (273).

One of the ways in which the novel builds on the traditional script of Dreamer narratives (despite not directly referring to the movement) is by grappling with complex issues that Mary Pat Brady has noted are lacking in much young adult literature, such as suicide and the exhaustion of being constantly surrounded by obstacles (382). In a collection of undocumented youths' testimonials, one speaker (Andrea, age sixteen) describes those obstacles as a "brick wall that never crumbles, the brick wall that we hit every time we believe a door has been opened for us" and speaks of "the exhaustion of always maintaining hope and being let down. The exhaustion of maintaining the thought of things turning out well in the end. The feeling of detachment from the rest" (Manuel 21). In Andreu's novel the paralysis that contributes to M.T.'s sense of a suspended and pointless life is disturbing because readers see what it means to want to give up on life. William Pérez notes that for undocumented youths, "the daily concern about vulnerability to detention and deportation can result in fear, depression and anxiety" (9); in the narrative, M.T.'s suicidal tendencies are the culmination of the trauma and fear that have been the undercurrent of much of her daily life during her late adolescence. Her fear of discovery is strongly physical too: in a casual conversation where Chelsea tries to convince M.T. to apply for a driver's test, M.T. finds that suddenly her "heart is pounding so hard I am afraid I might pass out" (84). Being without documentation makes every moment potentially dangerous, while being around her father makes every moment actually dangerous, so her normative state is one where her survival instinct is always activated. Such hyperalertness is physically draining, as is the weight of not speaking out; thus, M.T. frequently references being exhausted, particularly as her depression increases (232, 233, 277).

The story's exploration of depression and suicidal tendencies not only draws attention to the mental health crisis among the undocumented population but also conveys the severity of being undocumented through the more accessible language of mental health. By showing how the topics intersect, the narrative furthers the conversation about both in important ways. When M.T. tries to describe to Chelsea the feeling of being undocumented without mentioning her actual status ("minus the illegal thing" [258]), she sounds like someone contemplating suicide. She asks Chelsea, "What if there are lives like yours that go on into adulthood and others that . . . don't?" (260). Later, a social worker cautions M.T.: "You've got a lot of the signs [of harming herself]. Fatigue and loss of energy . . . withdrawal from family and friends. Loss of interest in activities. The way your grades are plummeting" (274). These are all also understandable responses to the situation an undocumented student faces at the end of their senior year, but although M.T. has hidden a razor blade in the bathroom, which she thinks of as her "escape hatch" for "one day maybe" (233), she is surprised to realize how closely her actions align with textbook warning signs of suicide risk, admitting, "I don't think about it like I actually want to do it. I just want a solution" (275). In her response, the two states (being undocumented, being suicidal) blend: she cannot definitively rule out being suicidal because that would entail ruling out the realities of being undocumented. Here, the narrative normalizes the shameful state of being undocumented as well as the shameful emotions sometimes associated with mental health challenges by showing how they overlap. Being undocumented, then, is not an abject foreign state but a more identifiable burden akin (and related) to common adolescent burdens: living without papers means living without hope.

Articulating the burden of being undocumented through the rhetoric of mental health thus allows the emotions associated with "illegality" to be doubly inflected: depression, the certainty of an empty future, and the desire to vanish are not only psychological states of mind but the consequences of a structurally abusive immigration policy. Because of this, the idea of vanishing (understood by M.T. somewhat metaphorically and somewhat literally) appeals to her, as it represents a solution to the seemingly insoluble state of being without documents; it represents taking control, taking action, and finally having an answer to her problem. Most of all, it represents a relief from the continuous ambiguity that threads itself through every experience. When she retreats from her activities (such as soccer), she is "perversely happy to cut one more little string holding me" (210) because doing so allows her "illegal" self to become aligned with her newly self-imposed cultural and social separation. Cutting connections to a life that she believes she has no right to resolves the inherent contradictions of her standing in the nation and provides relief and clarity because she can "make it all stop," "take action," be the one to leave (rather than being left by others), and have "nothing anymore. No more being afraid or tired or ashamed" (212–13).

The clarity—which M.T. might call enlightenment—that she finds in suicide rhetoric comes from the availability of that particular discourse and the unavailability of a Dreamer discourse. When a friend shares with her a song about suicide called "17 Ways to Say I'm Leaving," she feels a tug of recognition and a sense of being understood. The song "says something to me I've never heard before but which sounds weirdly like coming home. Like finding answers" (212). Hearing the song, "it's like someone turns a lightbulb on in my head" (212). The enlightenment trajectory normally associated with the Dreamer narrative (coming out into the light, feeling determined to live out loud and proud) is here turned around and redirected toward the idea of suicide, as M.T. finally feels a sense of community because someone, however abstract, shares her feeling of hopelessness and helplessness. To replace the collective draw of suicide with the collective draw of the Dreamer movement that might save her, M.T. has to engage in what Cummins terms "disclosure moments" that allow her to be public about her status ("Dreamers" 95). In lieu of moving toward silence and erasure, M.T. must move toward the confession story normalized by the Dreamer brand and the belief in her right to be here rather than elsewhere.

Disclosure and Closure: The Role of DACA

M.T.'s first moment of disclosure is in fact not entirely her own but her mother's. When her mother needs M.T. to translate for her in a meeting with Sister Mary, the school principal, about the increased tuition they cannot pay, M.T. reluctantly agrees. Her mother begins by apologizing to Sister Mary for involving her daughter in the conversation, and the apology has the effect of validating the mother's words (her confession of "illegality") while simultaneously separating M.T. from their authorial intent. M.T. is thus absolved of the "crime" of being undocumented even as she utters the words (her mother's words) that confess the family's status. Although M.T. and her mother share the act of speech, M.T. is a vehicle for the words and not the instigator of their meaning. Appropriately, then, here M.T. does not directly say that she is "illegal." Initially, she objects to translating her mother's disclosure ("As you know, we're illegals and we can't get very good jobs") but after her mother insists, M.T. acquiesces. The reader, however, does not get her direct utterance, only the statement "So I translate" (143), further preventing M.T. from explicitly speaking her status. This indirect confession does not empower M.T. personally; neither does it seem to inspire her; but because it ultimately allows her mother to work at the school in exchange for sending both M.T. and her brother there, it does show a newly assertive side to her mother and demonstrates the potential empowerment that can come from speaking out.

M.T.'s more intentional and direct disclosures toward the end of the story each prepare her for the possibility of reconnecting to the community and the nation and for being seen "for real. For the truth of me" (153). First, she utters the words *"I'm illegal"* (275) to the social worker she has been assigned, because she assumes that the social worker already knows about her status. This first confession is thus not intended to be a watershed moment, but it becomes one because of how the woman immediately decriminalizes the term. The fear "washes" out of M.T. when the social worker clarifies, "Illegal? You mean undocumented" and assures M.T., "I don't care about your immigration status. That's not a crime anyway" (276). Similarly, prior to confessing to Chelsea, M.T. had always imagined that her friend would literally pull back "in disgust" and distance herself from the "sneaky little illegal" that has been in her life all this time (91), seeing her as a contaminated, deceitful imposter. In her real disclosure moment to Chelsea, however, she says, "My parents came over when I was little, and they didn't have permission to stay. So we're illegals" (296), assigning the origin of the crime to her parents and herself as having to bear the burden of their actions. Chelsea's actual response also helps normalize the situation: she is immediately sympathetic and supportive and similarly shifts the focus of adolescent culpability onto the parents, as she offers up her own secret in return, "confessing" that her parents are getting divorced (297).

M.T.'s final disclosure moment is the most public, as she comes out to her peers when she orally presents her English paper during class. The difficulty of finding words with which to articulate her undocumented status is resolved by the framework of a school assignment, which offers her a safe (within the space of school) and creative way to contain and structure her confession. Her paper, entitled "Seventeen Ways to Say Illegal," is in fact a list of words that bring together the mental and emotional state of being undocumented and the state of feeling suicidal. This time, however, M.T. is explicit about the parallels between the two conditions and is able to carefully separate herself from the suicidal intent of the words as she moves away from the reductive connotations of the term *illegal* ("broken," "alone," "not allowed," "wrong," "trapped," "shunned," "not good enough") and toward a more expansive, hopeful identity: "still here anyway" (300). Some of the words have to do with her dislocation and with the abjection of the self, and some with concealment and silence, but the final statement indicates a determined intent to remain in place.

M.T.'s public assertion "still here anyway" has an undercurrent of value and visibility that sounds like a classic Dreamer statement. This assertion implicitly gestures beyond the parameters of her political vacuum because the coming-out moment is invariably part of the Dreamer movement's masterframe narrative. Speaking out gives M.T. the courage to call the police after a particularly violent scene with her father, and to find sanctuary at Chelsea's house, but this personal resolution to domestic abuse seems to depend on the unexpected benevolence and protection of the authorities. The policeman who drives her away from the apartment pointedly instructs her to "go out there and live a good life" (315). Prior to this, though, M.T.'s mother has worried that reporting the father's abuse to the authorities will result in deportation for the whole family (111), and M.T. also references reading online stories about domestic violence turning into deportation. At the end, when she and Chelsea discuss the likelihood of this happening, Chelsea says, "I'm sure it can't be true," and M.T. responds, "I don't even know what's true anymore" (296). Whether authorities report immigrants to ICE depends on whether state and local jurisdictions have agreed to proactively provide ICE with information about residents' immigration status (which in New Jersey, where the story is set, they have not), but the novel does not explain this. Instead, in keeping with its more personal scope, it implies that M.T.'s rescue is the lucky, chancy result of the sympathetic personalities that she encounters rather than (more likely) of policy. In a similar vein, Chelsea's mother helps M.T. get into an unnamed college in Connecticut, showing how, as Cummins notes, "the access held by people with power and secure legal status provides resources crucial to M.T.'s advancement" ("Dreamers" 97).

In her author's note at the end of the story, Andreu reassures readers that there is no shame in being the victim of abuse or in contemplating suicide and that one must always reach out for help. She cautions that even though in her novel things turn out all right, "in real life, you never know how things are going to go" and provides resources for domestic abuse and suicide prevention. Andreu's fictional space provides resolution for M.T. as a victim of domestic abuse, but its resolution of her immigration status is more incomplete. In a June 25, 2020, blog entry, Andreu writes that "we need to understand the many intersecting ways immigration in the United States is complicated" but that "fiction doesn't do that. That's for historians and political scientists and journalists to do. With *Secret Side*, I strove to do what fiction can do: put a human face on a situation many may never know personally" ("*The Secret Side of Empty* in Literary Analysis").

Although M.T. leaves her abusive household, the immigration problem is not as surmountable. In the final chapter of the book, M.T., Chelsea, and Chelsea's mother happen to come across Obama's speech on television about the DACA executive decision made in June 2012, and the ensuing scene "reflects the widespread joy experienced when DACA was first announced, and it gives a snapshot from the brief era until 2017 when the program was first stopped by the Trump administration" (Cummins, "Dreamers" 97–98). At best (and with inherent risks of disclosing one's undocumented status to government authorities), DACA offers temporary hope and a pause on some of the struggles of living in the shadows, and was the result of decades of youth organizing and work. Eileen Truax explains how the collective efforts of organizations such as United We Dream, National Immigrant Youth Alliance, and DreamActivist, as well as smaller local groups, resulted in DACA (14), while Julia Preston describes how young undocumented immigrants "have built an intensely organized political movement—speaking out, staging demonstrations, building alliances and hounding lawmakers to expand their legal foothold in the United States," eventually wresting a victory from Obama with DACA. In the story, though, DACA appears magically, with no reference to its context or history, implying (once again) that immigration relief is the result of chance and individual luck rather than collective activism and policy change.

In the same scene, Chelsea's mother makes the novel's first and only reference to the Dreamers, saying, "The president just made an executive decision on DREAMers. Teenagers who were brought over here when they were kids, like you, M" (328), and snippets of Obama's speech clarify that this is neither amnesty nor a path to citizenship but a "temporary stopgap measure" to give relief and hope to "talented, driven, patriotic young people" (328). Hearing this, M.T. "tries on" these Dreamer attributes to see whether they apply to her and decides that they do (329), dwelling not on the limitations of the measure but on its immediate potential. The president's utterance, which she realizes applies to her, recalls the earlier moment when the policeman gave her permission to live a good life: here too an even more significant authority figure validates her existence in the nation and grants her a form of belonging that is also firmly rooted in the Dreamer brand. It is only near the end of the story, then, after M.T. has disclosed her status to those around her, that the Dreamer movement's presence becomes briefly visible: on the television she notices some students holding a sign saying "No human being is illegal" (329). The narrative does not linger on this group nor address whether M.T. will embrace this community, but it implies that because she is no longer "wading a lake of silence," her future "begins to take a color . . . and . . . shines" (330) and that she will be able to use her voice to cement her presence in the nation. Having the Dreamer brand reflected back at her through the president's speech and the DACA policy does not give her American citizenship, but it does give her personhood, classification, legitimacy, and a categorical American identity with which to try to build a future.

It is, perhaps, impossible to overstate the significance of works such as Alberto Ledesma's and Maria E. Andreu's in the political and cultural climate of the first decades of the twenty-first century. Speaking about undocumented youths as leaders of a "cultural transformation that is sweeping the country," Favianna Rodriguez notes that they are "making huge gains for the immigrant rights movement. Unapologetic and unafraid, they are writing their own history." She foregrounds the youths' fundamental Americanness: "I see the vital importance of documenting these stories," which represent "what is enduring about the American spirit," and describes the stories as part of the "evolving" nature of the American nation (qtd. in Manuel et al. 84). The move to embrace and include immigrant experiences and stories into the continually changing landscape of America—so that they shape the nation even as it simultaneously reshapes them—is not new. A century ago, Jewish American writer Anzia Yezierska's narrator in "America and I" (1922) argued that it is "the glory of America that it was not yet finished," that it is "a world still in the making." Although there are important differences between European and Latinx immigration patterns and conditions at these two different moments in history, in both cases their proimmigration rhetoric points to the economic and social contributions of immigrants. Yezierska pleads with Americans not to keep newcomers knocking in vain "at their gates" with their "gifts unwanted" (2073). Then, as now, the context in which this plea was made is crucial: Yezierska's story was published just two years before the passing of the 1924 Immigration Act, which placed quota restrictions on refugees from eastern and southern Europe. Similarly, Dreamers have been operating against a constant backdrop—and foreground—of elected officials (at local, state, and federal levels) who, no matter their partisan loyalty, repeatedly fail to provide a comprehensive immigration policy.

Although Andreu's novel ends on a hopeful note, today's readers more fully understand the impact of Donald Trump's election and administration on DACA recipients just a few years after the events in the story. As Gabriela Monico writes, this time "unleashed a nativist wave of anti-immigrant rhetoric and draconian policy and enforcement." While the rhetoric and politics were familiar, the "intensity signal[ed] something specific about the new administration" (87). In 2017 the Trump administration (which had campaigned to drastically reduce immigration) tried to end the DACA program, and although the Supreme Court prevented them from doing so, the threat of this policy change contributed to Dreamers' fears about being driven back into the shadows. Ledesma's 2017 memoir ends with a sobering postscript entitled "Enter Trump" where he describes the "anxiety and disgust" churning in his stomach during the 2016 election results and contemplates "what tomorrow will bring" (*Diary* 113). His cartoon shows Trump standing in the foreground of a giant castle-like wall with a giant *T* on it, surrounded by protestors, police, and a Ku Klux Klan figure (112). On the next page he depicts Trump with giant hair filled with Ledesma's handwriting, where he explains that seeing Trump's popularity as a candidate is a reminder of "how thorough the commodification of xenophobia has become as a Republican election strategy" (115). In this neoliberal political climate, the only way to battle the xenophobia brand is to meet it head on with the Dreamer brand, which means that even though the Dreamers do not represent the majority of the immigrant population, their narratives do provide productive and accessible openings for recognizing the human face and the humanitarian crisis behind every sound bite and data point. Furthermore, even a commodified story can move and emote and create necessary change, which is why Ledesma ultimately decides that he will keep telling his experience "in such a way that others may find some resonance with it" because the only way to build community is "by exposing who I am and trusting that others will find some human connection with it" (113).

Conclusion

In *Unsettling Narratives* Clare Bradford makes the connection between literature and politics clear when she writes that "the language of children's books performs and embodies ideologies of all kinds, since children's texts purposively intervene in children's lives to propose ways of being in the world" (6). As I have illustrated in these chapters, the literary documenting and redocumenting of Latinx migrant children, as responses to and interventions in national anxieties about migration and as ways to reach child readers of the nation (Latinxs and others), show a gradual leaning toward nationalism as a form of belonging. The question now is, What do these various documentations mean for the future of the nation, in terms of its young citizen and noncitizen readers? In some respects, my theorization of this shift in Latinx children's literature over the first two decades of the twenty-first century echoes arguments made in 2002 by Manuel Luis Martinez about migrants' desirability for roots, place, and citizenship. He notes that borderlands criticism has tried to resist master-frame narratives of American nationalism by transforming the United States–Mexico borderlands into "the birthplace of hybrid subjects" and by valorizing the liminal status of such hybrid subjects (53, 54). This has various consequences. First, as Marta Caminero-Santangelo writes, "deterritorialization, movement, and transnationalism have severe *strategic* limitations . . . as forms of contestatory counterdiscourse within the circulation of anti-immigrant rhetoric" (*Documenting* 171). That is, anti-immigrant discourse that denies immigrants personhood in part because it understands personhood through national belonging is perhaps fueled by notions of hybridity. Second, valorizing the borderlands risks forgetting that the border is "something that kills" (M. Martinez 64). His directive, if we can call it that, is for texts to see the borderlands through the experience of the material border "in all its repressive, exploitative power" and to resist appropriating the borderlands as either a "nationalist symbol" or a "commodified object used to sell some new version of the melting pot," because no matter what resistance is imagined in the new hybrid versions of selfhood, the border "as a site for repressive state power remains intact" (64). And third, such hybridity leaves migrants with no firm foundation from which to engage in a form of empowering citizenry: in deconstructing "the idea of the national sphere, or of the 'nation' itself" we have turned away from the "necessity of a 'genuine' and 'legitimate' place from which and in which we might practice our rights to full inclusion and participation" (62).

Certainly, we have seen how the children's texts both present hybridity as an empowering state and also, as Martinez puts it, show a migrant's longing "to arrive, to get home, to make roots" (57). For Martinez, such works illustrate what he calls a renewed sense of *Americanismo*, which, for Mexican American writers of the 1930s and 1940s, recognized the importance of place, citizenship, and nationhood in "enacting radical democratic reform" (57). What matters for our analysis of Latinx children's literature is that this desire for stability is not a form of assimilation or of "selling out" but rather "direct political action to transform American national culture" (60). The texts increasingly advocate for U.S. belonging and simultaneously create and reshape what kind of nation the United States is: they thus exemplify "direct political action" in the very moment that a child (a future citizen) reads them. The hope is for the concept and practice of citizenship in a national entity to be "expanded, not dismissed" (63), and such expansion of the sociopolitical landscape, I claim, happens most effectively when children absorb stories. In contrast to the at times tokenized efforts of corporate diversity, equity, and inclusion initiatives, for example, the shifts and transformations that take place during a child's experience of reading are intuitive and organic.

We know, of course, that storytelling is a "powerful factor in ideology and education," but it also, according to Maria Nikolajeva, played a "significant role in our ancestors' survival strategies" ("Children's Literature" 313). Certain (minority) groups often operate in some kind of survival mode, but at times the need for survival is more heightened. Although that is not the only impetus for writing, most of the Latinx children's literature written in the last twenty years is unarguably responding to the intensified cultivation of fear brought about by various political strategies that have criminalized immigrants and attempted to drive them out of the nation. To this point, an article from CNN in 2019 notes, "Inspired by the political moment and their own experiences, a growing number of authors are writing children's books about immigrants" (Shoichet). Kirsten Cappy, executive director of I'm Your Neighbor Books, a Maine-based nonprofit group dedicated to promoting children's books about new arrivals and new Americans, says that "it's a total golden age . . . We have seen a serious uptick." According to their database, from 2000 to 2006, there were just a handful of children's books dealing with immigration or immigrant families published each year, while in 2016 there were a dozen, and by 2018 there were over one hundred (qtd. in Shoichet). Literary production as political action is evident when we see how one story begets another: Yuyi Morales states that she gave herself "permission" to tell her story "in the hopes that it would become an invitation for other people to tell their story . . . so that everyone knows, especially children, how valuable and important their stories are" (qtd. in Shoichet). Since 2018, which is the date of the most recent literary text I analyze in my book, multiple Latinx works (picture books, middle-grade works, and young adult novels) have been published that continue to imagine and validate the expanding citizenry of the U.S. sociopolitical landscape.

Diane de Anda's 2019 picture book *Mango Moon*, for example, which tells the story of a little girl whose father has been deported while she and her brother are at school, shows an anxious transnationalism that provides some sense of relief from her grief but ultimately does not provide real closure in terms of family reunification. While the little girl can vividly remember her father in various places (their porch, birthday parties), and while the text shows his former inclusion as member of the community (he was her soccer team's coach), his absence precipitates a series of material changes in her life and awakens new fears and a sense of loss and uncertainty. The story's transnational message—that Papa might be looking at the same "mango moon" that she looks at—works only as a symbolic reunification of family members. Unlike the characters of *Under the Same Sky* and *Return to Sender*, who seem confident about their proximity to absent ones based on the trope of a shared sky, here the protagonist can at best only "wonder" if Papa is looking at the same moon. In Alexandra Diaz's middle-grade novel *Santiago's Road Home* (2020), we see the three protagonists suffer a harrowing and nightmarish border crossing into the United States, followed by six months in a youth immigration holding center for the main character, Santiago. While there is family reunification and some hope of a future in the United States at the end, the sense of closure is uncertain because of the long-lasting traumatic effects of family separation ("being forcefully separated from a parent for a day can traumatize a child for life" [274]) and the knowledge that the asylum sought by the protagonists may not be granted (291).

Finally, in Marcia Argueta Mickelson's 2022 young adult novel *Where I Belong* (a Pura Belpré Honor Book), the main character, Milagros ("Millie"), a Guatemalan American high school senior, must, like Alberto Ledesma, navigate her former undocumented status and the long shadow it casts over her life. Although prior to her citizenship Millie was a legal resident (through her parents' successful asylum application) and then a green card holder, she remains ashamed because she was "technically" undocumented upon arrival (28). The narrative implies that Millie is somewhat justified in her fears that people "will hear *undocumented* and jump to their own conclusions" (28): when she accidentally becomes the public face for a proimmigration political candidate who is running for senate, she not only attracts negative stereotyping from online trolls but also becomes the victim of arson. Meanwhile, well-meaning proimmigration constituencies want to use her as a poster child to prove that undocumented immigrants are assets rather than threats, prompting her to note, "We have to be the hardest workers, the brightest students, the biggest achievers, if we want to belong here. We can't just be human beings who mean others no harm" (62).

Very gradually, however, Millie comes to accept her own use value as an ideal immigrant through a combination of factors: the bravery of an actual undocumented Dreamer she meets, who risks everything by speaking out; the news about children separated from their parents at the border; and the discomfort of going through the border patrol checkpoint. The novel combines, at the end, uncertainty about the fragile future of children who are now reunited with their parents, and an explicit statement about Millie's own innate and predestined Americanness. Readers have already learned that her mother's "greatest source of pride" was becoming, with Millie, a citizen (156) (Millie's younger siblings were born in the United States) and that her mother, who always "pull[s] herself up" (92), is heroic, persevering, and impeccably honest, despite the heavy burden of her multifold traumas. Although the Dreamer label is deeply commodifying and problematic, Milagros ultimately bears it by seamlessly blending her Spanish name and the American dream when she says, "My father was a dreamer when he named me Milagros; his dream for his family was that we would be Americans" (253).

Even a quick summation of these three texts shows the way that Latinx literature continues to document migrant children in complex and important ways. Together, the narratives fully face the trauma of the border, long for but remain uncertain about transnational connections with absent family members, and demonstrate belonging in the United States even when that belonging seems contingent upon being a "deserving" immigrant. More broadly, then, this expanding literary landscape addresses some of the concerns that Manuel Luis Martinez identified in terms of representations of hybrid borderlands: out of the traumatic materiality of the United States–Mexico border, the losses of migration, and the conditions for citizenship, it builds a foundation from which an "expanded citizenry" can shape the nation-state. And most important, it does all this for children, who are entitled to personhood and who, through the act of reading, are already participating as political agents and rehearsing and developing the voices they will need in order to document themselves and their communities in the nation.

NOTES

Introduction

1. At the time of this writing, YouTube has three versions of the commercial: the entire uncut version discussed here ("84 Lumber Super Bowl Commercial | The Entire Journey"), the version that was aired during the Super Bowl ("84 Lumber Super Bowl Commercial | The Journey Begins"), and its conclusion ("84 Lumber Super Bowl Commercial | Complete the Journey"). Incidentally, the domain Journey84.com is no longer owned by or affiliated with the company; by December 2017 the site had disappeared (Galarza and Stoltzfus-Brown 42).

2. The use of the ad by 84 Lumber to attract more (Mexican) workers and its simultaneous ambivalence about the need for such workers is part of the United States' long-ago institutionalized establishment of a Mexican migrant labor supply. Beginning in the 1920s, Mexicans began to be viewed as either temporary disposable workers or criminals. Because they were considered (unassimilable) laborers rather than immigrants (Orduña 34), they were excluded from restrictive immigration policies passed in the early 1920s, such as the 1921 Emergency Quota Act and the 1924 Immigration Act, which together curtailed the flow of southern and eastern European immigrants and eastern and southern Asians. However, during an immigration boom from Mexico in 1929, Congress passed new prohibitions on informal border crossings, prohibitions that have been interpreted as intentional attempts to criminalize, prosecute, and imprison Mexican immigrants (see Hernandez). In addition, the development of the regional political economy in the Southwest (which relied on active recruitment of Mexican migrant workers for railroads, ranching, and agriculture), the 1924 creation of the Border Patrol, and the 1942 Bracero Program all helped maintain a "revolving door" policy whereby mass deportations are concurrent with an overall, large-scale importation of Mexican migrant labor (De Genova and Ramos-Zayas 40).

3. The *Border Patrol Strategic Plan 1994 and Beyond* document explains that the agency cannot absolutely seal off the border, so instead it prioritizes efforts by geographic areas, which means "funneling people into the most remote, uninhabited expanse of the land" where "people then die" and are not always found (Orduña 154,

159). John Carlos Frey agrees that the harsh desert land and climate were believed to serve as a new prevention through deterrence (39). Prevention through deterrence, too, functions simultaneously as evidence that the United States is "serious about controlling its borders and as an assurance that some will survive and make it to the agricultural fields, the meat-packing factories, and the restaurants of El Norte" (Doty 136).

4. Grenby and Immel note that children's literature is "polymorphous" (xiii) because its readership is not just the intended child or teenager audience but also the adults that might read such works and those that mediate the material for the child (librarians, teachers, and parents).

5. Terrio describes this contradiction as "competing agendas of humanitarianism and security." In the first, the child is seen as a dependent victim in need of compassion and protection; in the second, the child is threatening and burdensome (12–13). Rhodes notes that with "victimized and passive Latinx child bodies a constant presence in the news and media" ("Carmelita Torres" 361), children's and young adult literature rethinks the way childhood agency is constructed for audiences that expect "both sanitized portraits of childhood and critical representations of undocumented immigration" ("Female Empowerment" 21).

6. I am using the term *undocumented* to refer to people without documents that legally authorize their current presence in the United States. While the term *undocumented* is not always accurate because those persons may possess other forms of documentation (for example, birth certificates or expired visas), it does denote the ways in which the "status of documents [has] gained primacy" as a measure of authorized presence (Caminero-Santangelo, *Documenting* 189).

7. Similarly, De Genova and Ramos-Zayas explain that "the figure of the 'illegal alien' itself has emerged as a mass-mediated sociopolitical category that is saturated with racialized difference" (3).

8. Carens argues that undocumented migrant children are "morally entitled to certain legal rights that are not granted to adults, the most important of which is the right to a free public education" (102). The 1982 *Plyler v. Doe* decision granted undocumented children the right to attend public school no matter their status and thus gives them (temporarily, in certain spaces) one of the benefits of legal personhood. It also signaled a larger principle, according to Olivas, of "how this society will treat its immigrant children" (8).

9. In 2014 tens of thousands of unaccompanied children arrived in the United States from the Northern Triangle of Central America (El Salvador, Guatemala, Honduras). Many had no parent or legal guardian to care for them or provide physical custody (Greenblatt). Terrio explains how this "vulnerable" population that for years had been absent from immigration debates was suddenly breaking news because of the shocking pictures of children in detention centers that circulated in the media (4). Public response was not always sympathetic, either, as "moral panic centered on the threat of criminality and disease [the children] posed" (10). Sayre also notes the steady increase in child detentions: in 2011 the U.S. Border Patrol detained around

6,800 undocumented children, in 2012 the number rose to 13,000, and in 2013 it was 24,000. Speaking in 2014, he says that "most estimates predict more than 60,000 minors will be detained this year alone."

10. We see a similar "good" versus "bad" immigrant binary with the construction of Dreamer youths. For example, when comprehensive immigration reform efforts gathered steam in Congress in 2013, Rep. Steve King of Iowa likened undocumented youths to livestock, insisting that for every Dreamer valedictorian there were one hundred drug mules who had "calves the size of cantaloupes" from "hauling huge bales of marijuana across the desert" (Terrio 10).

11. George J. Sánchez delineates three different antiforeign sentiments that mark racialized nativism at the end of the twentieth century and signal a decline of the nation: language (extreme antipathy toward non-English languages that might undermine the American nation), multiculturalism and affirmative action, and the belief that foreigners are a drain on public services (1021). The comparison between today and the 1920s is not uncommon: Terrio also argues that contemporary warnings about America's Latinx immigrants "recall early-twentieth-century anti-immigrant views" (9).

12. Valdivia notes that although the wave of mass deportations under Trump began during the Obama administration, under Trump "we are seeing changes in immigration policy and enforcement that yield a qualitatively different experience of what it means to be undocumented in the United States." Trump's 2017 memo, for example, placed "any and all undocumented immigrants who come into contact with immigration officers at equal risk of deportation and thus effectively heightened their vulnerability" (128). Trump's zero tolerance policy, which officially went into effect in the spring of 2018 and at its height attracted unprecedented media attention and public outcry, was part of the 2005 Operation Streamline initiative, based on the idea of "prevention through deterrence." Before Trump, parents traveling with children were generally exempt from prosecution under Operation Streamline, but this approach to securing the border did eventually result in family separation. Between July 2017 and January 2021, at least 3,900 children were separated from their parents at the border (Ward).

13. The Illegal Immigration Reform and Immigrant Responsibility Act made more immigrants (including legal residents) eligible for deportation, so that deportation went from being a "rare phenomenon" to being relatively common (Lind).

14. As Foer writes, "Before the birth of ICE, America had a bureaucracy that didn't treat [immigrants] as a policing problem. Immigration enforcement was housed in an agency devoted to both deportation *and* naturalization" (70).

15. Olivas observes that concurrent with the rise in anti-immigrant sentiment, there are efforts to incorporate migrant children and their families into the larger community, possibly as a result of wider acceptance by "citizen families" (3).

16. Transnationalism generally refers to the circular movement and temporary (rather than permanent) settlement of people, and also to the movement of cultures and capital across national borders. It also, therefore, implies maintaining contact

with the country of origin (and other nations), and perhaps less assimilation or loyalty to the new state (Huff).

17. The relationship between universal and nation rights is relevant here too. Some scholars argue that globalization and transnational immigration have challenged nation-centered accounts of citizenship and that the nation-state is no longer the only institution responsible for distributing rights. Thus, undocumented immigrants can be considered political actors with legitimate rights claims. But others propose that globalization has only sharpened nationalism. Walter Nicholls writes that membership in national communities is not only necessary for accessing "universal rights" but that national belonging is reinforced rather than weakened by the state's "exceptional" powers (180). Similarly, Cecilia Menjívar points that out the legal status of citizenship is revalorized and even reinvigorated as immigration policies become more restrictive (1005). At the same time, cultural membership and spaces of belonging that perhaps supersede legal citizenship invite the question, "Is residing within a community sufficient grounds for asserting membership, or does one first need to be recognized as a member?" (R. Gonzalez, *Lives in Limbo* 5). In other words, because universal rights are generally only accessible through national rights and laws, being a citizen of a nation is a necessary part of being a global citizen.

18. For discussions of Locke's notion of the child as a blank slate and the Enlightenment and Romantic views of childhood, see Reeves.

19. See Hintz and Tribunella for discussions of child archetypes.

20. For children's literature / Latinx studies intersections, see Serrato's "Working with What We've Got" and Jiménez García's "Side-by-Side"; for interdisciplinary studies in Chicanx children's literature, see Alamillo's introduction to *Voices of Resistance* (Introduction); for language in Latinx children's literature, see Ghiso and Campano, Barrera et al., and Barrera and Quiroa.

21. In 2017, for example, just under 6 percent of published books for children and young adults were written by Latinx writers. Such a lack of representation can have "negative impacts on how young Latinxs view themselves" (Boffone and Herrera 5).

22. Boffone and Herrera write that "as the Latinx population in the United States approaches becoming the majority by 2043, the need for scholarship centered on Latinx children's and young adult writing has become more pressing" (5).

23. For a discussion of audience and marketplace, see Capshaw's "Ethnic Studies."

24. As early as 2002, Capshaw Smith noted that as disciplines, both the fields of children's literature and ethnic studies have had to continually combat marginalization within the academy, but she saw this as an opportunity to position ethnic children's literature at the center of academic study rather than at its margins (8). In 2017, however, Jiménez García argues that children's literature still marginalizes Latinx literature and that its scholarship often seems to forget and exclude those voices ("Side-by-Side" 119).

25. One example of the effect of policy on social and educational marginalization can be seen in the 2010 Tucson Unified School District's banning of the Mexican American studies program. This led to the ban of many Chicanx-authored children's

books (disconnecting students from literature that was relevant to their cultural lives and their adolescence), which in turn led to reinvigorating undergraduate libraries of banned literature (Alamillo et al. xi).

Chapter 1

This chapter was adapted from an essay previously published as "Material Literacies: Migration and Border Crossings in Chicano/a Children's Picture Books," in *MELUS*, vol. 43, no. 4, 2018, pp. 148–74. *MELUS* is published by Oxford University Press.

1. For the formative importance of children's literature, see Kelen and Sundmark. For racial attitudes, see Thananopavarn and Davis. See Barrera and Cortez, Capshaw Smith, Cummins ("Education"), Naidoo, Serrato ("Conflicting Inclinations" and "Working"), Baghban, Mathis, and Horning on disproportionately low representations of Latinxs and other minority groups in children's literature.

2. See Landes, who argues that such traditional quest narratives satisfy a child's instinctive "literary logic" (53).

3. See also Cope and Kalantzis ("Multiliteracies"), Willis et al., Guo et al., and Mills.

4. I discuss orality, literacy, and multiliteracy in *Tomás* in my article "Material Literacies." See also Montaño and Postma-Montaño for an analysis of how the book builds bridges across societal divides, invites readers to value both orality and literacy, and functions as a "conocimiento mirror" for young Latinx readers who can be inspired toward activism.

5. Pilsen, home to the second-largest community of Latinxs in the United States outside of L.A., is situated in the Lower West Side community area of Chicago. Originally inhabited by German, Polish, and Czech immigrants in the late nineteenth century, it became home to an increasing number of Latinxs in the early 1960s and since then has seen some ethnic diversification and gentrification, together with efforts to curtail these and preserve Mexican American culture. In 2006 the Pilsen Historic District was listed on the National Register of Historic Places. See "About Chicago's Pilsen Neighborhood."

6. Nikolajeva notes that traditionally, school (as an institution) is absent or circumvented in children's literature ("Children's Literature" 322). For migrant child protagonists, the school is a place of heightened visibility but also often the locus of nation building. Reimer argues that in Foucauldian terms, school (in the context of school stories, but applicable here) is an important site for "the exercise of . . . surveillance," where the subject is in a state of "conscious and permanent visibility," but that the school setting can also persuade readers that they too have a place in the world, and sometimes offers a complete, self-sufficient, and contained system (211, 224).

7. The Mixtec are one of the Indigenous Mesoamerican peoples of Mexico, originally inhabiting the region of La Mixteca in Oaxaca and Puebla, and parts of Guerrero, but now one of the most numerous migrant groups to have moved to the United States. Mixtec communities are generally described as transborder because of their

ability to maintain and reaffirm social ties between their native homelands and their diasporic community. The "origin" community is multilayered, as hometowns are spread out throughout multiple sites in the United States and Mexico. See Kearney and Stephen.

8. Serrato questions the book's "tidy and uplifting" conclusion, which seems to be at odds with the narrative's commitment to depicting unpleasant realities. He argues that such an ending both speaks to the hesitancy in the world of children's publishing to put overly harsh or "depressing" books on the market and also shows the ambivalence on the part of Chicanx authors about how to best help contemporary youths negotiate the facts of their lives. Ultimately, this idealism allows the work to assume "a special relevance" and utility for its readers ("Conflicting Inclinations" 192, 193).

9. This visual may refer not to the border crossing itself but to the bus line after crossing. If so, it further supports the notion that the experience of border crossing defies easy representation.

Chapter 2

1. See Wald for a discussion of the influence of Locke on Jefferson's ideas about property, natural rights, and political rights, and for the racial history of wilderness and agricultural discourse.

2. Medical anthropologist Seth Holmes notes that the migrant farmworkers' experience is one of "physical sickness" as well as "mental, existential, and interpersonal anguish" (89).

3. DeFelice's non-Latinx identity (compared to Alvarez's Dominican American identity) might account for this. Beck notes that some critics "assert that it is impossible for a privileged person from outside a culture or class to authentically represent the experience of a racial or ethnic minority or oppressed class in a 'culturally authentic' or 'culturally conscious' manner" but that "when taken to its logical extreme . . . this position can lead to an absurd denial of the author's and artist's ability and creative prerogative to write or paint about anyone other than themselves" (101). He adds, "inevitably, some of these books will have to be written by cultural outsiders (because only a small minority are written by actual former migrants)" (102).

4. For example, agricultural interests in the first quarter of the twentieth century pressured the U.S. government to waive certain immigration laws (such as the head tax, literacy requirements, public charge provisions, and the Alien Contract Labor Law) to ensure the flow of Mexican farmworkers in the fields (Shea 124). In this respect, according to Olvera, legislation such as the 1986 Immigration Reform and Control Act or the 1996 Illegal Immigration Reform and Immigrant Responsibility Act is often just symbolic, putting immigration enforcement in the hands of employers rather than regulating immigration flows.

5. In one account (from the height of World War II) that explains the historical legacy of migrant farmwork today, a California farmer states, "We want Mexicans because we can treat them as we cannot treat any other living man. We can control

them at night behind bolted gates, within a stockade eight feet high, surmounted by barbed wire . . . We make them work under armed guards in the fields" (Mitchell 88).

6. Crèvecoeur also talks about the satisfaction of doing good work: his wife "praising the straightness of my furrows and the docility of my horses" (52). The skill and reward of labor earn you recognition and admiration.

7. It is important to note that Joe's father also resists prejudice toward the Mexicans, particularly in terms of their connection to his land. When the cars drive onto the farm, Dad stands in their direct path; when the authorities ask him "These migrant workers yours?" he replies, "These people work for us, yes" (75), correcting their rhetoric in order to force a recognition of the workers' humanity, hard work, and personhood.

8. See Caminero-Santangelo (*Documenting*), Cummins ("Border Crossings"), A. García, S. Martínez, Pitt, and Socolovsky ("Cultural (Il)literacy").

9. Caminero-Santangelo argues that while Mari provides the fictional "point of view" of a child "scarred by her family's separation and her own undocumented status," it is Tyler who "undergoes an education and enlightenment process in the course of the novel" (*Documenting* 138).

10. Pitt reads the novel as reframing conversations about immigration by considering the vulnerability of the immigrant and the food system and revealing "the extent to which recent immigrants have become central to the economic and cultural fabric of dairy farming communities far from the U.S. border with Mexico" (14). Pitt also notes that while historically fruit and vegetable harvesting, meatpacking, and food processing has been done by migrant laborers, the U.S. dairy industry joined that group later, due to the traditional geographies (regionally further from the border) and demographics (small, family-size farms) of the industry. By the late 1990s, however, "very few U.S.-born children raised on dairy farms were remaining there after high school and [farms] were struggling to find U.S. citizen employees willing to work early shifts, late nights, weekends, and holidays required for day-to-day milking operations" (20). See also A. García ("'We'") on the shortage of local farm labor in Vermont.

11. The novel's global perspective, and its intersection with child/adolescent protagonists, has drawn particular attention from scholars: Susana S. Martínez sees the children's transition into political beings and global citizens as giving them agency to work toward social change (112), Andrea Fernández García posits that they manage to "remake their identities by engaging with a global ethic of mutual recognition and justice embedded in . . . global citizenship" ("'We'" 111), and Marta Caminero-Santangelo argues that Tyler in particular is able to develop a moral and ethical outlook based on the novel's "partial cosmopolitanism" (*Documenting* 140).

12. For example, Mari describes the generational gap between herself and her parents as follows: "Sometimes . . . I felt a huge desert stretching between my parents and who I was becoming" (102); the transformation of place mirrors her own gradual maturation.

13. Crèvecoeur's (or rather, James's) farm is also ancestral and family oriented: it was left to him by his father; his wife "rendered [his] house all at once cheerful and pleasing . . . when I went to work in the fields, I worked with more alacrity and sprightliness; I felt that I did not work for myself alone, and this encouraged me so much" (52); and he also imagines many future generations to plow and toil the land (55).

14. Insofar as literacy can be defined as the ability to write, read, speak, and listen so as to communicate effectively and make sense of the world, one could argue that *Under the Same Sky* also demonstrates cultural literacy, as Joe learns to navigate the newly politicized farm landscape (as does Tyler, in Alvarez's novel: see Socolovsky "Cultural (Il)Literacy").

15. I am not claiming here that writing is equivalent to farm labor in terms of physical toil. Rather, this is a symbolic parallel that is also seen in later narratives such as Ledesma's, where the heavy legacy of farmwork manifests, for the Dreamer generation, as a weighty pressure to succeed academically and materially.

16. According to Shea, this act added to and consolidated the list of "undesirables" already banned from entering the country, including alcoholics, anarchists, contract laborers, criminals, convicts, epileptics, "feebleminded persons," "idiots," "illiterates," "imbeciles," "insane persons," "paupers," et cetera (132).

17. Writing letters, according to Crèvecoeur, is "nothing more than talking on paper" and is "only conversation put down in black and white" (41, 44).

18. With her use of letters, Alvarez foregrounds issues of literacy and education and creates what Linda S. Coleman calls a "community of readers" inside as well as outside the text. This strategy, according to Coleman, gives the writing subject the "needed authority and strength to negotiate or even to subvert external or internalized norms" that might be silencing her (1). The size and shape of the community of readers can vary: it can be a community of one or it can include places and people far beyond the writer's immediate experience, and it can be explicit or implicit, conscious or unconscious (1–2).

19. Note that even Mari's diary, a form that would generally be considered private property, also becomes a model of communal literacy and property in the story. Mari allows her sister to read it and imagines it one day becoming a public document; in addition, she includes in it notes written to her by her classmates, further expanding migrant/citizen experiences as plural, intersecting, and collective.

20. Other examples of failed or delayed reciprocity include Mari's letter to her deceased *abuela*; the letter to the president, where she cannot provide a return address; her first letter to her tío Felipe in jail; her letter to the Virgin of Guadalupe, which cannot be placed by the statues in her church in Mexico; and her letter to her grandparents in Mexico, which must be delivered in person because of the unreliability of the mail system.

21. Steven Wolk points out that "living in a democracy poses specific obligations for reading" because "while a nation of workers requires a country that *can* read, a democracy requires people that *do* read, read widely, and think and act in response to their reading." He adds that social responsibility (and schooling) must go "far beyond

basic citizenship: it is about shaping human beings with intellectual curiosity, a caring heart, and a belief in the common good" (665).

22. Even prior to the raid, the farm's landscape has absorbed trauma for Mari and her family, as after her mother's return, both her parents suffer stress and pain. After hearing her mother's stories, "her father walks around with a fierce look in his eyes, his jaw tense, and his hands in fists. Any little thing and he blows up at Mari and her sisters" (251). That is, the landscape is marked not only by the ICE raid but by the legacy of border disappearances and crossings.

23. See Marta Caminero-Santangelo for a discussion of Tyler's particular "brand of cosmopolitanism," which he sees through the lens of national myths, values, and history, still privileging his own nation's history (*Documenting* 143). It is Mari, Caminero-Santangelo points out, that introduces the connection between the trope of space and the global or cosmopolitan perspective in her letter to the president (144).

24. Nationalist sentiments, in fact, often accompany the narrative's global ideology, as seen in Papa's deep bond to their home in Mexico. Upon his return there, he picks up a handful of soil and sifts it through his fingers, explaining that "this has been our land for generations" (314). Here, nationalism is not a conceptual political entity and references not political borders or exclusionary practices but physical soil. In this respect, it is reconcilable with the novel's global ideology.

25. Although Mari fits the Dreamer demographic (arrival in the United States at the age of four, growing up in the United States), she generally expresses more longing for Mexico than the United States ("I always thought I would want to go back" [259]), and unlike her younger sisters, who were born in the United States, she rarely asserts confidence in her American cultural identity. See Caminero-Santangelo ("DREAMers") for more on the role of Mexico in Dreamer narratives.

Chapter 3

1. In this context, it is worth considering the marketing implied in the book's cover design. Despite the story's repeated mentions of Sofi's brown skin, the cover shows a white girl in profile staring off into the distance, with bare shoulders and a hat brim with seashell decorations. The image is sexualized and clearly vacation themed. At the same time, the framed boxes that contain the novel's title indicate firmness and immobility, while the arrows indicate a confused journey, suggesting a figurative and literal understanding of what it means to be lost. Overall, the cover's nod to the book's commercial value presents a whitewashed and eroticized image of Latina girlhood, while the more serious topic is implied in the title presentation.

2. Wood and Berger cite Jeffrey Pilcher, who says that Anglos' consumption "exoticizes *mexicanos* as objects of desire" (378).

3. Berger and Wood note that tourism "necessitates a marketed national identity that is sold, consumed, and negotiated" (5–6), and Berger explains how tourism development was "profitable and stabilizing" and played an important role in democratizing Mexico because "it is only viable in stable and hospitable conditions, requiring amiability in the domestic and foreign affairs of the host country" (108).

4. The value of documentation permeates even familial relationships. Later in the story, Sofi's Mexican grandmother explains that she is American born but lacks the documents to prove it. She is already estranged from her family, and in her mind, her lack of documents seems to cement this estrangement. She says, "I have nothing to help you. No birth certificate. No papers. Nothing . . . I am no good to you. I'm no good to anyone" (222). She sees herself as having no worth because she is paperless.

5. Latinx young adult narratives usually sympathize with border-crossing youths. See Cummins, "Border Crossings."

6. Alegría's fictional depiction of these productive possibilities reflects reality: in 2019 interviews with DACA beneficiaries in California and Arizona who had the opportunity to visit Mexico, Ruth et al. found that their visits to Mexico "allowed for a reflection on both places and, ultimately, accepting and embracing that they have both cultures" (307).

Chapter 4

This chapter was adapted from an essay previously published as "Borderland Ethics, Migrant Personhood and the Critique of State Sovereignty in Jairo Buitrago's *Two White Rabbits* and José Manuel Matéo's *Migrant: The Journey of a Mexican Worker,"* in *The Lion and the Unicorn*, vol. 46, no. 2, 2022, pp. 175–200. *The Lion and the Unicorn* is published by Johns Hopkins University Press.

1. Based on their written and visual narratives, *Two White Rabbits* and *Migrant* have different reading, listening, and viewing levels (the former is more likely to appeal to younger readers, while the latter might appeal to older children). However, both texts are legible as cultural products that resist easy commodification of the topic of border crossing and for this reason can be productively studied together. Further studies might explore in more detail whether the different strategies employed in the texts are more typically evoked because of the different ages of intended readers.

2. See especially Anzaldúa's *Friends from the Other Side* for the stigma and treatment of undocumented migrant bodies; Herrera's *Calling the Doves* for depictions of migrant farmwork; Jiménez's *La Mariposa* and Herrera's *The Upside Down Boy* for stories about school, belonging, and language; Mora and Martinez's *I Pledge Allegiance* for issues of citizenship; Morales's *Dreamers* for explorations of voice and literacy; and Herrera's *Super Cilantro Girl* for representations of border crossing and parental separation.

For scholarship on picture books, see Kiefer, Landes, Nikolajeva and Scott ("Dynamics" and *How Picturebooks*), and Capshaw Smith and Higonnet. For picture books and immigration, see Beck, López and Serrato, Naidoo ("Opening Doors"), Rebolledo, Serrato ("Conflicting Inclinations"), and Socolovsky ("Material Literacies").

3. Brady also warns against the design sensibility of "broadened, flattened illustrations echoing the traditions of . . . amate paintings," arguing that this kind of visual branding happens when artists are asked to produce "authenticity" (380). In this

paper, however, I offer a different reading of the function of the codex that interprets it as radically remapping national boundaries.

4. See Caminero-Santangelo (*Documenting*) for an extensive discussion of an ethics of recognition and responsibility.

5. See also "Enforcement Statistics."

6. See also Molly Bang on how picture structures affect readers' emotional responses.

7. Obviously, children who have themselves crossed the United States–Mexico border (or have some otherwise direct knowledge or experience of it) present a different type of child reader. Nevertheless, even with such knowledge, this "border" still looks like a simple wooden fence: it is a barrier that runs the full length of the double-page spread, nonmilitarized and not secured.

8. The book was published in Spanish in 2011 and in English in 2014. Current editions are bilingual, featuring English on one side and Spanish on the other.

9. For a discussion of Mesoamerican codices and chronicles and their descriptions of religion, history, society, and economy, see Batalla Rosado. For an analysis of pre-Columbian writing systems, see Boone.

10. Serrato notes that the book's cover works as an elegant artifact; it is "a work of art" that prompts in the reader "a mature approach to the subject of the book" ("Visual Brilliance").

Chapter 5

1. As Bradford notes, "tropes of travel and movement across space are endemic in children's literature" (14).

2. Several of the children on the journey engage in tricks of passing as Mexican, as they need hide their Central American identity: Ángela passes by adjusting to a Mexican accent (68–69), which she has learned from Mexican TV shows; Xavi wears a Mexican school uniform and passes as a student for the initial stage of the journey; Rafa has a fake letter addressed to him from his "Mexican" grandparents; and Joaquín has learned the Mexican national anthem.

3. This is also, of course, evidence of American globalization and consumerism. As Langer notes, "the colonization of children's lives by the entertainment product cycle has woven Disney, Hasbro, Mattel, and McDonald's into the fabric of everyday life for urban children across the globe" (263).

4. Pérez et al. note that in recent political debates and popular culture, Latinxs and Latin American immigrants are presented as "hypervisible" even though their daily lives (efforts to build community and to lay claim to full citizenship rights, community activism, and cultural production) remain "largely invisible and . . . mischaracterized" (1–2).

5. Gerber explains how the "contradictory directions" of immigration legislation in the 1990s "are evidence of the complexity of the problem that a world on the move has created for law makers and law enforcers," so that "in the first decade of the 21st

century, neither American political party was willing to directly take on the multiple policy challenges associated with immigration" (63).

6. Inda adds, "The body of the 'illegal' immigrant has served as an important terrain of governmental struggle. . . . Attempts to exclude the immigrant from the body politic imply that illegal lives are expendable" (135). Ngai builds on this by arguing that illegal immigration is a caste group categorically excluded from the national community, living in the shadows and never able to embark on the path to citizenship (xxiii). She notes that unauthorized immigration is inherent to a regime of immigration restriction (xxiv).

7. Inda writes, "Not only does the state construct illegal immigrants as undesirable and prevent them from entering the United States, it also implicitly judges them to be expendable, suggesting that their lives are not quite worthy of being lived" (149). Rosas also notes that under the logic of biopower, policing (expressed as extra surveillance and vigilance) draws on racialized perceptions of foreignness (410).

8. Ginsberg notes that "the cultural logic of passing suggests that passing is usually motivated by a desire to shed the identity of an oppressed group to gain access to social and economic opportunities" but that it can also be to fit in and forget one's past (3).

9. This is especially important given the text's emphasis, in other moments, on the remoteness of Guatemala because of how difficult it is to communicate with family there. The phone needs credit added to it, and although there is email, the family has to use a village computer that is slow and for which they're charged by the minute (40).

Chapter 6

1. The Fifth Circuit ruled in October 2022 that the original DACA program was illegal and remanded the case back to the Texas district court. In September 2023 the Texas district court ruled the Biden administration's DACA rule to be unlawful, and in November the Biden administration appealed that decision to the Fifth Circuit (Jeong). As of this writing, litigation is ongoing.

2. Menjívar attests that "even when . . . immigrants attain full legality and even citizenship . . . their early experiences in liminal legality continue to shape their views of their adopted country" (1030).

3. Although the DREAM Act has repeatedly failed to pass, the frequent attempts to pass it, particularly in the environment of the Dreamer activists, led to other important measures. In 2012 DACA provided temporary work permits and deportation relief to more than 664,000 young undocumented immigrants who had lived in the United States since childhood. It was expanded in 2014, so that the upper age ceiling (thirty-one) was eliminated, and a new program was introduced (Deferred Action for Parents of Americans and Permanent Residents) to provide deportation relief and work permits to about 3.5 million undocumented immigrants with U.S.-born children (R. Gonzales, *Lives* 1). DACA, too, has "highlighted the growing distance between the college educated and the rest of the undocumented youth population"

(26), but the hope has been that the Dreamer, as a "collective, personal and movement identity inverts and confounds negative images of undocumented immigrants by revealing the complexity of immigrant biographies, highlighting the similarities that come with acculturation, and by showing that the immigrants contribute to society" (de la Torre and Germano 465).

4. Even until recently, comics have been assessed comparatively as literature and not identified on their own terms. Comics are still seen as "a lesser narrative art than, say, a novel or short story or poem" (Aldama, "ReDrawing" 1).

5. Cheney's book was on the *New York Times* list of bestselling children's picture books for fifteen weeks in 2003. See Kakutani.

6. Ulanowicz reads the primer in light of Cheney's own controversial public career during the 1990s, when she worked toward the development of a set of national history standards to be implemented in primary and secondary education. For Cheney, American democracy was at stake, so children needed to learn anew about the nation's rights and celebrate them.

7. The novel, which began as a memoir, is rooted in some of Andreu's personal experiences: she notes that the story was "born out of my deepest, ugliest secret" of being undocumented (Camacho 31).

8. Indirectly referring to the novel's political vacuum, Cummins discusses M.T.'s attendance at a private Catholic school (because her parents do not trust "government schools") and notes that M.T. could have enrolled in public school without a social security number, and that Andreu, who herself entered school before the *Plyler v. Doe* decision, "does not convey any reference to the rights it established" ("Dreamers" 93). Similarly, although Andreu explains in her author's note how the 1986 Immigration Reform and Control Act changed her life, she makes no mention of DACA or the Dreamer movement as potential twenty-first-century equivalents to the Immigration Reform and Control Act.

9. Presumably, most educated readers would recognize that M.T. is a Dreamer, so it could be argued that at an extratextual level the novel is able to rely on our normative expectations for the brand.

10. Cummins notes that "the authorial decision to have undocumented people refer to themselves as 'illegal' still troubles readers by reifying the label" ("Dreamers" 90).

11. Prior to the story's events (which focus on M.T.'s depression and decline), M.T. has also been ambitious and entrepreneurial. Such overachievements and hyperdocumentation are classic Dreamer tropes: survey data has found that undocumented students perform academically at "superior levels" and show a "strong psychosocial orientation toward schooling" (W. Pérez 64).

12. For many undocumented youths, the transition moment from child to adulthood marks the beginning of their separation from belonging: "many of the symbolic events and liberties that mark the passage from childhood to adulthood simultaneously mark their increasingly different and difficult life trajectories as compared to documented peers" (de la Torre and Germano 454).

WORKS CITED

"84 Lumber Super Bowl Commercial | Complete the Journey." YouTube, uploaded by 84 Lumber, 6 Feb. 2017.

"84 Lumber Super Bowl Commercial | The Entire Journey." YouTube, uploaded by 84 Lumber, 6 Feb. 2017.

"84 Lumber Super Bowl Commercial | The Journey Begins." YouTube, uploaded by 84 Lumber, 2 Feb. 2017.

"About Chicago's Pilsen Neighborhood." Pilsen Environmental Rights and Reform Organization: *La Organización sobre Derechos y Reformas Ambientales de Pilsen.* Website. Accessed 7 Sep. 2018.

Alamillo, Laura, et al. Introduction. *Voices of Resistance: Interdisciplinary Approaches to Chican@ Children's Literature,* edited by Alamillo et al. Rowman and Littlefield, 2018, pp. ix–xv.

Alcoff, Linda Martín. Foreword. *Mestiz@ Scripts, Digital Migrations, and the Territories of Writing.* Palgrave Macmillan, 2008, pp. xi–xiii.

Aldama, Frederick Luis. "The Heart and Art of Latino/a Young People's Fiction." Introduction. *Latino/a Children's and Young Adult Writers on the Art of Storytelling,* edited by Aldama, U of Pittsburgh P, 2018, pp. 3–25.

Aldama, Frederick Luis. "ReDrawing of Narrative Boundaries: An Introduction." *Studies in 20th and 21st Century Literature,* vol. 42, no. 1, 2017, pp. 1–6.

Alegría, Malín. Interview with Frederick Luis Aldama. *Latino/a Children's and Young Adult Writers on the Art of Storytelling.* U of Pittsburgh P, 2018, pp. 35–40.

Alegría, Malín. *Sofi Mendoza's Guide to Getting Lost in Mexico.* Simon Pulse, 2007.

Alvarez, Julia. *Return to Sender.* Random House, 2009.

Amaya, Hector. *Citizenship Excess: Latinas/os, Media and the Nation.* New York UP, 2013.

Anda, Diane de. *Mango Moon: When Deportation Divides a Family.* Illustrated by Sue Cornelison, Whitman and Co, 2019.

Anderson, James. "84 Lumber's Super Bowl Ad Stirs Immigration Debate." *LBM Journal,* 7 March 2017.

Andreu, Maria E. *The Secret Side of Empty.* Running Press, 2014.

Andreu, Maria E. "*The Secret Side of Empty* in Literary Analysis." MariaEAndreu. com, 25 Jun 2020.

Anzaldúa, Gloria. *Borderlands / La frontera*. 3rd ed. Aunt Lute Books, 2007.

Anzaldúa, Gloria. *Friends from the Other Side / Amigos del otro lado*. Illustrated by Consuelo Méndez, Children's Book Press, 1993.

Auchter, J. "Border Monuments: Memory, Counter-Memory, and (B)Ordering Practices Along the U.S.–Mexico Border." *Review of International Studies*, vol. 39, 2013, pp 291–311.

Baca, Damián. *Mestiz@ Scripts, Digital Migrations, and the Territories of Writing*. Palgrave Macmillan, 2008.

Baghban, Marcia. "Immigration in Childhood: Using Picture Books to Cope." *The Social Studies*, vol. 98, no. 2, March/April 2007, pp. 71–76.

Bang, Molly. *Picture This: How Pictures Work*. Revised and expanded 25th anniv. ed., Chronicle Books, 2016.

Barrera, Rosalinda B., and Oralia Garza de Cortes. "Mexican American Children's Literature in the 1990s: Toward Authenticity." *Using Multicultural Literature in the K-8 Classroom*, edited by Violet J. Harris and Christopher Gordon, 1997, pp. 129–154.

Barrera, Rosalinda, and Ruth E. Quiora. "The Uses of Spanish in Latino Children's Literature in English: What Makes for Cultural Authenticity?" *Stories Matter: The Complexity of Cultural Authenticity in Children's Literature*, edited by Dana Fox and Kathy G. Short, National Council of Teachers of English, 2003, pp. 247–65.

Barrera, Rosalinda, et al. "Spanish in Latino Picture Storybooks in English: Its Use and Textual Effects." *Multicultural Issues in Literacy Research and Practice*, edited by Arlette Ingram Willis et al., Lawrence Erlbaum Associates, 2003, pp. 145–65.

Batalla Rosado, Juan José. "The Historical Sources: Codices and Chronicles." *The Oxford Handbook of the Aztecs*, edited by Deborah L. Nichols and Enrique Rodríguez-Alegría, Oxford UP, 2017, pp. 29–40.

Beck, Scott A. "Children of Migrant Farmworkers in Picture Storybooks: Reality, Romanticism, and Representation." *Children's Literature Association Quarterly*, vol. 34, no. 2, 2009, pp. 99–137.

Bender, Daniel, et al. Editors' introduction. *Radical History Review*, vol. 129, October 2017, pp. 1–9.

Bender, Steven W. *Mea Culpa*. New York UP, 2015.

Berger, Dina. "Goodwill Ambassadors on Holiday." *Holiday in Mexico: Critical Reflections on Tourism and Tourist Encounters*, edited by Dina Berger and Andrew Grant Wood, Duke UP, 2010, pp. 107–29.

Berger, Dina, and Andrew Grant Wood. "Tourism Studies and the Tourism Dilemma." Introduction. *Holiday in Mexico: Critical Reflections on Tourism and Tourist Encounters*, edited by Berger and Wood, Duke UP, 2010, pp. 1–20.

Boffone, Trevor, and Cristina Herrera. "Weirding Out Latinx America." Introduction. *Nerds, Goths, Geeks, and Freaks: Outsiders in Chicanx and Latinx Young Adult Literature*, edited by Boffone and Herrera, UP of Mississippi, 2020, pp. 3–11.

Bomey, Nathan. "84 Lumber Owner Is Pro-Trump, Pro-Wall Despite Super Bowl Ad." *USA Today*, 7 Feb. 2017.

Boone, Elizabeth Hill. "Writing and Recording Knowledge." Introduction. *Writing Without Words: Alternative Literacies in Mesoamerica and the Andes*, edited by Elizabeth Hill Boone and Walter Mignolo, Duke UP, 1994, pp. 3–26.

Bourgois, Philippe. "The Symbolic Violence of Primitive Accumulation in the United States." Foreword. *Fresh Fruit, Broken Bodies: Migrant Farmworkers in the United States*, by Seth M. Holmes, U of California P, 2013, pp. xi–xvii.

Bradford, Clare. *Unsettling Narratives: Postcolonial Readings of Children's Literature*. Wilfrid Laurier UP, 2007.

Brady, Mary Pat. "Children's Literature." *The Routledge Companion to Latino/a Literature*, edited by Suzanne Bost and Frances R. Aparicio, Routledge, 2012, pp. 375–82.

Brochin, Carol, and Carmen L. Medina. "Critical Fictions of Transnationalism in Latinx Children's Literature." *Bookbird: A Journal of International Children's Literature*, vol. 55, no. 3, 2017, pp. 4–11.

Bromann, Katrina. Review of *Sofi Mendoza's Guide to Getting Lost in Mexico*, by Malín Alegría. *Bulletin of the Center for Children's Books*, vol. 60, no. 11, July/August 2007, pp. 450–51.

Brown, John Seely, and Paul Duguid. "Organizational Learning and Communities of Practice: Toward a Unified View of Working, Learning and Innovation." *Organization Science* vol. 2, no. 1, 1991, pp. 40–57.

Buitrago, Jairo. *Two White Rabbits*. Illustrated by Rafael Yockteng, translated by Elisa Amado, Groundwood Books, 2015.

Butts, Dennis. *Stories and Society: Children's Literature in Its Social Context*. Edited by Butts, St. Martin's Press, 1992.

Cabrera, Gabrielle. "Disrupting Diversity: Undocumented Students in the Neoliberal University." *We Are Not Dreamers*, Duke UP, 2020, pp. 66–83.

Cacho, Lisa Marie. *Social Death: Racialized Rightlessness and the Criminalization of the Unprotected*. New York UP, 2012.

Calloway-Thomas, Carolyn. *Empathy in the Global World: An Intercultural Perspective*. Sage, 2010.

Camacho, Haydee. "From Memoir to Fiction: Maria Andreu Talks About *The Secret Side of Empty*." *Voya Magazine*, June 2015.

Caminero-Santangelo, Marta. *Documenting the Undocumented: Latino/a Narratives and Social Justice in the Era of Operation Gatekeeper*. UP of Florida, 2016.

Caminero-Santangelo, Marta. "DREAMers: Youth and Migration: American DREAMers and Mexico." *Modern Mexican Culture: Critical Foundations*, edited by Stuart A. Day, U of Arizona P, 2017, pp. 25–45.

Caminero-Santangelo, Marta. "The Lost Ones: Post-Gatekeeper Border Fictions and the Construction of Cultural Trauma." *Latino Studies*, vol. 8, no. 3, 2010, pp. 304–27.

Caminero-Santangelo, Marta. "Making a Place: Life Narratives of Undocumented Youth." *Critical Insights: The Immigrant Experience*, edited by Maryse Jayasuriya, Salem Press, 2018, pp. 166–80.

Cantú, Norma Elia. "Our Stories Matter and We Matter." Preface. *Latino/a Children's and Young Adult Writers on the Art of Storytelling*, edited by Frederick Luis Aldama, U of Pittsburgh P, 2018, pp. xvii–xx.

Capshaw, Katharine. "Ethnic Studies and Children's Literature: A Conversation between Fields." *The Lion and the Unicorn*, vol. 38, 2014, pp. 237–57.

Capshaw Smith, Katharine. "The Landscape of Ethnic American Children's Literature." Introduction. *MELUS*, vol. 27, no. 2, 2002, pp. 3–8.

Capshaw Smith, Katharine, and Margaret R. Higonnet. "Bilingual Books for Children: An Interview with Nicolás Kanellos, Director of Piñata Press." *MELUS*, vol. 27, no. 2, 2002, pp. 217–24.

Carens, Joseph H. *The Ethics of Immigration*. Oxford UP, 2013.

Chacón, Jennifer M. "The Security Myth: Punishing Immigrants in the Name of National Security." *Governing Immigration Through Crime: A Reader*, edited by Julie A. Dowling and Jonathan Xavier Inda, Stanford UP, 2013, pp. 77–93. *ProQuest*.

Chávez, Alex E. "Intimacy at Stake: Transnational Migration and the Separation of Family." *Latino Studies*, vol. 15, no. 1, 2017, pp. 50–72.

Chávez, Leo R. "'Illegality' Across Generations: Public Discourse and the Children of Undocumented Immigrants." *Constructing Immigrant 'Illegality': Critiques, Experiences, and Responses*, edited by Cecilia Menjívar and Daniel Kanstroom, Cambridge UP, 2013, pp. 84–110.

Chávez, Leo R. *The Latino Threat: Constructing Immigrants, Citizens, and the Nation*. Stanford UP, 2013.

Cheney, Lynne. *America: A Patriotic Primer*. Illustrated by Robin Preiss Glasser, Simon and Schuster, 2002.

"Childhood in Literature." Wikipedia. Accessed 31 May 2023.

Clark, Meredith. "Super Bowl 2023: The 10 Most Controversial Super Bowl Ads Ever." *The Independent*, 9 Feb. 2023.

Coleman, Linda S. Introduction. *Women's Life-Writing: Finding Voice/Building Community*, edited by Coleman. Bowling Green U Popular P, 1997, pp. 1–7.

Cope, Bill, and Mary Kalantzis. "Multiliteracies: The Beginnings of an Idea." Introduction. *Multiliteracies: Literacy Learning and the Design of Social Futures*, edited by Cope and Kalantzis, Routledge, 2000, pp. 3–8.

Cope, Bill, and Mary Kalantzis. "Multiliteracies: New Literacies, New Learning." *Pedagogies: An International Journal*, vol. 4, no. 3, 2009, pp. 164–95.

Crèvecoeur, Hector St. John de. *Letters from an American Farmer and Sketches of Eighteenth-Century America*. 1782. Edited by Albert E. Stone, Penguin, 1986.

Croucher, Sheila. *The Other Side of the Fence: American Migrants in Mexico*. U of Texas P, 2009.

Cummins, Amy. "Border Crossings: Undocumented Migration Between Mexico and the United States in Contemporary Young Adult Literature." *Children's Literature in Education*, vol. 33, 2013, pp. 57–73.

Cummins, Amy. "Dreamers: Living Undocumented in Contemporary Young Adult Fiction." *Theory in Action*, vol. 13, no. 2, 2020, pp. 80–103.

Cummins, Amy. "Education in Children's Picture Books Portraying Mexican American Immigrants and Written by Mexican American Authors." *The Dragon Lode*, vol. 33, no. 2, spring 2015, pp. 82–90.

Cummins, Amy. "Refugees and Immigrants in Children's Fiction: New Books to Build Understanding Across Borders." *English in Texas*, vol. 46, no. 2, 2016, pp. 24–29.

Dávila, Arlene. *Latino Spin: Public Image and the Whitewashing of Race.* NYU Press, 2008.

Davis, Rocío G. "Metanarrative in Ethnic Autobiography for Children: Laurence Yep's *The Lost Garden* and Judith Ortiz Cofer's *Silent Dancing*." *MELUS*, vol. 27, no. 2, summer 2002, pp. 139–56.

DeFelice, Cynthia. *Under the Same Sky.* Macmillan, 2003.

De Genova, Nicholas, and Ana Y. Ramos-Zayas. *Latino Crossings: Mexicans, Puerto Ricans, and the Politics of Race and Citizenship.* Routledge, 2003.

de la Torre, Pedro, III, and Roy Germano. "Out of the Shadows: DREAMer Identity in the Immigrant Youth Movement." *Latino Studies*, vol. 12, no. 3, 2014, pp. 449–67.

Del Castillo, Adelaida R. "Illegal Status and Social Citizenship: Thoughts on Mexican Immigrants in a Postcolonial World." *Women and Migration in the U.S.-Mexico Borderlands: A Reader.* Duke UP, 2007, pp. 92–105.

Demata, Massimiliano. "'A Great and Beautiful Wall': Donald Trump's Populist Discourse on Immigration." *Journal of Language Aggression and Conflict*, vol. 5, no. 2, 2017, pp. 274–94.

Deppen, Colin. "What Is 84 Lumber Saying About Its Controversial Super Bowl Ad? The Answer Might Surprise You." *Pennsylvania Real-Time News*, 6 Feb. 2017.

Diaz, Alexandra. *The Crossroads.* Simon and Schuster, 2018.

Diaz, Alexandra. *The Only Road.* Simon and Schuster, 2016.

Diaz, Alexandra. *Santiago's Road Home.* Simon and Schuster, 2021.

Doty, Rozanne Lynn. "Bare Life: Border-Crossing Deaths and Spaces of Moral Alibi." *Governing Immigration Through Crime: A Reader*, edited by Julie A. Dowling and Jonathan Xavier Inda, Stanford UP, 2013, pp. 129–43.

Edkins, Jenny. "Time, Personhood, Politics." *The Future of Trauma Theory: Contemporary Literary and Cultural Criticism*, edited by Gert Buelens et al., Routledge, 2014, pp. 127–39.

"Enforcement Statistics FY 2019. U.S. Customs and Border Protection." U.S. Customs and Border Protection, 20 May 2019.

Fairchild, Henry Pratt. "The Literacy Test and Its Making." *The Quarterly Journal of Economics*, vol. 31, no. 3, 1917, pp. 447–60.

Fass, Paula S. "Is There a Story in the History of Childhood?" *The Routledge History of Childhood in the Western World*, edited by Fass, Routledge, 2014, pp. 1–14.

Fernández-Kelly, Patricia, and Douglas S. Massey. "Borders for Whom? The Role of NAFTA in Mexico-U.S. Migration." *The ANNALS of the American Academy of Political and Social Science*, vol. 610, no. 1, 2007, pp. 98–118.

Flores-González, Nilda. *Citizens but Not Americans: Race and Belonging Among Latino Millennials*. New York UP, 2017.

Foer, Franklin. "How ICE Went Rogue." *The Atlantic Monthly*, September 2018, pp. 56–70.

Frey, John Carlos. *Sand and Blood: America's Stealth War on the Mexico Border*. Bold Type Books, 2019.

Galarza, Litzy, and Lars Stoltzfus-Brown. "84 Lumber's Constrained Polysemy: Limiting Interpretive Play and the Power of Audience Agency in Inspirational Immigrant Narratives." *International Journal of Communication*, vol. 15, 2021, pp. 41–60.

García, Andrea Fernández. "'We Are Not Just Patriots of a Country, but Citizens of the Planet': Children's Identity Negotiations in Julia Alvarez's *Return to Sender*." *Odisea* vol. 17, 2016, pp. 101–18.

García, Georgia Earnest. "Giving Voice to Multicultural Literary Research and Practice." Introduction. *Multicultural Issues in Literacy Research and Practice*, edited by Arlette Ingram Willis et al., Lawrence Erlbaum Associates, 2003, pp. 1–9.

Gerber, David A. *American Immigration: A Very Short Introduction*. Oxford UP, 2011.

Ghiso, María Paula, and Gerald Campano. "Ideologies of Language and Identity in Children's Literature." *Bookbird: A Journal of International Children's Literature*, vol. 51, no. 3, July 2013, pp. 47–55.

Ginsberg, Elaine K. "The Politics of Passing." Introduction. *Passing and the Fictions of Identity*, edited by Ginsberg, Duke UP, 1996, pp. 1–18.

Goodnow, Jasmine M., and Edward Ruddell. "An Illustration of the Quest Genre as Spiritual Metaphor in Adventure Travel Narratives." *Leisure/Loisir*, vol. 33, no. 1, 2010, pp. 241–67.

González, Christopher. "Latinx Lives, in Living Color." *American Book Review*, vol. 40, no. 2, Jan./Feb. 2019, pp. 5–6.

Gonzalez, Eduardo. "Stereotypical Depictions of Latino Criminality: U.S. Latinos in the Media During the MAGA Campaign." *Democratic Communique*, vol. 28, no. 1, 2019, pp. 46–62.

Gonzales, Roberto G. *Lives in Limbo: Undocumented and Coming of Age in America*. U of California P, 2016.

Greenblatt, Alan. "What's Causing the Latest Immigration Crisis? A Brief Explainer." NPR, 9 Jul. 2014.

Grenby, M. O. "The Origins of Children's Literature." *The Cambridge Companion to Children's Literature*, edited by Grenby and Andrea Immel, Cambridge UP, 2009, pp. 3–18.

Grenby, M. O., and Andrea Immel. Preface. *The Cambridge Companion to Children's Literature*, Cambridge UP, 2009, pp. xiii–xv.

Guo, Libo, et al. "Multiliteracies: Introduction to the Special Issue." *Pedagogies: An International Journal*, vol. 4, no. 3, 2009, pp. 159–63.

Guskin, Emily, and David Nakamura. "Poll: Percentage of Democrats Who See Border 'Crisis' Jumps 17 Points Since January amid Spike in Migrant Families." *Washington Post*, 30 Apr. 2019.

Gutman, Marta. "The Physical Spaces of Childhood." *The Routledge History of Childhood in the Western World*, edited by Paula S. Fass, Routledge, 2014, pp. 249–66.

Hanley, Jane. "International Solidarity, Volunteer Tourism and Travel Writing: Mexico and Central America in Spanish and English." *TEXT*, vol. 56, October 2019, pp. 1–15.

Heath, Thomas. "84 Lumber and the Big-Budget Super Bowl Ad to Nowhere." *The Washington Post*, 6 Feb. 2017.

Hernandez, Kelly Lytle. "How Crossing the US-Mexico Border Became a Crime." *The Conversation*, 30 Apr. 2017.

Herrera, Juan Felipe. *Calling the Doves / El canto de las palomas*. Illustrated by Elly Simmons, Children's Book Press, 1995.

Herrera, Juan Felipe. *Super Cilantro Girl / La superniña del cilantro*. Illustrated by Honorio Robledo Tapia, Children's Book Press, 2003.

Herrera, Juan Felipe. *The Upside Down Boy / El niño de cabeza*. Illustrated by Elizabeth Gómez, Children's Book Press, 2000.

Hintz, Carrie, and Eric Tribunella. *Reading Children's Literature: A Critical Introduction*. 2nd ed., Broadview Press, 2019.

Holmes, Seth. *Fresh Fruit, Broken Bodies: Migrant Farmworkers in the United States*. Berkeley: U of California P, 2013.

Horning, Kathleen T. "Still an All-White World?" *School Library Journal*, vol. 60, no. 5, May 2014.

Horst, Megan, and Amy Marion. "Racial, Ethnic and Gender Inequities in Farmland Ownership and Farming in the U.S." *Agriculture and Human Values*, vol. 36, no. 1, 2019, pp. 1–16.

Hoyt, Homer. "The Relation of the Literacy Test to a Constructive Immigration Problem." *Journal of Political Economy*, vol. 24, no. 5, 1916, pp. 445–73.

Huff, Richard. "Transnationalism." *Encyclopedia Britannica*, 15 Aug. 2014.

Ibarraran-Bigalondo, Amaia. "When the Border Educates: Malín Alegría's *Sofi Mendoza's Guide to Getting Lost in Mexico* (2007)." *International Journal of English Studies*, vol. 16, no. 1, 2016, pp. 19–32.

Inda, Jonathan Xavier. "The Value of Immigrant Life." *Women and Migration in the U.S.-Mexico Borderlands: A Reader*, edited by Denise A. Seguar and Patricia Zavella, Duke UP, 2007, pp. 134–57.

Jefferson, Thomas. *The Papers of Thomas Jefferson*. Edited by Julian P. Boyd, vol. 8, Princeton UP, 1950.

Jeong, Andrew. "Federal Court Rules Obama-Era DACA Program Still Unlawful." *The Washington Post*, 14 Sep. 2023.

Jiménez, Francisco. *La mariposa*. Illustrated by Simón Silva, Houghton Mifflin, 1998.

Jiménez García, Marilisa. "En(countering) YA: Young Lords, Shadowstoppers, and the Longings and Possibilities of Latinx Young Adult Literature." *Latino Studies*, vol. 16, 2018, pp. 230–49.

Jiménez García, Marilisa. "Side-by-Side: At the Intersections of Latinx Studies and ChYALit." *The Lion and the Unicorn*, vol. 4, 2017, pp. 113–22.

Johnson, Joanna Webb. "Chick Lit Jr.: More Than Glitz and Glamour for Teens and Tweens." *Chick Lit: The New Women's Fiction*, edited by Suzanne Ferriss and Mallory Young, Routledge, 2006, pp. 141–57.

Joseph, Gilbert M. "Close Encounters: Toward a New Cultural History of U.S.–Latin American Relations." *Close Encounters of Empire: Writing the Cultural History of U.S.–Latin American Relations*, ed. Gilbert M. Joseph, Catherine C. LeGrand, and Ricardo D. Salvatore, Duke UP, 1998, p. 3–46.

Kakutani, Michiko. "To Stars, Writing Books Looks like Child's Play." *The New York Times*, 23 Oct. 2003, p. E1.

Kaplan, Caren. *Questions of Travel*. Duke UP, 1996.

Kauffman, Gretel. "Does the 84 Lumber Ad Really Mean What You Think It Means?" *Christian Science Monitor*, 7 Feb. 2017.

Kearney, Michael. "Transnationalism in California and Mexico at the End of Empire." *Border Identities: Nation and State at International Frontiers*, edited by Thomas W. Wilson and Hastings Connan, Cambridge UP, 1998, pp. 117–41.

Kelen, Christopher, and Bjorn Sundmark. "First Things: Introduction." *The Nation in Children's Literature: Nations of Childhood*, edited by Kelen and Sundmark, Routledge, 2013, pp. 1–8.

Kiefer, Barbara. "What Is a Picturebook? Across the Borders of History." *New Review of Children's Literature and Librarianship*, vol. 17, 2011, pp. 86–102.

Klocker, Natascha, et al. "Exploring Migrants' Knowledge and Skill in Seasonal Farm Work: More than Laboring Bodies." *Agriculture and Human Values*, vol. 37, 2020, pp. 463–78.

Landes, Sonia. "Picture Books as Literature." *Children's Literature Association Quarterly*, vol. 10, no. 2, 1985, pp. 51–54.

Langer, Beryl. "The Business of Branded Enchantment: Ambivalence and Disjuncture in the Global Children's Culture Industry." *Journal of Consumer Culture*, vol. 4, no. 2, 2004, pp. 251–77.

Ledesma, Alberto. *Diary of a Reluctant Dreamer*. Mad Creek Books, 2017.

Ledesma, Alberto. "Doodling as Activism: How I Produced My Diary of a Reluctant Dreamer." *Latinx in Kid Lit: Exploring the World of Latinx YA, MG and Children's Literature*, 3 May 2018.

Lima, Lázaro. *The Latino Body: Crisis Identities in American Literary and Cultural Theory*. New York UP, 2007.

Lind, Dara. "There Is a Crisis at the Border, It's Just Not What Trump Says It Is." *Vox*, 29 Jan. 2019.

Lind, Dara. "The Disastrous, Forgotten 1996 Law That Created Today's Immigration Problem." *Vox*, 28 Apr. 2016.

Loewen, James. *Lies My Teacher Told Me: Everything Your American History Book Got Wrong.* Touchstone, 1995.

López, Tiffany Ana, and Phillip Serrato. "A New *Mestiza* Primer: Borderlands Philosophy in the Children's Books of Gloria Anzaldúa." *Such News of the Land: U.S. Women Nature Writers,* edited by Thomas S. Edwards and Elizabeth A. De Wolfe, UP of New England, 2001, pp. 204–16.

MacArthur, Elizabeth Jane. *Extravagant Narratives: Closure and Dynamics in the Epistolary Form.* Princeton UP, 1990.

Machado-Casas, Margarita. "*Pedagogías del camaleón* / Pedagogies of the Chameleon: Identities and Strategies of Survival for Transnational Indigenous Latino Immigrants in the U.S. South." *The Urban Review,* vol. 44, 2012, pp. 534–50.

Magaña, Rocío. "The Border Effect." *American Anthropologist,* vol. 116, no. 1, 2014, pp. 146–59.

Mallonee, Laura C. "A Contemporary Codex Teaches Children About Migration." *Hyperallergic,* 17 Feb. 2005.

Manning, Susan. Introduction. *Letters from an American Farmer,* by Hector St. John de Crèvecoeur, edited by Susan Manning, Oxford UP, 1997, pp. vii–xxxvii.

Manuel, José, et al., editors. *Papers: Stories by Undocumented Youth.* Illustrated by Julio Salgado, Graham Street Productions, 2012.

Márquez, John D. "Latinos as the 'Living Dead': Raciality, Expendability, and Border Militarization." *Latino Studies,* vol. 10, no. 4, 2012, pp. 473–98.

Martínez, Manuel Luis. "Telling the Difference Between the Border and the Borderlands: Materiality and Theoretical Practice." *Globalization on the Line: Culture, Capital, and Citizenship at U.S. Borders,* edited by Claudia Sadowski-Smith, Palgrave, 2002, pp. 53–68.

Martínez, Susana S. "Patriots and Citizens of the Planet: Friendship and Geopolitics in Julia Alvarez's Young Adult Fiction." *Inhabiting La Patria: Identity, Agency and Antojo in the Work of Julia Alvarez,* edited by Rebecca L. Harrison and Emily Hipchen, State U of New York P, 2013, pp. 109–30.

Massey, Doreen. "Globalization: What Does It Mean for Geography?" *Geography,* vol. 87, 2002, pp. 293–96.

Mateo, José Manuel. *Migrant: The Journey of a Mexican Worker.* Illustrated by Javier Martínez Pedro, translated by Emmy Smith Ready, Abrams Books, 2014.

Mathis, Janelle B. "Literacy Possibilities and Concerns for Mexican-American Children's Literature: Readers, Writers, and Publishers Respond." *Celebrating the Faces of Literacy: The Twenty-Fourth Yearbook,* edited by Patricia E. Linder et al., College Reading Association, 2002, pp. 189–205.

Menjívar, Cecilia. "Liminal Legality: Salvadoran and Guatemalan Immigrants' Lives in the United States." *American Journal of Sociology,* vol. 111, no. 4, 2006, pp. 999–1037.

Mercado-López, Larisssa M. "Entre tejana y chicana: Tracing Proto-Chicana Identity and Consciousness in Tejana Young Adult Fiction and Poetry." *Voices of Resistance: Interdisciplinary Approaches to Chican@ Children's Literature,* edited by Laura Alamillo et al., Rowman and Littlefield, 2018, pp. 3–15.

Mercer, Kobena. "Welcome to the Jungle: Identity and Diversity in Postmodern Politics." *Identity: Community, Culture, Difference*, edited by Jonathan Rutherford, Lawrence Wishart, 2003, pp. 43–71.

Mermann-Jozwiak, Elisabeth. "Writing Mexico: Travel and Intercultural Encounter in Contemporary American Literature." *Symploke* vol. 17, no. 102, 2009, pp. 95–114.

Mickelson, Marcia Argueta. *Where I Belong*. Lerner Publishing, 2021.

Mickenberg, Julia L., and Philip Nel. "Radical Children's Literature Now!" *Children's Literature Association Quarterly*, vol. 36, no. 4, 2011, pp. 445–73.

Mills, Kathy A. "Multiliteracies: Interrogating Competing Discourses." *Language and Education*, vol. 23, no. 2, 2009, pp. 103–16.

Miroff, Nick. "From the Border, More Frustrating Immigration Numbers for President Trump." *Washington Post*, 8 May 2019.

Mitchell, Don. *The Lie of the Land: Migrant Workers and the California Landscape*. U of Minnesota P, 1996.

Monico, Gabriela. "American't: Redefining Citizenship in the U.S. Undocumented Immigrant Youth Movement." *We Are Not Dreamers*, Duke UP, 2020, pp. 87–105.

Montaño, Jesus, and Regan Postma-Montaño. *Tactics of Hope in Latinx Children's and Young Adult Literature*. U of New Mexico P, 2022.

Mora, Pat. *Tómas and the Library Lady*. Illustrated by Raul Colón, Dragonfly Books, 1997.

Mora, Pat, and Libby Martinez. *I Pledge Allegiance*. Illustrated by Patrice Barton, Alfred A. Knopf, 2014.

Morales, Yuyi. *Dreamers*. Neal Porter Books, 2018.

Moreno-Orama, Rebeca. "Creating Social Justice: A Conversation with Julia Álvarez." *Latin American Literary Review*, vol. 44, no. 87, 2017, pp. 73–77.

Naidoo, Jaime C. "Magical Encounters with Latino Children's Literature." Foreword. *Latino/a Children's and Young Adult Writers on the Art of Storytelling*, edited by Frederick Luis Aldama, U of Pittsburgh P, 2018, pp. xi–xv.

Naidoo, Jaime C. "Opening Doors: Visual and Textual Analyses of Diverse Latino Subcultures in América's Picture Books." *Children and Libraries*, vol. 6, no. 2, 2008, pp. 27–35.

Nel, Philip. "Migration, Refugees, and Diaspora in Children's Literature." Introduction. *Children's Literature Association Quarterly*, vol 43, no. 4, 2018, 357–62.

Ngai, Mae M. *Impossible Subjects: Illegal Aliens and the Making of Modern America*. Princeton UP, 2014.

Nicholls, Walter J. *The DREAMers: How the Undocumented Youth Movement Transformed the Immigrant Rights Debate*. Stanford UP, 2013.

Nikolajeva, Maria. "Children's Literature." *The Routledge History of Childhood in the Western World*, edited by Paula S. Fass, Routledge, 2014, pp. 313–27.

Nikolajeva, Maria, and Carole Scott. "The Dynamics of Picturebook Communication." *Children's Literature in Education*, vol. 31, no. 4, 2000, pp. 225–39.

Nikolajeva, Maria, and Carole Scott. *How Picturebooks Work*. Garland, 2001.

Nodelman, Perry. *Words Without Pictures: The Narrative Act of Children's Picture Books*. U of Georgia P, 1989.

Olivas, Michael A. *No Undocumented Child Left Behind:* Plyler v. Doe *and the Education of Undocumented School Children*. New York UP, 2012.

Olvera, Jacqueline. "The State, Unauthorized Mexican Migration, and Vulnerability in the Workplace." *Sociology Compass*, vol. 10, no. 2, 2016, pp. 132–42.

Olwig, Kenneth. "Sexual Cosmology: Nation and Landscape at the Conceptual Interstices of Nature and Culture; or What Does Landscape Really Mean?" *Landscape: Politics and Perspectives*, edited by Barbara Bender, Oxford UP, 1993, pp. 307–43.

Ong, Aihwa. "The Gender and Labor Politics of Postmodernity." *The Politics of Culture in the Shadows of Capital*, edited by Lisa Lowe and David Lloyd, Duke UP, 1997, pp. 61–97.

Orduña, José. *The Weight of Shadows: A Memoir of Immigration and Displacement*. Beacon Press, 2016.

O'Reilly, Lara. "The 84 Lumber Super Bowl Ad's Creative Director Explains the Thinking Behind the Mexican Immigration–Themed Ad." *Business Insider*, 5 Feb. 2017.

Orner, Peter. "Permanent Anxiety." Introduction. *Underground America: Narratives of Undocumented Lives*, edited by Orner, McSweeney's Books, 2008, pp. 5–13.

Paul, Lissa. "Learning to Be Literate." *The Cambridge Companion to Children's Literature*, edited by M. O. Grency and Andrea Immel, Cambridge UP, 2009, pp. 127–42.

Pekala, Nancy. "Lessons Learned from 84 Lumber's Super Bowl Fail." *Nancy Pekala*, 8 Feb. 2017.

Pérez, Amada Irma. *My Diary from Here to There / Mi diario de aqui hasta allá*. Illustrated by Maya Christina Gonzalez, Children's Book Press, 2002.

Pérez, Gina, et al. Introduction. *Beyond El Barrio: Everyday Life in Latina/o America*. Edited by Pérez et al., New York UP, 2010, pp. 1–23.

Pérez, Joanna B. "Undocuartivism: Latino Undocumented Immigrant Empowerment Through Art and Activism." *Chiricú Journal*, vol. 2, no. 2, 2018, pp. 23–44.

Pérez, William. *Americans by Heart: Undocumented Latino Students and the Promise of a Higher Education*. Teachers College Press, 2012.

Pitt, Kristin E. "The Vulnerable Harvest: Farmworkers, Food, and Immigration in the Contemporary United States." *Aztlán: A Journal of Chicano Studies*, vol. 41, no. 2, 2016, pp. 13–36.

Preston, Julia. "How the Dreamers Learned to Play Politics." *Politico*, 9 September 2017.

Radoff, Sara. "Crossing the Border of *Plyler v. Doe*: Students Without Documentation and Their Right to Rights." *Educational Studies*, vol. 47, 2011, pp. 436–50.

Ramirez, Pablo A. "Toward a Borderland Ethics: The Undocumented Migrant and Haunted Communities in Contemporary Chicana/o Fiction." *Aztlán: A Journal of Chicano Studies*, vol. 35, no. 1, 2010, pp. 49–67.

Rebolledo, Tey Diana. "Theories and Methodologies: *Prietita y el otro lado*: Gloria Anzaldúa's Literature for Children." *PMLA*, vol. 121, no. 1, 2006, pp. 279–84.

Reeves, Margaret. "A Prospect of Flowers: Concepts of Childhood and Female Youth in Seventeenth-Century British Culture." *The Youth of Early Modern Women*, edited by Elizabeth S. Cohen and Margaret Reeves, Amsterdam UP, 2018, pp. 35–58.

Reimer, Mavis. "Traditions of the School Story." *The Cambridge Companion to Children's Literature*, edited by M. O. Grenby and Andrea Immel, Cambridge UP, 2009, pp. 209–25.

Review of *Migrant: The Journey of a Mexican Worker*, by José Manuel Mateo, illustrated by Javier Martínez Pedro. *Kirkus Reviews*, 16 Mar. 2014.

Rhodes, Cristina. "Carmelita Torres and Bodies of Resistance: Reclaiming Young Latinas' Bodies Within Hegemonic Discourse." *Latino Studies*, vol. 19, 2021, pp. 358–73.

Rhodes, Cristina. "Female Empowerment and Undocumented Border Crossing in Bettina Restrepo's *Illegal.*" *Bookbird: A Journal of International Children's Literature*, vol. 55, no. 3, 2017, pp. 20–26.

Rodriguez, Luis J. *Always Running: La Vida Loca: Gang Days in LA*. Simon and Schuster, 1994.

Rodriguez, Luis J. *América Is Her Name*. Illustrated by Carlos Vásquez, Curbstone Press, 1998.

Rodriguez, Sanjuana C., and Eliza Gabrielle Braden. "Representation of Latinx Immigrants and Immigration in Children's Literature: A Critical Content Analysis." *Journal of Children's Literature*, vol. 44, no. 2, pp. 2018, 46–61.

Rosas, Gilberto. "The Managed Violences of the Borderlands: Treacherous Geographies, Policeability, and the Politics of Race." *Latino Studies*, vol. 4, 2006, pp. 401–18.

Rostankowski, Cynthia. "A Is for Aesthetics: Alphabet Books and the Development of the Aesthetic in Children." *The Journal of Aesthetic Education*, vol. 28, no. 3, 1994, 117–27.

Rottenberg, Catherine. *Performing Americanness: Race, Class, and Gender in Modern African-American and Jewish-American Literature*. Dartmouth College Press, 2008.

Ruiz, Jason. *Americans in the Treasure House: Travel to Porfirian Mexico and the Cultural Politics of Empire*. U of Texas P, 2014.

Ruth, Alissa, et al. "Soy de aquí, soy de allá: DACAmented Homecomings and Implications for Identity and Belonging." *Latino Studies*, vol. 17, 2019, pp. 304–22.

Salinas-Moniz, Felicia. "Narratives of Latina Girlhood in Malín Alegría's *Estrella's Quinceañera* and *Sofi Mendoza's Guide to Getting Lost in Mexico.*" *Theorizing Ethnicity and Nationality in the Chick Lit Genre*, edited by Erin Hurt, Routledge, 2019, pp. 87–101.

Sánchez, George J. "Face the Nation: Race, Immigration, and the Rise of Nativism in Late Twentieth Century America." *The International Migration Review*, vol. 31, no. 4, 1997, 1009–30.

Sánchez, Rosaura. "The Toxic Tonic: Narratives of Xenophobia." *Latino Studies*, vol. 9, no. 1, 2011, pp. 126–44.

Sati, Joel. "'Other' Borders: The Illegal as Normative Metaphor." *We Are Not Dreamers*. Duke UP, 2020, pp. 23–44.

Sayre, Wilson. "Riding 'the Beast' Across Mexico to the U.S. Border." *NPR*, 5 June 2014.

Schantz, Eric M. "Behind the Noir Border." *Holiday in Mexico: Critical Reflections on Tourism and Tourist Encounters*, edited by Dina Berger and Andrew Grant, Duke UP, 2010, pp. 130–60.

Schmidt, James. "Children and the State." *The Routledge History of Childhood in the Western World*, edited by Paula S. Fass, Routledge, 2014, pp. 174–90.

Serrato, Phillip. "Conflicting Inclinations: Luis J. Rodriguez's Picture Books for Children." *Ethnic Literary Traditions in American Children's Literature*, edited by Michelle Pagni Stewart and Yvonne Atkinson, Palgrave Macmillan, 2009, pp. 191–204.

Serrato, Phillip. "Working with What We've Got." *Arte y loqueras*, 16 February 2013.

Serrato, Phillip. "Visual Brilliance / Narrative Deficiency." *Arte y loqueras*, 14 May 2019.

Shea, Anne. "'Don't Let Them Make You Feel You Did a Crime': Immigration Law, Labor Rights, and Farmworker Testimony." *MELUS* vol. 28, no. 1, 2003, pp. 123–44.

Shoichet, Catherine E. "These Authors Don't Like the Immigration Stories They're Hearing from Washington. So They're Writing Their Own." *CNN*, 21 Dec. 2019.

Siegler, Kirk. "A 'Mainstreaming of Bigotry' as White Extremism Reveals Its Global Reach." *NPR*, 16 Mar. 2019.

Sipe, Lawrence R. "How Picture Books Work: A Semiotically Framed Theory of Text-Picture Relationships." *Children's Literature in Education*, vol. 29, no. 2, 1998, pp. 97–108.

Smallman, Etan. "Drawing on Childhood: New Exhibition Examines Why So Many of Our Most Cherished Fictional Heroes Are Orphans." *The Independent*, 10 Jan. 2016.

Socolovsky, Maya. "Cultural (Il)literacy: Narratives of Epistolary Resistance and Transnational Citizenship in Julia Alvarez's *Return to Sender*." *Children's Literature Association Quarterly*, vol. 40, no. 4, 2015, pp. 386–404.

Socolovsky, Maya. "Material Literacies: Migration and Border Crossings in Chicana/o Children's Picture Books." *MELUS*, vol. 43, no. 4, 2018, pp. 148–71.

Soeiro, Liz Phipps. "Dear Mrs. Trump." *Family Reading*, 26 Sep. 2017. *The Horn Book*.

Spener, David. *Clandestine Crossings: Migrants and Coyotes on the Texas-Mexico Border*. Cornell UP, 2009.

Stephen, Lynn. *Transborder Lives: Indigenous Oaxacans in Mexico, California, and Oregon*. Duke UP, 2007.

Stone, Albert E. Introduction. *Letters from an American Farmer and Sketches of Eighteenth-Century America*, by Hector St. John de Crèvecoeur, edited by Albert E. Stone, Penguin, 1986.

Terrio, Susan J. *Whose Child Am I? Unaccompanied, Undocumented Children in U.S. Immigration Custody*. U of California P, 2015.

Terrones, Lettycia. "Águila: Personal Reflections on Reading Chicanx Picture Books from the Inside Out." *Voices of Resistance: Interdisciplinary Approaches to Chican@ Children's Literature*, edited by Laura Alamillo et al., Rowman and Littlefield, 2018, pp. 47–57.

Thananopavarn, Susan. "Negotiating Asian American Childhood in the Twenty-First Century: Grace Lin's *Year of the Dog, Year of the Rat*, and *Dumpling Days*." *The Lion and the Unicorn*, vol. 38, no. 1, 2014, pp. 106–22.

Thomas, Piri. *Down These Mean Streets*. Vintage Books, 1997.

Truax, Eileen. *Dreamers: An Immigrant Generation's Fight for Their American Dream*. Beacon Press, 2015.

Ulanowicz, Anastasia. "Preemptive Education: Lynne Cheney's *America: A Patriotic Primer* and the Ends of History." *Children's Literature Association Quarterly*, vol. 33, no. 4, 2008, pp. 341–70.

Valdivia, Carolina. "Undocumented Young Adults' Heightened Vulnerability in the Trump Era." *We Are Not Dreamers*, Duke UP, 2020, pp. 127–43.

Vargas, Jose Antonio. "We Are Americans, Just Not Legally." *TIME*, vol. 179, no. 25, 25 June 2012.

Villa-Nicholas, Melissa. "Latinx Digital Memory: Identity Making in Real Time." *Social Media + Society*, vol. 5, no. 4, 2019, pp. 1–11.

Wald, Sarah D. *The Nature of California: Race, Citizenship and Farming Since the Dust Bowl*. U of Washington P, 2016.

Ward, Myah. "At Least 3,900 Children Separated from Families Under Trump 'Zero Tolerance' Policy, Task Force Finds." *Politico*, 8 June 2021.

Weaver, Lila Quintero. Review of *Diary of a Reluctant Dreamer*, by Alberto Ledesma. *Latinx in Kid Lit: Exploring the World of Latinx YA, MG and Children's Literature*, 30 Apr. 2018.

Wides-Muñoz, Laura. *The Making of a Dream: How a Group of Young Undocumented Immigrants Helped Change What It Means to be American*. HarperCollins, 2018.

Willis, Arlete, et al., editors. *Multicultural Issues in Literacy Research and Practice*. Routledge, 2002.

Wolk, Steven. "Reading for a Better World: Teaching for Social Responsibility with Young Adult Literature." *Journal of Adolescent and Adult Literacy*, vol. 52, no. 8, 2009, pp. 664–73.

Wood, Andrew Grant, and Dina Berger. "Should We Stay or Should We Go?" Conclusion. *Holiday in Mexico: Critical Reflections on Tourism and Tourist Encounters*, edited by Berger and Wood, Duke UP, 2010, pp. 371–84.

Wylie, Andrea Schwenke. "Expanding the View of First-Person Narration." *Children's Literature in Education*, vol. 30, no. 3, 1999, pp. 185–202.

Yezierska, Anzia. "America and I." *The Heath Anthology of American Literature, Concise Edition*, edited by Paul Lauter, Houghton Mifflin, 2004, pp. 2066–73.

INDEX

ABOUT THE AUTHOR

Maya Socolovsky is an associate professor of English and Latinx literature at University of North Carolina at Charlotte and the author of *Troubling Nationhood in U.S. Latina Literature: Explorations of Place and Belonging* (Rutgers University Press, 2013). She has published numerous articles in peer-reviewed journals on race, memory, and citizenship in Latinx literature. More recently, she has written three publications on Latinx children's literature, for the journals *MELUS*, *Children's Literature Association Quarterly*, and *The Lion and the Unicorn*.